THE
HISTORY OF
HAITI

THE
HISTORY OF
HAITI

Steeve Coupeau

The Greenwood Histories of the Modern Nations
Frank W. Thackeray and John E. Findling, Series Editors

Greenwood Press
Westport, Connecticut • London

Library of Congress Cataloging-in-Publication Data

Coupeau, Steeve.
  The history of Haiti / Steeve Coupeau.
    p. cm.—(The Greenwood histories of the modern nations, ISSN 1096–2905)
  Includes bibliographical references and index.
  ISBN 978–0–313–34089–5 (alk. paper)
  1. Haiti—History.   I. Title.
  F1921.C68 2008
  972.94—dc22   2007037490

British Library Cataloguing in Publication Data is available.

Library of Congress Catalog Card Number: 2007037490
ISBN: 978–0–313–34089–5
ISSN: 1096–2905

First published in 2008

Greenwood Press, 88 Post Road West, Westport, CT 06881
An imprint of Greenwood Publishing Group, Inc.
www.greenwood.com

Printed in the United States of America

The paper used in this book complies with the
Permanent Paper Standard issued by the National
Information Standards Organization (Z39.48–1984).

10 9 8 7 6 5 4 3 2 1

Contents

Contents

Series Foreword

The Greenwood Histories of the Modern Nations series is intended to provide students and interested laypeople with up-to-date, concise, and analytical histories of many of the nations of the contemporary world. Not since the 1960s has there been a systematic attempt to publish a series of national histories, and, as editors, we believe that this series will prove to be a valuable contribution to our understanding of other countries in our increasingly interdependent world.

Over thirty years ago, at the end of the 1960s, the Cold War was an accepted reality of global politics, the process of decolonization was still in progress, the idea of a unified Europe with a single currency was unheard of, the United States was mired in a war in Vietnam, and the economic boom of Asia was still years in the future. Richard Nixon was president of the United States, Mao Tse-tung (not yet Mao Zedong) ruled China, Leonid Brezhnev guided the Soviet Union, and Harold Wilson was prime minister of the United Kingdom. Authoritarian dictators still ruled most of Latin America, the Middle East was reeling in the wake of the Six-Day War, and Shah Reza Pahlavi was at the height of his power in Iran. Clearly, the past 30 years have been witness to a great deal of historical change, and it is to this change that this series is primarily addressed.

With the help of a distinguished advisory board, we have selected nations whose political, economic, and social affairs mark them as among the most important in the waning years of the twentieth century, and for each nation we have found an author who is recognized as a specialist in the history of that nation. These authors have worked most cooperatively with us and with Greenwood Press to produce volumes that reflect current research on their nations and that are interesting and informative to their prospective readers.

The importance of a series such as this cannot be underestimated. As a superpower whose influence is felt all over the world, the United States can claim a "special" relationship with almost every other nation. Yet many Americans know very little about the histories of the nations with which the United States relates. How did they get to be the way they are? What kind of political systems have evolved there? What kind of influence do they have in their own region? What are the dominant political, religious, and cultural forces that move their leaders? These and many other questions are answered in the volumes of this series.

The authors who have contributed to this series have written comprehensive histories of their nations, dating back to prehistoric times in some cases. Each of them, however, has devoted a significant portion of the book to events of the last thirty years, because the modern era has contributed the most to contemporary issues that have an impact on U.S. policy. Authors have made an effort to be as up-to-date as possible so that readers can benefit from the most recent scholarship and a narrative that includes very recent events.

In addition to the historical narrative, each volume in this series contains an introductory overview of the country's geography, political institutions, economic structure, and cultural attributes. This is designed to give readers a picture of the nation as it exists in the contemporary world. Each volume also contains additional chapters that add interesting and useful detail to the historical narrative. One chapter is a thorough chronology of important historical events, making it easy for readers to follow the flow of a particular nation's history. Another chapter features biographical sketches of the nation's most important figures in order to humanize some of the individuals who have contributed to the historical development of their nation. Each volume also contains a comprehensive bibliography, so that those readers whose interest has been sparked may find out more about the nation and its history. Finally, there is a carefully prepared topic and person index.

Readers of these volumes will find them fascinating to read and useful in understanding the contemporary world and the nations that comprise it. As series editors, it is our hope that this series will contribute to a heightened sense of global understanding as we embark on a new century.

Frank W. Thackeray and John E. Findling
Indiana University Southeast

Timeline of Historical Events

1492 Christopher Columbus lands in Haiti.

1791 Beginning of a bloody insurrection in the night of August 22–23, which marks the opening of the war for independence.

1793 Proclamation of general freedom, which is seen as a rapid culmination of the insurrectional movement initiated two years earlier.

1803 Death of Toussaint Louverture in Fort de Joux, France.
Victory of indigenous forces over French troops at the battle of Vertières.

1804 Haiti proclaims its independence from France on January 1.

1806 Assassination of Dessalines, the commander of the independence army. Upon Dessalines' death, Haiti splits into two rival states from 1806 until 1820. A western republic emerges under the leadership of Aléxandre Pétion. In the North, Henry Christophe founds a republic, which becomes a kingdom in 1811.

1820 Jean-Pierre Boyer, a mulatto general, unifies Haiti and then rules over the island until 1843.

1825 A convention is signed between Haiti and France under which France recognizes the Republic of Haiti. In return, Haiti agrees to pay an indemnity of 150 million francs. Haiti does not finish paying the debt until 1938.

1844 Division of the eastern part of the island under the presidency of Rivière Hérard. The Dominican Republic emerges as an independent state.

1849 Haiti becomes an empire under Faustin Soulouque, who has ruled the country since 1847 and continues to rule until 1859.

1860 An agreement called the Concordat is signed in Rome on March 28, 1860, and ratified by the Haitian senate on August 1, 1860.

1915 Landing in Haiti of American forces, which occupy Haiti until 1934.

1946 The Revolution of 1946 culminates in the departure of Élie Lescot.

1957 The Central Census Bureau (Bureau Central du Recensement) declares François Duvalier the winner of the September 22 election.

1964 François Duvalier proclaims himself president-for-life with self-attributed right to designate his successor.

1971 Transfer of power from François Duvalier to his son, Jean-Claude. The junior Duvalier pursues the dictatorial policies of his father.

1980 Visit in Haiti of Pope John Paul II, who advocates for change: "Some things have to change here."

1986 The Duvalier dynasty ends with the departure for France of Jean-Claude Duvalier.
Ascension to power of the military-dominated National Governing Council.

1990 Election of Jean-Bertrand Aristide as President of Haiti.

1991 A military coup deposes President Aristide in September.

1994 President Aristide is restored in office with the support of American troops.

1995 Election of René Préval as President of Haiti.

2000 Aristide is elected anew as President of Haiti.

2004   Aristide flees the country after weeks of uncertainty caused by dem-
         onstrations by unarmed students coupled with a separate armed in-
         surrection.
         After Jean Bertrand Aristide's departure for exile on February 29, 2004,
         judge Boniface Alexandre, the President of the Court of Cassation,
         Haiti's supreme court, took oath at the Office of the Prime Minister, in
         presence of the retiring prime minister, as Provisory President of the
         Republic of Haiti.

2007   Aristide remains in exile in South Africa. Under the presidency of
         René Préval, the country moves slowly toward stability. Widespread
         poverty fuels human insecurity and political violence.

1

The Pearl of the Antilles

SAINT-DOMINGUE

Haiti shares with other societies of the Caribbean some similar historical experiences. Migration is one of the founding elements of the population of the Caribbean. The Caribbean islands are largely populated by people from other places. The first inhabitants, the Arawak and the Caribs, came from the mainland of America. In the fifteenth century, the indigenous peoples welcomed the Europeans seeking to escape the economic problems of their continent and seeking new wealth in the Americas and the Caribbean.

Haiti differs from its Spanish and English Caribbean neighbors in its preservation of Haitian Creole as the language of the majority of the population, with French spoken by the educated minority.

Haiti is a small country of some 17,398.39 miles 28,000 km², including the island of La Tortue and La Gonâve. The country occupies the western third of the island of Quisqueya, which it shares with the Dominican Republic. It is located in the Caribbean Sea between Cuba and Puerto Rico. The terrain is mostly mountainous, and only 15 percent of the territory is relatively flat.

Haiti ranks among the world's poorest countries. Rural living standards have been declining because of the decline of agriculture. There are huge inequalities in wealth distribution between the countryside and the capital city

Map of Haiti. [Cartography by Bookcomp, Inc.]

of Port-au-Prince. The country is divided into nine departments: (1) the west; (2) the north; (3) the northwest; (4) the northeast; (5) the Artibonite; (6) the center; (7) the south; (8) the southeast; and (9) the Grand'Anse.

Haiti ranks among the countries with the highest densities in the world. The country enjoys climatic variations. The anticyclone systems known as Acores located in the North Atlantic represent the most important epicenter influencing the country as well as the rest of the Antilles. A seasonal anticyclone centered on the central plains of North America sends, during the boreal winter, a cool flux from the north to the south, known as *nordé* in Haiti. The *nordé* usually blows from November to March. This wind that translates the intervention of polar wind makes itself felt essentially in the north region of

Haiti. At the opposite direction, cyclones and tropical depressions represent seasonal manifestations of the rise of equatorial wind. Haiti finds itself in the zone prone to cyclones, of a primary direction East–West, which are formed and move themselves in the Caribbean basin. However, because of the high altitudes of central areas of the island and the small distance between mountain chains, the south, southeast, and the Grande Anse departments of Haiti are the most directly affected regions.

Among all of the administrative departments of Haiti, the northwest department suffers the greatest physical constraints on its development. Its underground is primarily composed of permeable limestone, and its rainfall is the lowest of the whole republic. As a result, this region is the driest of the country, a feature that often causes droughts and famine among the poorest communities. Already during the colonial era, it was difficult to convince settlers to inhabit this region (Saint-Méry, 1958, 713). The northwest region includes the land west of the crest of the Massif du Nord and of the northern tip of the Montagnes Noires (Chaîne des Cahos), including the Tortue Island.

Les Trois-Rivières is the most important river of the region and the second most important in the republic. The drainage of the river basin runs toward the northwest.

To the first inhabitants of the island, Saint-Domingue was an earthly paradise. At the arrival of Christopher Columbus, the island was covered with dense forests. The colony later produced immense wealth for the metropolis. Mining has yielded bauxite and some precious stones. Haitian forests provide hardwoods, dyewood, and charcoal. Two centuries ago, during the colonial era, Haiti was better known as the Pearl of the Antilles, a fertile paradise that brought its French plantation owners immense wealth produced by the sweat and suffering of enslaved Africans. In the era of French colonization, the precious woods of Saint-Domingue (acajou, campeachy, and Brazil wood) began to be exploited. This practice continued until the resources were more or less exhausted, around World War II. Tree cutting for the production of charcoal continues today. As a result, Haiti is a deforested nation with denuded mountainsides and many hungry citizens, desperate enough to take flimsy boats to try their luck elsewhere.

At the time of the discovery of the island, Quisqueya, whose territorial divisions were inspired by the hydrographic system, comprised several chiefdoms. La Magua, or the kingdom of the plain, contained all of the northeastern parts of the island. Le Marien, to the north, included the small provinces of Guayaba and Cayaha and was traversed in its western limits by the Hatiboniko River. The Xaragua included the west and the south. Le Managua occupied the center of the island.

At the dawn of the French Revolution, Saint-Domingue was the most prosperous colony in the Antilles. Its plantation economy gave priority to incomes and therefore to export crops such as sugar. In fact, by 1789, it had about 8,000 plantations producing crops for export (Geggus, 1989, 21). Saint-Domingue was the first producer of sugar in the entire world. In 1883 the sugar production of Saint-Domingue was almost equal to that of all the British Caribbean colonies put together (Lundhal, 1997, 62). Saint-Domingue was also producing roughly 60 percent of the coffee sold in the Western world, and by the end of the century, it held the worldwide production record for both sugar and coffee (Trouillot, 1990, 37). In addition to sugar and coffee, cacao, indigo, and precious wood flowed in a steady stream to France through port-towns. Following the French and American revolutions, the Haitian Revolution was the third major social cataclysm in the Western world that culminated in a permanent change in the national balance of power in favor of the exploited majority.

Despite its prerevolutionary affluence, its glorious revolutionary beginning, Haiti has become the poorest nation of the Western Hemisphere. Haiti is the site of the only successful slave revolt in the history of the Americas and was crucial in the development of the New World. However, since the Haitian Revolution, Haiti has been portrayed only as the place where tragedies take place. The media transmit news of violence to confirm their points of view that the Haitians can only poorly govern themselves. Foreign observers often use Haiti to lament the consequences of emancipation of African slaves. Conservatives allude to Haiti to interfere with independence movements, racial desegregation, and minority rights. Yet not enough scholarship is published examining the processes that hinder the advancement. Understanding of the current state of poverty requires taking cognizance of the larger social, political, and economic factors that shaped the colonial and post-independence periods in Haiti. This is the main task of this book.

The country's nine geographic departments are precariously linked. Roads are inadequate. The provision of public services reflects the kind of state that manages them. The Haitian state is weak. Its reach is minimal in the hinterland. It is especially implanted along road networks. The capital witnessed two periods of urban railroad: a horse-drawn network between 1878 and 1888 and a second period that started with steam-powered locomotives in 1897 and finished with the internal combustion in 1932. The first concession for the construction of a tramway was granted in 1876 to a group of financiers from New York, who founded the Railroad Company of Port-Au-Prince. The company ordered six open cars from the J. G. Brill Company of Philadelphia in October 1877 and inaugurated tram service on January 17, 1878. The first line, which linked the Croix des Bossales to Champ de Mars, was deemed the first railroad of the country.

On April 18, 1897, the Society of the Port-au-Prince Trams inaugurated the first line of its steam-powered tram, from the Portal of St.-Joseph through the streets of Quai and Miracles to the depot at Champ de March, and then to the Rue des Casernes. In the first six months, the tram transported 250,000 passengers. In 1905 the National Railroad of Haiti inaugurated a railroad between Port-au-Prince and Saint-Marc, located 62.13 miles or 100 kilometers to the north of the capital (U.S. Bureau of Foreign & Domestic Commerce, 1925, 283–284).

The majority of nonfood items are brought from Port-au-Prince to be sold in the countryside. Mountainous areas are nearly impossible to reach. The lack of freight trucks renders transport costs prohibitive for peasant producers. Most farmers sell their products to spéculateurs (licensed buying agents for coffee export companies) or merchants who have the cash to pay transport fees. Coffee spéculateurs are usually all men, and the transport system is run exclusively by men. Women are particularly active in trade. Although Creole is universally spoken, an educated minority speaks fluent French.

In the course of the nineteenth century and the beginning of the twentieth century, Haiti gradually lost its economic independence. The Haitian economy recorded long periods of stagnation because of economic isolation, foreign debts, the eruption of social conflicts, and ensuing political instability.

THE POLITICAL SYSTEM

Haiti is roughly equivalent in size to the state of Maryland and as of 2007 has a population of 8.5 million inhabitants. The majority of the urban population resides in the capital city of Port-au-Prince, where the main industries and employment are concentrated. In order to better understand the political system, it is necessary to consider the distribution of power between the three branches of government.

The Office of the President

The main source of executive power lies in the office of the president, which controls distribution of resources and public authority.

The Judiciary System

The Haitian legal system stems from Roman law as modified by French civil law of the Napoleon period. The judiciary system is divided into four main levels: justices of the peace, court of first instance, court of appeal, and the Supreme Court. At the first level, the Office of Justices of the Peace issues warrants and takes depositions. Judicial officials at this level enjoy jurisdiction over policy, adjudicate minor infractions, and refer major cases to higher judicial authorities. Haitian laws provide for a Justice of the Peace in each commune. Magistrates and public prosecutors are trusted with investigation of major cases, which are subsequently tried by judges in the first instance courts. Appellate courts hear cases referred from the first instance court. The highest level of the judicial system, the Supreme Court, handles constitutional and procedural issues and concerns.

The Legislature

The legislature makes the country's laws and ratifies the national budget and international treaties and conventions. Although Haiti's bicameral structure was first provided by the Constitution of 1816, the executive branch has consistently denied the legislature the independence and resources necessary to the fulfillment of their responsibilities. Overall, the legislature plays an important role only during periods of presidential succession and political transition.

Political Transition. A major political transition occurred on February 7, 1986. The Duvalier dynasty was finally hunted out of Haiti, after 30 years of a reign of terror, corruption, and mistrust toward the state. The Haitian population was jubilant. A state would be rebuilt on the ashes of the dictatorship of the Duvaliers. The Haitian people, empty-handed, but with the determination to live differently, with respect and dignity, defeated one of the most ferocious dictatorships in Haitian history. All hopes were permitted.

After the departure of Jean-Claude Duvalier in 1986, hopes for a democratic society were widespread, and a tacit consensus emerged around the commander-in-chief of the army who led the government of transition. Unfortunately, the illicit practices of oppression and enrichment of the leaders don't change. A post-authoritarian transition started with the fall and the departure of Jean-Claude Duvalier. Transition implies a change in the nature of the power, a new way of exercising, sharing, distributing power. It implies a new set of rules of the game. The new rules of the game were not accepted by the parties. Moreover, the mode of transition severely impacted democratic consolidation. Jean-Claude Duvalier passed along power to a military-dominated regime to starve off a popular uprising. The absence of a negotiated transition pact, though reflective of Haitian political culture, severely undermined democratic consolidation.

For 20 years the people of Haiti have wished for a sociopolitical regime to put an end to the mistrust of the population towards the state. Since 1986, civil society and popular sectors in Haiti have been pressing for greater efficiency and transparency in governance. Yet such goals have not been reached. This marks a departure from a mode of thinking prior to February 7, 1986, when it was thought that a dictator's departure would be sufficient to give birth to irreversible conditions for the emergence of a democratic and prosperous society. Reforming the Haitian state proved more difficult than expected. When asked about the prospects of institutional reforms in Haiti, many Haitians display both skepticism and fatalism. Others display profound skepticism of government and political parties, especially national government and national parties. These entrenched beliefs depress voting rates in national and local elections.

Since 1986, majority-based politics have strengthened the position of popular sectors. Rural dwellers increasingly participate in the electoral process. Thousands of civic groups have formed with the main raison d'être of assuming the management of the essential collective needs in the cities and the countryside. But in spite of their significant efforts, they have not managed to replace the state in its functions. Their failure is largely attributable to the extent of the needs, a lack of resources, and an inability to coordinate actions. The poverty of the population undermines the very foundation needed to institute a new manner of participation in the political life.

In spite of their tremendous contributions, civic groups have not solved the fundamental problems of the country. This makes it more pressing to strengthen the state not at the central, but at the local level. The restoration of the state therefore implies the strengthening of the local state as a necessary step to promote the general interest of the country.

Populism stirred briefly in the 1990s, when Aristide was elected as president. But his term was quickly interrupted by the army acting on behalf of elite interests. Conflict with the Haitian elite characterized this period. Aristide was returned to office in 1994 by the United States after pledging to engage in reconciliation, but conciliation was limited. Many Haitians who challenged the system have been repressed, at times brutally.

THE ECONOMIC SYSTEM

From 1492 to 1804, the colonial economy catered to the interests of metropolitan Spain and France. The colony produced items that could not be made in the old world, particularly sugar, coffee, cacao, and indigo. Sugar, for many centuries, remained the most profitable crop. However, sugar plantations and sugar-grinding mills were destroyed during the war of independence.

The indigenous population quickly dwindled, decimated by disease and hard manual labor. Seeking a highly remunerative plantation system, the French imported African slaves to replace the dying indigenous population.

Two Types of Economy

Today, there are two types of economy: a market economy that is crumbling and an increasingly precarious subsistence economy that is benefiting from the downfall of the market economy. This conflict opposes market-based operations and practices of the small independent farmer, who cultivates just enough for the survival of his own family. Signs of this dual market system emerged during the colonial period. Away from the plantations, the landowners permitted the establishment of gardens controlled by the slaves to produce food crops for the slaves' own survival *(places à vivres)*. The practice of *vivres communs* was necessary for the production of food crops. The land of the plains was generally reserved for the production of sugarcane, and the production of food crops took place in the mountains. However, even before the revolution, many *affranchis* (free people of color) and even slaves became attached to the *places à vivres* and demanded their own. For instance, one inspector noted in 1774 that the wives of those enrolled in the Legion of Equality (Légion de l'Egalité) created by the colonel Rigaud no longer wanted to work but demanded *places à vivres* like the others. It became very clear that liberty was linked to possession of a small plot of land.

In the post-independence era, a shift occurred from plantation agriculture to small, family-based landholdings. Many farmers continue to grow both cash crops for export and subsistence crops. The multiple crop system reflected the farmer's way to minimize risk by working to ensure that at least one crop would provide a decent harvest.

Today, more than 250,000 farmers grow coffee, although most grow a variety of other crops as well. Millions of Haitians make a living out of growing and marketing export and food crops.

The marketing of coffee is divided into two separate channels. The first channel is characterized by a large number of market ladies called Madam Saras who travel through communities in the plains and the mountains to purchase agricultural commodities, which are then sold in urban markets. These traders purchase coffee from producers and spéculateurs to resell in the local domestic market. The second track involves purchase of cash crops for export. The spéculateurs purchase from producers for resale to exporters. As a rule, exporters provide affiliated spéculateurs with cash advances at the beginning of the coffee harvest for the purchase of coffee from peasant producers.

The coffee exporters typically maintain their base of operation in the port cities, notably the capital city of Port-au-Prince. In addition to working with coffee exports, export houses can be involved in the processing of edible oil, textile manufacturing, production of beer and soft drinks, and some production of light industrial goods.

Although manufactured goods and imported products are brought and sold every day by small traders and shopkeepers, the majority of the trade takes place once or twice a week in a town's marketplace. Some vendors come far away to sell their goods.

THE SOCIAL SYSTEM

Newspapers play important roles in Port-au-Prince and other cities. Few, however, promote investigative journalism, partly because of the succession of civilian and military dictatorships. Haitian Creole programming played an important role in the awareness movement of the 1970s and 1980s, which contributed to the end of the Duvalier regime.

The civil registry includes two types of citizens with two different statuses: the city-dwellers and the peasants. The peasants live in the countryside and form the majority of the population, although urbanization is growing. The rural farm is typically very small. The 1971 census showed that 70 percent of farms measured less than 3.21 acres, and only 5.22 percent of farms measured more than 9.56 acres. For the Haitian farmer, access to land represents a considerable stake.

State and Society

In the middle of the twentieth century the state went through a difficult process of integrating new layers of Haitian society into the political system. These citizens seek participation in the game established by the entrenched elites. Their integration is made necessary by the crisis of legitimacy of the state. In 1946 and again in 1957, the emerging black middle class articulated demands and raised themes of skin color and black power. Debates on color questions and national unity between blacks and mulattoes were treated in ways that would not threaten the contours of the established state structures. This meant accommodation of the new elite by the entrenched one and monopoly of military and political resources by the new aspiring elite. The black movement of 1957 used generalized violence to lead to the elimination of political competitors such as Déjoie, Jumelle, and Fignolé and to a renewal of the political, administrative, and military personnel. This meant the replacement of traditional political cadres who enjoyed control over their own base by individuals of the petty bourgeoisie who did not have their own political means but depended politically on Duvalier. This also resulted in the inclusion in elite spheres of a group of people traditionally excluded from entry. These individuals were integrated through Duvalier's militia. The militia permitted individuals from popular classes to access a possibility of social promotion. This social promotion was financed mostly not by small group of entrenched elites, but by the poor majority. In the end, the crisis of the state was accommodated by the inclusion of the petty bourgeoisie in political structures rather than the economic systems. The political integration of the new actors occurred not through market expansion but through the bloated state apparatus.

Due to the heterogeneity of elite interests and the reliance on coercion in the political system, a structure is necessary to arbitrate differences between competing sectors. The Haitian presidency has historically been the main structure to arbitrate conflicts between sectors of the Haitian elite. At the same time, it serves as the highest political structure of the country. This authoritarian political regime was characterized by the absolute character of the political

power of the president. The methods of governing are arbitrary: physical coercion, torture, corruption. The system of one political party—and the prohibition of real political party opposition capable of articulating the interests
of social classes—limits mechanisms of political participation; participation
is restricted to the small group of the elite. Political power is embodied in the
power of an all-powerful personality. Many leaders build a following with the
hope of securing a cabinet post or some other advantage. This explains how
they perpetuate themselves in power.

CULTURAL CHARACTERISTICS AND RELIGION

Historically, the religion of the majority of Haitians has been voodoo, which
at times competed with and at other times adapted to Catholicism. Slaves hid
their religious beliefs, twinning their gods with Roman Catholic saints to give
an appearance of following the religion of their masters.

During the colonial era, voodoo was most prevalent in the west. It was a
cult that the colonizers associated with slaves from Aja-Fon, which they called
"Arada." It is true that the Arada, with the Nagos or Yoruba, were more numerous in the west than in the two other provinces. Indeed, the Haitian voodoo traces its origin from the polytheism Fon of the culture of Benin and other
African ethnicities, primarily Bantu, from Togo and Cameroun. It is the Rada
rhythm of Benin that constitutes the base of Haitian voodoo.

Moreover, the two voodoo songs preserved by Moreau de Saint-Méry and
Drouin de Bercy were in the Kikongo tongue. Slaves from Congo were the majority in the northern and southern provinces, where both Moreau and Drouin
lived. The Petro cult that acquired popularity in the era before the revolution
has some affinities with the Kongo culture. These two cults reflect the origins
of the two waves of slaves brought to Saint-Domingue. The first and largest
wave of slaves came primarily from Benin. The second wave of slaves came
primarily from the coast of Congo and Angola. These slaves were known
under the generic term of Congo.

Various authors sought to preserve the independence of Haiti by advising
earlier presidents against the interference of the pope. One such author, Henri
Grégoire, published *De la Liberté de conscience et de culte en Haïti* in 1824. In this
book he warned of the propagation of the Catholic religion in Haiti and the
difficulties and obstacles that this religion creates notably because of multiple
superstitions and the separation of the Christian churches in several competitive sects in Haiti. Grégoire dreamt of securing the emergence in Haiti of an in-
dependently constituted Church of Rome, based on the model of the Civilian
Constitution of the clergy, which was abolished by Consul Napoleon in 1802
and of which Grégoire was an advocate. As a result, he warned the President

of the Republic of Haiti, Boyer, against seizure by the papal church. In *De la Liberté*, Grégoire wrote, "Let us hope that the time will come where Haiti will have a sufficient clergy which is truly national, under the direction of the venerable archbishop of Santo Domingo and that of its collaborators. A free Haiti is an elevated beacon on the Antilles towards which the slaves and their masters, the oppressed and the oppressors turn their sights, the first sighing, and the other roaring."

The first protestant missionary arrived at Hispaniola in 1816 (Romain, 1985, 43). Later, the Protestants who migrated to Haiti resided and promoted the religion in the main towns of the country. The Protestants got involved in education in the sectors of the bourgeoisie. They created schools in the capital city of Port-au-Prince as well as in the largest Haitian towns.

Boyer instituted a system in which religion was strictly controlled and was often used as a political instrument in the hands of leaders. Civilian authorities named and revoked priests and decided the affairs of the cults. The French language was used by the church in administering sermons, which showed that the church was an instrument of established powers. Many of the foreign priests sought to deter the religion of the majority, voodoo. According to Bernard Maupoil (1988, 53–54), the African term *vodû* belongs to the Fon language of Dahomey and refers to the unknown, the mysterious.

In 1860 an agreement was signed between the Haitian state and the Vatican, which brought the Catholic Church back in the lap of the Roman hierarchy. The agreement further marginalized the position of voodoo in the public sphere. On the eve of the signing of the treaty between the Haitian government and the Vatican, the leadership of the country was entrusted to a small black and mulatto minority that was attached to exotic values and detached from the common folks while the vast majority of the people were confined in ancient traditions. There were few ties between the two groups, a factor that impeded mobilization of national forces for economic development.

The American occupation witnessed the expansion of Protestantism at the expense of both voodoo and Catholicism. Until 1928, Protestant Christianity was practiced by only a few notorious families and had been brought to only a few regions of Haiti. Since that time, the number of converts has increased considerably. To this was added the thousands of Haitians repatriated from Cuba who converted to reformed religions while abroad.

Various religious groups penetrated Haiti during the Duvalier era. Local religious persuasions ranged from voodoo, the indigenous Haitian religion, to Catholicism (which can be combined with voodoo) to Protestant sects. American missionary activity in Haiti significantly increased the number of Haitians converted to Protestantism. In recent years, Protestantism has been making significant inroads in the country. Many Haitians are flocking to fundamentalist churches. Protestant denominations, most of them evangelical or Pentecostal, have been winning converts. This means austerity in dress codes, abstinence from alcoholic beverages, and rejection of pleasures such as Carnival celebrations.

Various religious themes formed the basis of inscriptions on Tap Taps, the local transport system in Haiti. Although the cars are imported, a local industry has emerged to build the tops, seating areas, and decoration of the tap taps. Carpenters turn out handsome furniture not just for car seating but also for home use. The traditional architecture of many houses, particularly in Port-au-Prince, includes gingerbread houses. The beautiful interiors of the churches include incredibly detailed representations of saints on stained glass and expensive statues and icons, all heavily gilded.

The Haitian public school system provides free or low-cost education through the university level, but public schools are hindered by overcrowding, low salaries for teachers, and related relatively low teacher performance. The better-staffed private schools are attracting many Haitians who can afford to pay. Students typically have to pass difficult final exams for the bachelor's degree (baccalauréat) to enter the university.

THE HAITIAN CULTURE

One element that makes Haiti so attractive is its culture. Holy Week festivities, which occur annually, last several days and nights and attract thousands of national and international visitors. Pre-Lenten Carnival in Port-au-Prince and smaller cities are the most festive occasions in Haiti. As such, they have become a major tourist attraction. By Good Friday, the streets of cities small and large are replete with parade floats or bands on foot. In either case, dancers wear brightly colored, exuberant costumes, party all night, and escape the difficulties of their daily lives. Celebrants walk behind dance troops, singing the refrains of the special Carnival songs, while improvising. Others beat on impromptu percussion instruments. The lyrics can be harsh satires targeting prominent politicians with social commentaries.

Marching Rara bands walk from their turfs to other parts of the town. Although the Rara bands may look chaotic, they follow directives from the leader of the band, who chooses the route, blows on a whistle, and carries a special whip, which he hits from time to time to clear the path ahead. Another officer in each group is the *Majò Jon,* who performs a spectacular dance while twirling a baton. Each Rara band attracts followers of all ages as it parades along, and the groups compete with each other. The drum is always present in the Carnival celebration, and drummers play rhythms reflecting one of the three traditions: (1) Dahomey, (2) Rada, or (3) Petwo. The costumes reflect the traditions of the music and the Rara bands.

Haitians celebrate on many other occasions as well, such as New Year's Eve and the first of January in commemoration of the day of independence. The grand celebrations of New Year's Eve have always attracted and mesmerized even the most traveled tourist. The grandeur of the celebration reflects the depth of Haitian culture. Major celebrations take place in major cities and tourist sites. The smooth transition from the old to the new year is counted as a blessing. Most Haitians start the new year with specially prepared pumpkin soup (*soup joumou*). Haitians wear their best clothes, visit each other, and share best wishes for the year to come. Haiti has a centuries-old tradition called Krik Krak, in which Haitians share oral traditions. The storyteller begins with a ritual of warming up the audience by asking "Krik?" and the audience responds "Krak!"—and this is the cue to begin. This storytelling tradition embodies a collection of stories of wisdom that have been transmitted from generation to generation.

From the flamingoes of Lake Saumatre to the pine forests, to the fortress of the Citadel and Sans Souci, and to the deep Caribbean beauty of Haiti's beaches and cultural assets, the "pearl of the Antilles" has a wealth of delights and insights for the world to explore.

NOTE

1. Translation from documents published in French and Spanish will be my own unless otherwise noted.

REFERENCES

Geggus, David Patrick. 1989 "Sex ratio, age and ethnicity in the Atlantic slave trade: Data from French shipping and plantation records." *Journal of African History* 30, 23–44.

Grégoire, Henri. *De la Liberté de conscience et de culte en Haïti.* Paris: Baudouin, 1824.

L'Inspecteur des habitations du Sud aux commissaires civils, 20 mai 1774 A.N. DXXV-25 (261–31).

Lundhal, Mats. "The Haitian Dilemma Reexamined: Lessons from the Past in the Light of Some New Economic Theory." In Robert I. Rotberg, ed., *Haiti Renewed: Political and Economic Prospects.* Washington, DC: Brookings Institution Press and Cambridge, MA: The World Peace Foundation, 1997.

Maupoil, Bernard. *La géomancie à l'ancienne côte des esclaves.* Paris: Institut d'ethnologie, 1988.

Romain, Poisset C. *Le Protestantisme dans la Société Haitienne.* Port-au-Prince, Haiti: Henri Deschamp, 1985.

Saint-Méry, Moreau de. *Description topographique, physique, civile, politique et historique de la partie française de l'Isle de Saint-Domingue.* Volume 2. Paris: Société de l'Histoire des Colonies Françaises et Librairie Larose, 1958.

Trouillot, Michel-Rolph. *Haiti, State against Nation: The Origins and Legacy of Duvalierism.* New York: Monthly Review Press, 1990.

U.S. Bureau of Foreign and Domestic Commerce. "Haiti: General Features of the Republic." In *Trade Promotion Series,* no. 5, pp. 283–284. Washington, DC: U.S. Bureau of Foreign and Domestic Commerce, 1925.

2

Early Haiti (1492–1804)

The first period of Haitian history, which extends from the arrival of Christopher Columbus to the independence of Haiti, is the period of initial settlement. The Republic of Haiti and the Dominican Republic share one island in the Greater Antilles. The first inhabitants of the island, the native peoples of various tribes, notably Arawak and Taino, once called it Haiti, Bohio, or Quisqueya, which meant "Great Land" or "Mountainous Land." The reference to mountains derives from the domination of the territory by rugged mountain chains, which are interspersed with plains and valleys. Variations exist in the distribution of rainfalls because of the country's principal mountains.

The island was later designated Hispaniola by Christopher Columbus. When Columbus, at the time of his first journey in 1492, took possession of the island in the name of the king of Spain, this territory was home to, according to various estimates, about a million Amerindians (Saint-Méry, 1958, 6). The native peoples were tragically decimated by Spanish colonization (through coerced labor, persecution, and various illnesses). Christopher Columbus was particularly brutal in the subjugation of the island. The "discoverer" of America ruled the colony in a tyrannical fashion and demonstrated significant greed. In the decades following Columbus' arrival, between 12 and 20 million native peoples were killed or fell victim to diseases brought in by the Spaniards. Smallpox ended the lives of some 200,000 people. After the massacre perpetuated by

Ovando in 1507, the population was reduced to 60,000 Amerindians, who did not take long to succumb under the weight of servitude.

Anxious to enrich themselves as quickly as possible before returning to Spain, the first Spanish colonizers took over landed properties and coerced into labor the native peoples who lived on such land under the principle of *repartimiento*, a system of coerced labor in which the indigenous population was subjected to low-paid and unpaid work during a set period of time every year. The indigenous worker would work under the supervision of a Spanish overseer to complete work in agriculture, public infrastructure or gold mining. In particular, the extraction of gold by means of coerced labor proved rewarding for Spain, yielding 500,000 gold ecus per year. As the Indian population was being decimated, the Spaniards brought in African slaves from Guinea, the Congo Dahomey, and Senegal as early as 1502 to replace the native peoples in the plantations and gold mines. The slave trade brought new blood to the plantations at the rate of 33,000 slaves imported annually (Saint Méry, 198). Through this pattern of forced migration, Hispaniola was repopulated

Most of the slaves can be traced back to Dahomey, the present Benin. They were brought in as the autochthonous population was being decimated. Some native peoples mixed with the new arrivals from Europe and Africa. By 1530, the autochthonous population had practically disappeared as a distinct group. The wealth of continental colonies such as Mexico and Peru quickly overwhelmed the interests of the Spaniards in the Antilles. As a result, in spite of the arrival of several thousands of Spanish immigrants and the introduction of dozens of thousands of African slaves in the nineteenth century, the population of Hispaniola around 1600 remained at under 20,000 inhabitants, who were concentrated on the oriental part of the island, which is today the Dominican Republic.

The Spaniards founded several towns in Hispaniola, including Bayaha in 1503 (today the Haitian town of Fort Liberté). This town was later renamed Puerto Real. Under French colonization, the town bore other names, including Fort-Royal and Fort-Dauphin, and it is the captivating historic site of Fort-Liberté. Constructed around 1731 by order of Louis XV, King of France, the fort still reflects a perfect combination of aesthetic genius, utility, and efficiency. Successive changes in the name of this town reflected the shift of power from Spanish to French colonization. It was in this town that Haiti's first declaration of independence was redacted on November 29, 1803.

In the seventeenth century, some French buccaneers began to settle on the island neighboring La Tortue. These were pirates and corsairs who routinely attacked the Spanish galleons that escorted precious metals from the rich province of Mexico to Spain. As Spanish settlers' interest in the declining productivity of their gold mines began to decline, the French colonists began to outnumber them on the western part of the island. The first French were preoccupied by the natural salt marshes, which could be found on the coast of Saint-Domingue. They prepared the salt and bartered it with the English for other goods. Their main establishment was created at the mouth of the Artibonite River in a location called Grande-Saline. The Amerindians once called the Artibonite River Hattiboniko. Its total basin was 26,246.71 feet At Grande-Saline, throughout the eighteenth century, they maintained a community of salt processors, recruited haphazardly and living without any contact with the society of planters (Aubin, 1910, 282).

A burgeoning population of some 3,000 French buccaneers became very visible, attracting the attention of the French government. On August 31, 1640, the French buccaneers expelled their rival Englishmen from La Tortue and disembarked on the northern section of the island of Hispaniola. The following year, a Huguenot named Le Vasseur occupied the Island of La Tortue at the behest of France. The following year, the knight of Fontenay took possession of the western section of Hispaniola in the name of King Louis XIII. The plantations of coffee, tobacco, cocoa, and indigo prospered under the tropical climate of the island. However, the culture of sugarcane, the real white gold of the XVIII century, prevailed. Coffee would not be introduced until 1725 (D'Ans, 1987, 155). The variety was *Arabica typica,* and this remains the dominant plant cultivated to date. Coffee is grown at altitudes ranging from 984.25 to 5,249.34 feet above sea level, mostly in humid mountains. Coffee plants are usually intercropped with fruit trees and food crops. The arrival of Brazil in the international market and the related decline of coffee prices served to depress production as of the late 1800s.

In 1697 King Louis XIV secured the western part of Hispaniola legally through the treaty of Ryswick, which ended the war of the League of Augsburg. The treaty of Ryswick divided the island into two colonies, Saint-Domingue and Santo Domingo.

During the French period, the western part of the island was at the outset divided into three distinct divisions, the north, west, and south. The French colonizers first became interested in the south of Haiti when the occupation of the north (particularly the Cap) and west (the cul-de-sac) of Haiti was already very advanced. Every division was subdivided in quarters (*quartiers*), and every quarter into parishes, and each parish into canton. The territorial divisions were clearly delineated, and therefore the surface of each division was clearly known.

The colony of Saint-Domingue represented in the eyes of metropolitan France a purely economic value. The plantations exported their agricultural products through port-towns to France and received merchandise, manufactured products, and machinery in return.

The culture of sugarcane on large estates and the growth of coffee production yielded economic prosperity and resulted in the expansion of the colony of Saint-Domingue, which quickly became the most prosperous of the French overseas possessions. However, the colony served the interests of foreign consumers, not its own. The social structure of the colony was attuned to metropolitan needs and objectives.

Many researchers of sugar plantations believe in inextricable links between production, capital concentration, and coercive labor practices. The introduction of slavery to meet labor-intensive process in the sugarcane production was important because it constituted a matrix of the practice of power that remained entrenched in Haitian society after independence.

There were two forms of dividing the colonial territory: the territorial dimension and the religious-administrative division. Under the territorial dimension, three provinces were created: the north, the west, and the south. A parallel religious-administrative division emerged with the establishment of the parish, For instance, the parish of Les Cayes was created in 1720 in the southern province. (A parish is a territorial division of the Roman Catholic Church, without any relation to political or administrative units.) This parish included at the end of the eighteenth century some 1,536 whites, 300 freed slaves, and 12,000 slaves (Hua-Buton, 1983, 7). These figures exclude, however, the population of the town of Cayes. At the dawn of the French Revolution, Saint-Domingue was the most prosperous colony in the Antilles and the world's largest sugar producer. On the eve of the French Revolution, Saint-Domingue produced close to three-fourths of the world trade of sugar. In 1788 the colony's external trade, estimated at 214 millions francs, was superior to that of the United States.

Saint-Domingue was also the most populated colony. A census was conducted on Saint-Domingue, which became French through the Treaty of Ryswick. From 8,000 inhabitants, of which 4,500 were whites, in the first census implemented in 1687, the population of Saint-Domingue reached 173,000 in 1753 and 520,000 in 1791. The distribution of this population was 40,000 whites, 30,000 *Affranchis* (free people of color), and 450,000 slaves, which reflected the expansion of the plantations that relied on slavery. Therefore, the social structure was made up of three social groups: the colonizers, the *Affranchis*, and the slaves.

However, the social stratification of Saint-Domingue was based on race, which meant that the *Affranchis* shared with the African slaves a common interest in changing this system. They were excluded from many professions, forbidden from wearing certain clothes and from carrying a sword, and prohibited from sitting among whites in public places such as theaters and churches. In many part of Saint-Domingue, the *Affranchis* outnumbered the whites. Wealthy *Affranchis* possessed many plantations and slaves. Yet they lacked political equality with the white colonists.

There were also the Petits Blancs. The term Petits Blancs refers to the poor, working class white population of Saint-Domingue. They were the immediate competitors of the much wealthier *Affranchis*. However, the wealth of the *Affranchis* did not translate into power. This stratification system became a source of the trouble that would later ruin the colony.

The *Affranchis* formed a coordinated group, which defended its group interests. They worked in all sorts of small professions or held small commerce in colonial towns for they lacked access to capital to enter the commercial production of crops. This group fought for equality with the whites. An uprising of *Affranchis* occurred in Saint-Marc, Verrettes, and Petite-Rivière de l'Artibonite. Instigated by Savary, the main leader of the *Affranchis* in this period, the uprising aimed, as declared in a text titled "Resistance to Oppression," to "ensure the continuation of the system of shops (système des ateliers), the repression of all actions contrary to the maintenance of this system, the maintenance of respect that slaves owe to free men and obedience to their masters" (Ardoin, 1958, 65).

The refusal of the dominant class of colonizers to grant equality led the *Affranchis* to form an alliance with the slaves to overthrow French rule.

The growth of the population of *Affranchis* is the result of an important French immigration, which grew by at least 60,000 from 1740 to 1791. It also reflected the mixing of the population due to low proportion of women in the white population and the massive introduction of African slaves in the colony. The number of Africans imported in Saint-Domingue between 1681 and 1791 is estimated at 860,000 (Curtin, 1975). The importation of slaves in the eighteenth century not only contributed to the important growth of the servile population, but also countered the excess of deaths over births that seems to have characterized for a long time the demographic regime of African slaves.

France imposed severe restrictions on commerce between Saint-Domingue and British commercial outlets in Jamaica, Dutch buyers in Curacao, and North American trade houses. Saint-Domingue could trade only with France, which held the exclusive power to set prices.

In the period between 1763 and 1770, there were sporadic uprisings of coffee growers against trade restrictions imposed by France. The governor of Saint-Domingue then reinstated the colonial militia dominated by sugar-growing officers. The trade restrictions were not lifted until 1784, after intense mobilizations of white merchants and landowners. The increasing involvement of white planters and merchants reflected not a consciousness of the interests of Saint-Domingue per se but an awareness of their own collective interests as planters. In this sense, the white planters differed from the freed men and Creole-born slaves whose only home was Saint-Domingue. The Creole ideology is marked above all by the conscience of the adherence to one soil: that of Saint-Domingue. This feeling of identity, originating in birth in the islands, was at the origin of the first nationalist demands by the whites, to which the *Affranchis* and Creole slaves later adhered too. The Creole persons proclaimed that the colony belonged to them more than to the whites because they would not leave after they made their fortunes. Among the *Affranchis*, there was also this obsession with property, which in addition to being desirable, was also a guarantee of freedom and social standing. In particular, the mulattoes of this group wanted the independence to control the monopoly over property. They were the first to raise inheritance rights and to attempt to purchase land at low prices or to acquire it through often falsified papers.

The African-born slaves were mistrustful of the Creoles, who were more able to obtain the status of *Affranchis*. This suspicion was also grounded in the fact that the *Affranchis* were the guarantor of individual safety against insurrections against slavery. The *Affranchis* were part of the militia and the army of Saint-Domingue, which often hunted down the black maroons (fugitive slaves). Their role was to defend the system. It is only when the defense of their collective interests dictated an alliance to overthrow slavery that the *Affranchis* and Creole-born slaves found allies among surviving Amerindians and African-born slaves to engage in the war of independence. Pre-revolutionary Haiti is replete with stories of survival and strength. Discontent with the metropolis was also rising among Indian survivors and African slaves. It bears noting here that slavery necessarily results in constant resistance of the slaves from the first moment of captivity. This resistance can take multiple forms. An Indian chief (cacique) named Hatuey was witness to the atrocities committed by the Spanish Conquistadors against his people, the Arawak and Taino Amerindians. Hatuey and his followers fled to Cuba to escape persecution and a death sentence imposed upon him by the Spanish crown. After some years of living clandestinely in Cuba, Hatuey was captured and sentenced to death. Cacique Hatuey is honored in Cuba. The story of Cacique Hatuey's execution, as originally recorded by Father Bartolommeo de las Casas, is part of the oral tradition in the eastern provinces of Cuba.

The Spanish colonial forces established on the eastern side of Quisqueya several commercial towns as commerce and industry blossomed. The Spanish economy was also based on the rearing of cattle and horses. On both sides of the island, the Spaniards overthrew the political hegemony of the chiefs, or cacique. This reversal met with some opposition. In the Artibonite region of Haiti, an Amerindian chief named Cacique Kaonabo launched a holy resistance against foreign oppression.

Another indigenous leader named Henri took refuge in the mountains with Indian and black comrades and succeeded in maintaining his independence for 13 years. This marked the beginning of marronnage, which refers to the flight of slaves to the forest (a derivative of the Spanish term *cimarron*, which means wild). These maroons established in the mountains a type of rural economy based on family farms. For the maroons, freedom meant control of their gardens, agricultural tools, and herds. They left the plains, where they had engaged in plantation work, for the hills, where they carved out secure individual parcels and engaged in farming of foodstuff and coffee. The movement from sugar production in the plains to coffee farming in the mountains was driven by the search for secure ownership titles.

The colony had close to 600,000 inhabitants, of which 40,000 were *Affranchis*, essentially mulattoes, and 500,000 were black slaves. The *Affranchis* did not have the same rights as the colonists but enjoyed a certain ease and were sometimes slaveholders. The inability of the *Affranchis* to secure political rights in proportion of their wealth and tax burdens ultimately led to an alliance with the slaves to overthrow slavery. It is now appropriate to examine the relations between Saint-Domingue and France.

Saint Domingue's plantations produced enormous profits for the colonists while satisfying the rising European demand for sugar. Plantation agriculture was a commercial endeavor exclusively aimed at massive exports to French and European markets. It concentrated on a small number of rare products that were highly profitable. This colonial plantation system was highly capitalized and required investments in infrastructure such as the establishment of indigo, coffee, and most importantly, sugar mills, which produced semi-refined sugar. Owners of plantations and processing infrastructures made huge profits, which were often sent to Europe. The slaves, who produced enormous wealth, lived in abject poverty. They were allowed to engage in a parallel system of small-scale subsistence agriculture for their own survival. In the end, the slaves mobilized to establish self-governance on their own terms and to reap the fruits of their own labor.

In 1791 there were roughly 40,000 whites, 30,000 freed slaves, and 450,000 slaves in the colony of Saint-Domingue. The number of slaves has been historically underreported because of a colonial tax that was imposed on this group. Not only were the colonizers always declaring fewer slaves than they had, but also they led the slaves to be afraid of the census and to not participate through various tricks. In spite of these clarifications, this racial distribution clearly indicates the expansion of the plantations, which accounted for the prosperity of Saint-Domingue.

The fate of the island was influenced by the French Revolution. The French Revolution raised very quickly the problem of the equality of free colored people with the whites and then the issue of the abolition of slavery. On May 15, 1791, in Paris, the National Assembly timidly granted the right to vote to some free men of color. The decree of April 4, 1792, provided citizenship to property-owning free men of color. These measures worried the white colonists of Saint-Domingue, who dreamed of proclaiming their independence to preserve their island from seditious ideas coming from Paris. The measure did not satisfy either free men of color like Vincent Ogé, who were demanding equality with the colonists. In 1790 the *Affranchis* engaged in political agitation. Ogé organized a political movement of mixed-blood men who overtly aspired to political equality. The colonial government refused to release the real number of the *Affranchis* as a means to undermine their political claims.

The wealthy and propertied slaveholders often referred to as the *grand Blancs* in the colony, provoked an insurrection with the executions of mulatto rebels Ogé and Chavannes. These executions led the *Affranchis* to radicalize their positions. Utter confusion reigned among the white colonizers as the *Affranchis* in a meeting at Mirebalais and the slaves at Bois Caiman succeeded in acquiring a certain level of organization.

The magician named Boukman, surrounded by lieutenants, presided over a ceremony that marked the beginning of a bloody insurrection in the night of the August 22–23, 1791. The main historical text that mentioned Boukman himself was that of Ardouin, which like the work of Dalmas, demonstrated that by the time of the ceremony, the conspiracy was well-organized. The importance of the ceremony was that it anointed a political movement that had reached maturity. After Boukman, the most important leader of the ceremony was Jean-François.

David Lee Child captured this series of events in these terms: "The mulattoes flew to arms, and they were soon joined by the slaves generally. Then, indeed, commenced a bloody revolution" (Child, 1971, 68). Many Southern states in the United States banned the importation of slaves from Saint-Domingue in fear that slaves from that colony would pass on the values of black emancipation to their own slaves.

The free men of color who were angered by the execution of several of their peers, including the famous Ogé, combined forces with the black insurgents. They soon received the support of Toussaint Louverture, who joined the camp of the rebel as a medical officer.

Toussaint was born in Saint-Domingue, on the Bréda plantation at Haut-du-Cap on May 20, 1746. Therefore, Toussaint was not a *bossale (Africa-born slave)*, but a Creole. In this sense, he shared many of the concerns of the Creoles for increasing autonomy from France. Alfred de Lacaze (1860, 38–44) reports that a rigorous punishment drove Toussaint to flee his first master. As a result a captain of the French merchant marine named Bailly bought him to make him his coachman. Lacaze added, "His master taught him how to read, and in response to his integrity and humanity, made him commander of his estate. This is how one day a black man would appear with mission to revenge his offended race. Toussaint was freed in 1776."

In a short period of time, Toussaint's ability to strategize and lead troops became apparent. He was elevated from aide-de-camp to the rank of general, first fighting under Biassou, a major leader of the army of independence and then serving as a commander of his own troops. Dissatisfied with French rule, Toussaint later moved to the eastern side of the island and made an alliance with the Spanish crown, which was also at war against France.

Portrait of Toussaint L'Ouverture (1743–1803), Haitian revolutionary and statesman. Photo by Time Life Pictures/Mansell/Time Life Pictures/Getty Images.

After the news of the execution of Louis XVI and Paris' declaration of war against Madrid, Toussaint accepted the colonel's rank in the Spanish army, which had joined the fight of blacks against the French republic (July 9, 1793). He became general of the king's armies and established his headquarters at Marmalade.

On March 28, 1792, the Legislative Assembly of France granted equality of right to all free men but this half measure came too late to stop the insurrection. The insurrection turned into a social revolution. Toussaint led his troops to repeated victories over French forces. Toussaint resisted the temptation to join the French forces until given leave after his duty to Spain was honorably fulfilled.

The British invasion, in September 1793, hastened the pace of events. When Toussaint learned that the French government had enacted general liberty for all slaves (August 29, 1793), he sought to take advantage of the situation. Meanwhile, a notorious citizen of Jérémie, Saint-Domingue, deplored the British occupation. Thomas-Alexandre Dumas was born on March 25, 1762, in Jérémie, Saint-Domingue, as the natural son of Citizen Alexandre Antoine Davy de la Pailleterie, former extraordinary commissioner of artillery, and Marie-Césette (a black woman). After moving to France, Dumas never returned to his country, but it was always on his mind. At the end of 1795 he wrote to the Minister of war Aubert du Bayet, "As head of household without any fortune in France, I sympathize with the destiny of those who have been burnt and who lost it all, which is my case as the British are in my house in Jérémie." In the first half of the twentieth century, inhabitants of Jérémie went on pilgrimage in the steps of Dumas every January 6 (the day of feast of the kings in Haiti), and they liked to bathe in the river La Guinaudée, at the location called "the bath of the Dumas."

LE COMTE DE MONTE-CRISTO

The confinement of Dumas in the Calabrian jails upon his return from Egypt, the ingratitude of the general's friends, the remaining life of his father le Marquis of the Pailleterie, who returned to France to recover his castle and his lands, are the sources of the novel *The Count of Monte-Cristo* by Dumas's son and namesake, Alexandre Dumas. It is important to note that the brother of the Marquis, the great uncle of Thomas-Aléxandre Dumas, owned a pier *(embarcadère)* at Monte-Christi, to the east of Cap-Haitian.

When a convention abolished slavery in all French lands by means of decree on February 4, 1794, many local planters did not hesitate to call on the English for help. Three months later, in May 1794, 7,500 British soldiers invaded Saint-Domingue from the neighboring Jamaica and seized the capital city of Port-au-Prince the following month. The British forces secured an alliance with the white planters with the understanding that the British would reinstate slavery and strip property-owning men of color of citizenship in exchange for white planter support. According to Buckley (1979), abolitionists were aware of the British campaign in Saint Domingue and were duly embarrassed. One pamphlet by abolitionist Garrison (cited in American Anti-Slavery Society, 1839, 4) noted that the English "came not to assist [blacks] in maintaining their rights, but to drive out the French, to claim the colony, and to endeavor... to re-establish and perpetuate the system of [slavery] which was at this moment abolished."

In the face of the English landing, the French official Polvérel, who had delegated authority in the south to André Rigaud and in the west to Hughes

Monbrun and Pinchinat, all three men of color, relied on the oldest freed men to resist for some time with success. On June 3, 1794, he resolved to abandon Port-Au-Prince, besieged by the English, to escape in the company of Léger-Félicité Sonthonax to Jacmel. Sonthonax was sent to the colony of Saint-Domingue as part of the Revolutionary Commission. In spite of his command of 7,000 French troops he could not control the situation, which ultimately evolved in favor of the slaves.

The English were soon defeated and were nearly decimated by a yellow fever epidemic to which the blacks seemed almost invulnerable. Hundreds of sugar and coffee plantations were destroyed. Toussaint Louverture's army rapidly gained territory by fighting a guerilla war with lightning attacks. The colonists were slaughtered by the thousands. This was the beginning of a long and murderous war of liberation. In total, the Revolution of Saint-Domingue would kill 45,000 British soldiers (during their occupation, from the end of August 1793 until August 1798), 46,000 French soldiers, and 10,000 colonists. As for the nonwhites, a third of some 530,000 slaves and freemen of 1789 probably disappeared in 1804 (Gragnon-Lacoste, 1877, 202).

By 1795, Toussaint had returned to the French forces, where he was promoted to the rank of colonel. In March 1796, the city of the Cape having rebelled, the French general, prisoner of the mulattoes, was delivered by Toussaint. As a result, Toussaint was elevated to lieutenant's rank to the general government of the colony (March 31, 1796) and then to general of the division (August 17, 1796). He then became the instrument of colonial power: at his order, all blacks laid down their weapons. The English still held some outposts in the north and the west, but he hunted them out. Peace with Spain and the expulsion of Jean-François marked the return to calmness on the island.

The historical evidence reveals the behavior of Toussaint and the events that led Toussaint to expel Jean-François from Saint-Domingue. At some point, Toussaint was indeed a pro-Spanish royalist. At that time, the slaves believed that Louis XVI wanted to grant them three days off every week and that only the colonizers refused to allow this to occur. This pushed the black chief to the Spanish camp. When he realized that he had made a mistake and when he became disenchanted with the schemes of Jean-François, he had the stroke of genius to declare himself for France and the Republic, an act that marked the beginning of his career. He then proceeded to expel Jean-François from the island.

The history of Jean-François is interesting itself. Before he joined Spanish forces, he was a maroon in 1791. In a Spanish document dated 1793, Biassou painted Jean-François as a poor fugitive (Archivo General de Indias).

Jean-François continued his career in the Spanish army. The Garífunas of Livingston, which is also called Labuga, assigned the foundation of their city to Marcos Sanchez Diaz, French-speaking black officer from Saint-Domingue, who arrived in 1802 at the head of a black Caribs group, to settle in this site. Rey (2001, 2005) has recovered at Livingston the traces of the Franzua and Francisco families, who are the direct descendents of Jean François, one of the fathers of the Haitian Revolution. The founding French Negro of Livingston, Marcos Sanchez Diaz, was seen as a Haitian mystical figure. His direct descendants even specify that he was a highly positioned officer in Saint-Domingue with the grade of major.

In Saint-Domingue, the insurgents of the north (named as French negroes by the Spaniards) taken by Jean François and Biassou after the death of Boukman enrolled in the service of the Spanish crown in 1793, against revolutionary France, which then held power on the island. Sonthonax, sent by the convention to establish the authority of the French Revolution, finally took the initiative to abolish slavery in August 1793 and was facing an increasingly deleterious situation: English invasion on the island; harassment by Spanish troops and their black allies; and royalist colonists, or Jacobins, opposed to equal rights for the mulattos and the blacks.

Toussaint joined the abolitionist Sonthonax and France while abandoning black chiefs Jean François and Biassou and their Spanish allies. He hunted these men out of the island in 1795 on the account of France and didn't linger in affirming his power on the island. He dealt secretly with the English so that they would also leave the place in 1798. On the orders of the crown of Spain, Jean François and Biassou reached the coast of Cuba, to take service there. But the Spanish authorities on this island refused to let them disembark in fear that they would ally with the blacks of Cuba against the crown. While entering with the boats of Aristizabal in the port of the Havana in January 1796, General Las Casas ordered, on request from the Township of La Havana, that the boats that transported François, Biassou, and Narciso throw the anchor as far as possible to avoid all contact with the blacks and their leaders, with the aim of stationing them in an isolated place between Casa Blanca and the Castillo del Morro, at the entry of the port (Franco, 1963, 10; 1965). The Spaniards then decided to use them in Central America, where the black presence was nearly nonexistent in comparison with the Antilles, to defend the coasts of the Reino of Guatemala against English incursions launched from Belize and Jamaica. These black chiefs from Saint-Domingue and their troops, named French Negroes, were incorporated in 1796 to the militia of Trujillo, Honduras. Such black elite troops accustomed to armed struggles against colonial powers in the Antilles, particularly against the French in Saint-Domingue, proved themselves very quickly in the service of Spain in Central America.

In 1797, Sonthonax named Toussaint governor for his loyalty. This promotion made Toussaint the effective commander in chief. This gave Toussaint the opportunity to work toward a new world order, one with authority, work, and order but led by black power. The whites refused to have an upheaval of the hierarchy of power. They wanted to have the whites above the blacks, property owners above the agricultural workers, the metropolis above the colony. Toussaint wanted a different distribution of power in Saint-Domingue, where the black man would become his own master.

Contrary to Laveaux, Toussaint Louverture was keen to develop trading relations with England and the United States as a means to reduce colonial dependence on France. His position was widely shared by white planters who routinely engaged in illegal and profitable trade with the United States. The newly independent United States paid a relatively competitive price for goods from Saint-Domingue, while not insisting on exclusive trade.

When the French Directoire considered the consignment of armed forces to restore colonial order, Toussaint answered these threats by making it clear that if the French government intended to restore slavery, the blacks of Saint-Domingue would defend themselves.

State policy sought to discourage the fragmentation of large properties. Local courts promoted enforcement of a decree passed by Toussaint Louverture on May 7, 1801, that forbade the legalization of sales or transfers of ownership on properties of less than 159.38 acres. The Toussaint Louverture regime received the support of an emerging social class in the colony: the newly freed. This new group witnessed class ascendancy by means of their positions as renters of state land (*fermiers de l'état*). Moreover, several black generals acceded to property ownership in addition to their positions as renters of state land. These included Dessalines, Magny, and Toussaint.

Toussaint also published a regulation in 1800 concerning the operation of the plantations that subordinates viewed as a return to the slavery because it reintroduced coerced labor. Toussaint sought to implement an organized system of cultivation, which depended on coerced labor. In this system, enlisted soldiers became freeholders but engaged in small-scale farming on large estates controlled by their former superiors in the Haitian army. This resulted from the enactment of a coercive practice, the "caporalisme agraire," which subjected the emerging peasantry to a system of social organization where cultivators were assimilated to soldiers in a regiment and were, therefore, prohibited from leaving assigned plantations.

This practice derived from a military conception of society, which resulted in a true division of the territory into sections for close supervision. In this system, society was assimilated to the military model. National laws also prohibited a Haitian from traveling outside the province of birth without permission from superiors. Cultivators were often working under the surveillance of a military guard. Agricultural work was transformed into an obligation. The inherent limitations attached to this form of liberty were presented as a consequence of assuming freedom: intense work by farmers who remained tied to agricultural production; rigid discipline for farmers; and restrictions imposed on freedom of circulation and exchange. All of these restrictions were justified in a statement in the preamble of the "règlements de culture" issued by Toussaint on October 12, 1800: "the safety of liberty demands it." This is a crucial period in Haitian history. The omnipresence of the army meant the invasion of the state by the Haitian military. The genesis of the state against civil society began here. The purported superiority of the military over the civilian quickly generated hatred of military activities among the peasantry. This hostility of the civilian toward the military was also founded in the controversial role of the army as the guarantor of social discipline. The social order was repressive. The colonial army had two main tasks: surveillance and punishment. It guaranteed the existence of the state.

Toussaint reproached a large number of farmers on the agricultural dwellings. The proclamation of November 25, 1801, stipulated, "It is necessary that everyone knows that there is no other means to live peacefully and respectfully than through work, an assiduous work."

The war of the south contributed to further weaken discipline on the plantations, and the defeat of Rigaud, which occurred in August 1800, led the winners to impose on the farmers of the south the regimen established in the rest of the colony. Those living in the towns were forcibly returned to the plantations under the surveillance of the gendarmerie and military authorities.

These measures, which were against the interests and habits already entrenched in the customs, were poorly received, and an opposition quickly developed. Those formerly mobilized and armed by the mulattoes in 1792 were little inclined to retake work on the plantations. Less than two months after his arrival in Cayes, Toussaint Louverture, who sought to address the abandonment of production and the decline of the economy, enacted a new rule for production that assimilated managers, conductors, and cultivators to military personnel (Règlement de culture 12 Octobre 1801).

In Toussaint's view, the independence of the country necessarily required its enhancement: "agriculture is the support of the governments, because it procures the trade, the ease and abundance, the birth of the arts and the industry as it occupies all arms" (Règlement de culture 12 Octobre 1801).

Many cultivators submitted to this new regimen. However, these coercive practices upon newly freed slaves provoked the recrudescence of marronage in post-independence Haiti. The irresistible tenacity with which farmers asserted their rights to settle wherever they want posed a challenge to Toussaint and later to Dessalines. In the end, the vast majority of the farmers opted for small-scale production corresponding to their own needs. In the end, from all of the cash crops of their heydays of the colony, only coffee survived in the typical Haitian peasant economy. The repeated outbursts of a prolonged war of independence undermined the application of restrictive laws as farmers view individual freedom as embodied in self-ownership of a parcel of land.

Later, the agrarian laws of Pétion and Boyer confirmed this triumphant agrarian individualism.

By August 1800, Toussaint had concretized his project then to unify the island. At the head of an army of 40,000 men, surrounded by his favorite lieutenants Dessalines and Christophe, he occupied the Spanish part without major use of force on January 26, 1801. The Spanish formally ceded the side of the island previously under their control over to the French in the Treaty of Bale on July 22, 1795. However, the Spanish never turned over the colony to the French. In 1800 Toussaint set out to claim France's authority and also his own over the entire island of Hispaniola.

Three main reasons explain Toussaint's decision to occupy both sides of the island: (1) implementation of the Treaty of Bâle of 1795, which made the Spanish side of the island a French territory; (2) the desire by Toussaint to protect his flanks; and (3) implementation of the decree of February 4, 1794, which called for the implementation of all of the clauses of the Treaty of Bâle. A precedent was established with the French's decision to nominate successively Kerverseau, Chanlatte, Roume, and Agé as agents of French interests in the eastern side of the island. This presence, merely symbolic, did not prevent the Spaniards from practicing slavery. Indeed, Roume, who was transferred from the side of the island previously controlled by the Spanish to Cap as agent of the French government (*Directoire*) at Saint-Domingue, spoke with his successor Chanlatte with the aim of approaching Don Garcia, president of the Spanish command, to end the abusive practices of kidnapping, selling, and treating as slaves French citizens who were taken to the eastern side of the island. Therefore, not only did slavery exist in the oriental part, but the slave *trade* was also prevalent. The urgency of the situation led Chanlatte to act promptly. In a letter dated February 14, 1800, to Don J. Garcia, Chanlatte expressed the views of the French government on this thorny issue. However, it would take more than a letter to get Don J. Garcia to budge. On April 27, Chanlatte passed a decree by means of which the army of Saint-Domingue was authorized to stop the slave trade and slavery, two behaviors highly prejudicial to human dignity, and therefore contrary to the values of the revolution.

On the basis of this decree, the General-in-Chief dispatched to Santo Domingo a superior officer, the Général Agé, who carried a letter from Roume and another letter from Toussaint Louverture, dated the same day as the decree, addressed to Don J. Garcia, to whom they announced "the motives of the possession founded on the trade of blacks." This notification could only increase the pressures on the authorities of the east. The arrogance of the Spanish authorities led Agé to shorten his stay on the eastern side of the island. He hastily returned to the western side of the island. The army of Saint-Domingue felt insulted by the treatment given General Agé, and this required reparation and more direct actions. Toussaint Louverture was then compelled to act. In

January 1801, he ordered General Moyse to move toward Santo Domingo. On January 28, 1801, Toussaint sent another letter to Don J. Garcia that reinforced the thesis of the protection of human rights, without retracting the thesis of application of the clauses of the Treaty of Bâle.

This letter stated clearly that "the French government won't sit idle while one removes from it under your authority more of 3000 farmers, whom I have been instructed have been already moved to other Spanish countries."

In any case, Spanish Captain General Don Joaquim Garcia y Moreno refused to cede command to black Haitians. He prepared for a resistance. Toussaint massed his troops for the invasion of Santo Domingo. The soldiers considered him a being of a superior nature; the officers, including the terrifying Dessalines, trembled in his presence.

Toussaint encountered minor resistance and entered the capital triumphantly on January 26, 1801. Toussaint quickly consolidated power and emerged as the governor-general of Hispaniola. This led François-Marie Périchou, otherwise known as Kerverseau to observe, "It is impossible to find other motives for the invasion other than his persistence to achieve this chimera of independence of which he is proud, the desire to close to the metropolis all access to its island and to refuse even one port where it can bring in safely its dispatch-boat, its agents and its troops when the time will come of send them."

Kerverseau was correct in seeing this action within a broader framework of independence by Louverture, in which Toussaint sought to protect his right flank against all French intervention. The conquest of the east consolidated the regime of Toussaint over a territory that he controlled, rendering more viable the tasks of national defense and economic administration. The landing of Hédouville and Vincent at Santo Domingo proved to Toussaint the crucial importance of this port to the metropolis.

During his stay in Santo Domingo, Toussaint Louverture proclaimed the abolition of slavery in presence of the population assembled in the big venue. While the rule of Toussaint Louverture over the whole island reinforced his power, it also fulfilled the intent of the revolt of 1791, which was the abolition of slavery. In the enthusiasm surrounding Toussaint's rule, a new constitution was approved in 1801, whose first article named him governor for life (art. 28), with the right to choose his successor (art. 30) and to name personnel to all jobs. Toussaint established his government sometimes in Cape, and at other times in Port-au-Prince. Finally, he divided the island into six departments by means of law on July 6, 1801. The governor proceeded anew to carve the western part of the island. He transformed the three existing provinces into four departments: (1) the north, (2) the west, (3) the south, and (4) Louverture. This new geographic formation, while including the Artibonite region, stretched until the Saint-Nicolas Môle. With its own departments in the eastern section of the island, the island had six departments, whose administrative and military organizations were not neglected. Thus, the Constitution of 1801 legalized a done deal, the institutionalization of an established power and acquired rights. It defined the type of cooperation proposed to the First Consul in the context of French colonial empire. The constitution established a community of interests, granting the governor his choice of interior policy as well as the right to continue trade with England and the United States. Toussaint signed several treaties, one with Maitland at the time of the evacuation of the British soldiers in 1798 and the other with Stevens in 1799, Maitland and Stevens being mandated representatives of, respectively, Great Britain and the United States of America. Toussaint viewed these commercial treaties as tools for the consolidation of general freedom.

Last, the Constitution of 1801 emphasized liberty and spoke very little of equality. The preamble of the Constitution of 1801 stated, "Liberty is a right given by nature. Equality is a continuation of this liberty." The constitution went as far as to break with France, instituting a new court, the cassation court (article 45 of the Constitution of 1801).

Due to the arrogance of the Catholic clergy, the inhabitants of the Spanish side of the island, which contained many white colonists and immigrants, became as devoted to Toussaint as were the blacks. In an exercise of state power, Toussaint displayed cleverness: in order to rally the whites to his cause, he recalled the emigrants and declared that the Catholic religion was the religion of the state, to the detriment of voodoo, on July 3, 1801, the date of the approval of the constitution.

Aside from the constitution, other laws were adopted to ensure the proper operation of public life. These testified to the spirit of independence as well as the organizational capacity of the governor.

Toussaint hoped that new financial levies would be sufficient to cover equipment expenditures and to ensure the payment of the army and public functionaries. Consistent with his policy of promoting large properties, Toussaint enacted a decree *(arrête)* on March 3, 1801, that prohibited the cutting of specialty trees such as the Bois de Gayac and Bois d'Acajou in the eastern part of the island, to avoid the development of this alternative form of production at the expense of the production of crops.

In France the ascension to power of Napoleon Bonaparte and the establishment of a new government (the Consulat) spelled trouble for Toussaint. After the signing of a peace treaty at Amiens between France and England (October 18, 1801), a more confident Bonaparte sent two expeditionary forces: one to Saint-Domingue under the orders of the General Charles Leclerc, his brother-in-law, and Pauline's husband and the other to Guadeloupe under the orders of Antoine Richepanse. Bonaparte gave general Leclerc the command of a fleet of 54 ships, 27 frigates, and 17 corvettes with 13 generals of division, 27 generals of brigade, and some 12,000 soldiers, with orders to restore French sovereignty by containing the revolt and removing the "gilded African." Two Polish legions that were incorporated into Napoleon Bonaparte's expeditionary army sent out in 1802 to restore slavery to Saint-Domingue (Patchonski and Wilson, 1986).

Bonaparte considered the creation of a French America out of Saint-Domingue and Louisiana (which would later be sold to the United States, with the French population abandoned, after the failure at Saint-Domingue). Jefferson advised Bonaparte to abandon his project to annihilate Saint-Domingue. (Matthewson 1996, 22). Toussaint was not inclined to give up the supreme power. Besides, his hard work was finally paying off. The exports of Saint Domingue reached 64.7 million francs in 1801 (Annales 1853).

He sent his general Christophe to notify Leclerc and admiral Villaret that "their hundred vessels and hundred thousand men would not enter the City and that the earth would burn before the squadron entered in roadstead." (Debien, 1974, 422; Ardouin 1958, 8) Leclerc disembarked in Cap Haitian in February 1802 with the aim to annihilate the military power of the blacks. The fate of the battle turned against Louverture in spite of brilliantly executed battles. The Cape was put to fire, Toussaint called for an insurrection on February 7.

Upon the arrival of the Leclerc expedition, Toussaint put together some important sums of money. He ordered Commander Aignan to transport them to the Cahos in the Artibonite. The fortune of Toussaint was estimated at 20 million francs, and the fortune is said to be still buried in the mountains of the Cahos section of the Artibonite (Chauvet et Prophète, 1894, 103). In February 1892, Toussaint also reunited with his two sons, Placide and Isaac, in the town of Ennery, in the Artibonite region (Debien 1974, 430; Ardouin, 1958, 12).

The Leclerc expedition was fatal to Toussaint, whose capture terminated a brilliant political and military career. The goals as given to the expedition were clear: (1) the instauration of a strong military power; (2) the arrest and deportation of Louverture; (3) the disarmament of farmers; and (4) the restoration of slavery and the slave trade.

Manipulating André Rigaud and Aléxandre Pétion, Leclerc succeeded in capturing Toussaint Louverture. The general Brunet invited Louverture to his headquarters to confer on the general situation of the country. After presenting himself to the French general on June 7, Louverture was immediately arrested and thrown aboard the frigate *The Creole* to be driven to the Cape (Dorsainville, 1974, 14). On *The Creole,* Toussaint predicted to the chief of division, Jean Savary, "In overthrowing me, they have cut down in Saint-Domingue only the trunk of the tree of liberty for the Negro; it will re-grow by the roots, because they are deep and numerous" (Dorsainville, 1974). Indeed, Leclerc died of yellow fever on November 2, 1802, without following up on Bonaparte's instructions that enjoined him, after occupation of ports and places, to capture the

Negro ringleaders and to reestablish his rule. Leclerc's successor, Rochambeau, did not succeed in containing the insurgents, whom Toussaint called to battle under the theme of liberty or death. Toussaint was ultimately deported to Fort de Joux, a cold prison in border between France and Switzerland. Toussaint later died in Fort de Joux on April 7, 1803. The autopsy revealed the pleural and pulmonary attacks as indicators of apoplexy, the main cause of his death.

In the end, the vision of Toussaint was far ahead of the maturity of new social forces. It did not adequately take into account social cleavages. Only with the establishment of a revolutionary alliance in 1803 compelled ethnic unity did all forces unite to achieve general liberty. In some ways, the Leclerc expedition and the cruelty of the French repression served to galvanize indigenous forces and temporarily create a much-needed unity that ushered in the Haitian nation. In this sense, the Leclerc expedition did not achieve its expected outcomes and yielded instead an alliance between divergent forces and social categories to fight for the constitution of a nation-state.

The vision of Toussaint was implemented by his lieutenants, who allied themselves with old enemies to launch the black state. The capture of Toussaint, his deportation to France, and subsequently death added fuel to the fire. The slaves were further determined to win independence under the command of a dark-skinned leader named Jean-Jacques Dessalines.

Dessalines first served as an officer in the French army and later rose to become a commander in the revolt against the same colonial power. After the betrayal and capture of Toussaint Louverture in 1802, Dessalines switched sides and made an alliance with Aléxandre Pétion to free the slaves from colonial oppression. In recognition of his military ingenuity, Dessalines became the leader of the Haitian Revolution at a rebel meeting in Arcahaie. The leaders also selected the red and blue flag as their banner.

Dessalines was as revered by his soldiers as he was feared. He was proclaimed supreme general of the indigenous army in 1803. He then made an alliance with Britain, which provided arms and naval support to the slave insurrection. Under his leadership, the slaves set fire to the plantations and massacred most colonialists. On November 19, 1803, Rochambeau, the replacement for General Leclerc, begged for a 10-day truce to permit the evacuation of Le Cap, thus liberating Haiti from French rule. The uprising culminated in the independence of Saint-Domingue after 13 years of struggle. The war of independence and the proclamation of independence marked the decline of sugar as an export crop. Most of the plantations were dismembered, and the sugar-processing facilities were abandoned.

The indigenous forces were united by the blind repression exerted by French troops. The French intervention provoked the resistance of an entire people, which finally established its independence and sovereignty. The ardent strength of the country was mustered to assail the French troops on all sides.

Cut off from France after the disruption caused by the Peace at Amiens, the expeditionary force was forced to capitulate, abandoning the country to patriotic forces, which proclaimed Haiti's independence.

After the defeat of French troops in November 1803 at the battle of Vertières, Dessalines declared Haiti independent on January 1, 1804, in Gonaives. Upon proclaiming its independence from France, the first independent nation in the Western Hemisphere took back the Amerindian name of Haiti. Dessalines assumed the office of Governor General in 1804 and became emperor of Haiti in 1805 to signal a sharp break from the French imperialist regime. Dessalines governed with an iron fist. As a result of the war and the mass departure to Cuba, Jamaica, and the United States of the majority of the white population who survived the war, the population of the new state was reduced to roughly 500,000. The general massacre ordered by Dessalines allowed only a small number of notorious French to escape. He also allowed the Poles who came as part of Napoleon's expedition to remain if they so wished and gave them pathway to Haitian citizenship. But of the 400 Poles who did remain, few had specific skills, and most ended up as agricultural plantations laborers. The majority of the population of the new nation was composed of former African slaves and freed people or mulattoes.

The Haitian case is unique in its abolishment of slavery through revolutionary means. There have been, however, other means of achieving the abolition of slavery as well. Another case, equally unique, is that of the United States, where it took a civil war to terminate the slavery regime. Abolition of slavery elsewhere generally came in the form of metropolitan decrees, as was the case of the British Antilles, the former French and Dutch colonies. In other cases, it took a combination of external pressures against the slave trade and the slow internal decomposition of the slave-based system of production, as occurred in countries such as Cuba, Brazil, and other states of Latin America.

An entirely new elite dominated by Haitian mulattoes (of mixed African, French, and Spanish descent) arose to replace the French and to wield disproportionate political and economic power. The nascent republic encountered significant political and economic barriers in the path of nation building. The major world powers of the time—Britain, Spain, the United States, and France— were all nervous about the existence of a black republic. They feared that the Haitian independence might set a precedent for slave-based colonies. Haitian merchants were denied official representation in foreign nations with which the country traded. Liberated from the French colonial orbit, the Republic of Haiti and its products had to compete with the competition of plantations based in the Antilles and Central America, where colonizers continued to practice slavery.

At the same time, the Haitian Revolution left an indelible mark on the liberation movement of many continents. Antislavery militants hoped that the Haitian Revolution would force whites to accept blacks' humanity and presented

Haiti as the guardian of the rights and privileges of African Americans in the New World.

REFERENCES

American Anti-Slavery Society. *St. Domingo: Compiled, Chiefly, from Recent Publications.* New York: American Anti-Slavery Society, 1839.

Annales du Commerce Extérieur Numéro 644, Novembre 1852. *Paris et reproduit par l'Annuaire de l'Economie Politique et de la Statistique.* Paris: Guillaumin, 1853.

Archivo General de Indias. Sevilla, Aud. Santo Domingo 956, No. 152/6.

Ardouin, Beaubrun. *Études sur l'histoire d'Haïti suivies de la vie du général J.-M. Borgella,* 11 vols. Port-au-Prince, Haïti: Editions François Dalencour, 1958.

———. *Études sur l'histoire d'Haïti,* Tome II. Port-au-Prince, Haïti, Dalencourt 1958.

Aubin, Eugène. *En Haïti: Planteurs d'Autrefois, Nègres d'Aujourd'hui.* Paris: Librairie Armand Colin, 1910.

Buckley, Roger N. *Slaves in Red Coats: The British West India Regiments, 1795–1815.* New Haven, CT: Yale University Press, 1979.

Chauvet, Henri, and Raoul Prophète. *A Travers la République d'Haïti: Relations de la Tournée Présidentielle dans le Nord* (Première Série). Paris: Imprimerie Vve Victor Goupy, 1874.

Child, David Lee. *The Despotism of Freedom or the Tyranny and Cruelty of American Republican Slave-Masters.* Boston, 1833; Freeport: Books for Libraries Press, 1971.

Curtin, Philip D. *Economic Change in Pre-colonial Africa; Senegambia in the Era of the Slave Trade,* Madison: University of Wisconsin Press, 1975.

D'Ans, André-Marcel. *Haïti: Paysage et Société.* Paris: Éditions Karthala, 1987.

Debien, Gabriel. *Les Esclaves aux Antilles Françaises.* Basse-Terre and Fort-de-France: Société d'Histoire de la Martinique, Fort-de-France, 1974.

Dorsainville, J. C. *Histoire d'Haïti.* Port-au-Prince, Haïtí: Edition Henri Deschamps.

Franco, J. L. *La Conspiración de Aponte.* La Habana: Consejo Nacional de Cultura, Publicaciones del Archivo Nacional, 1963.

———. *La Batalla por el dominio del Caribe y el Golfo de México,* 3 vols. La Habana: Academia de Ciencias, 1965.

Gragnon-Lacoste (Thomas Prosper). *Toussaint Louverture, Général en chef de l'armée de Saint-Domingue, surnommé le Premier des Noirs.* Paris: A. Durant et Pedone-Lauriel, 1877.

Hua-Buton, Nadine. *Étude des Relations Ville-Campagne dans le sud D'Haïti (région des Cayes),* Thèse en vue du Doctorat de 3ème cycle, UER de Géographie, Université de Bordeaux III, Décembre 1983.

Lacaze, Alfred de. *Nouvelle biographie générale depuis les temps les plus reculés jusqu'à nos jours (..), sous la direction de M. le Dr HOEFER.* Paris: Firmin Didot Frères, 1860, t. 32.

Matthewson, Tim. "Jefferson and the Nonrecognition of Haiti." *Proceedings of the American Philosophical Society.* 140 (1) (March 1996): 22–48

Patchonski, Pan, and Wilson, Reuel K. "Poland's Caribbean Tragedy: A Study of Polish Legion in the Haitian War of Independence, 1802–1803." *East European Quarterly* (July 1986).

Périchou, François-Marie dit Kerverseau. Rapport sur la partie ci-devant espagnole de Saint-Domingue P.R. carton No 2, doc. No 77.

Règlement de culture rendu par Toussaint Louverture au Port Républicain le 20 vendémiaire an IX (12 Octobre 1801), cité par Beaubrun Ardoin, Etudes sur l'Histoire d'Haïti, 1958. Cinquième époque pages 54–55.

Rey N. *Les ancêtres noirs "révolutionnaires" dans la ville caribéenne d'aujourd'hui: L'exemple de Livingston, Guatemala,* thèse de doctorat en sociologie sous la direction de M. Haubert, Paris 1 Panthéon-Sorbonne, Décembre 2001.

———. *Caraïbes noirs and negros franceses: Les "oubliés de l'Histoire." Des guerres coloniales aux indépendances du Nouveau Monde.* Paris: Karthala, 2005.

———. "Les Garifunas: Entre "mémoire de la résistance" aux Antilles et transmission des terres en Amérique centrale." in *Cahiers d'Etudes Africaines,* 45: 178, (March 2005).

Saint-Méry, Moreau de. *Description topographique, physique, civile, politique et historique de la partie française de l'Isle de Saint-Domingue.* Paris: Société de l'Histoire des Colonies Françaises et Librairie Larose, 1958.

3

Independence and Empire (1804–1843)

The major powers of the time refused to recognize Haiti's independence from France. The United States took 60 years to grant diplomatic recognition. Meanwhile, in Brazil, one referred to disorder and violence as "haitianism." Slave owners there escaped haitianism until 1888. That year, Brazil abolished slavery. It was the last country in the world to proclaim abolition.

Decades of foreign isolation for Haiti fueled a sense of habituation with international blockades, which shaped the evolution of this nation, which was seeking a different path in a world dominated by the Great Powers. The new nation was driven by pride, a sense of sovereignty, and a staunch capacity for resistance to foreign reoccupation. In fact, this nation of Creoles and African descendents still resists foreign penetration, seeking to set into motion a collective national project of its own. The Haitian nation was founded on the principles of black dignity and equality of the races. Noted Haitian writer Edmond Paul (1863, 59) found that the Haitian state was founded on the belief of racial equality and human dignity.

The threat of foreign intervention to reestablish slavery gave ammunitions to authoritarian governments to centralize powers. One of the first steps of the Dessalines administration was to enlarge the Haitian state domain by nationalizing properties of the kingdom of France and individual colonizers (Saint-Remy, 1846, 56). The state refers to institutions of centralized rule-making and sovereign power, including officials in control of those institutions. The decree of January 2, 1804, annulled all previous leases on plantations. Through these measures, the Haitian state became the largest landowner in the country.

The enlargement of the state domain coincided with administrative centralization. The Haitian constitution of May 20, 1805, stipulated in its article 13 that all Haitians who secured property from former colonizers and who remitted only a portion of the price would be responsible for defraying to the state the remaining amount.

Contrary to the indiscriminate clauses of the decree of January 2, 1804, this article of the constitution recognized property rights dating from the antebellum era. With the occurrence of abuses of titles, a decree of the Ministry of Finance dated July 24, 1805, prescribed a new verification of land titles. Difficulties in the enforcement of this decree forced the Dessalines administration to enact a new decree on September 1, 1806, enjoining local tribunals to submit land titles to the central administrators in the Ministry of Finance before making a decision on the validity of titles.

The constitution of 1805 retained the old colonial division of the country into parishes. The administration of Jean-Jacques Dessalines trusted the administration of each parish to an officer of the indigenous army. It was not until 1816 that the term "commune" became synonymous to parish. One year later, a Council of Notable was established in the parish, which was renamed a commune.

The country's first president nationalized colonial properties. The law of April 20, 1807, recognized the existence of the colonial practice of subsistence agriculture. It recognized the right of farmers to maintain or reconstitute plots that they had cultivated as a family in the colonial era (Moral, 1961, 33). Many slave families became attached to these small plots. Psychologically, freedom became associated with ownership of family plots. For the newly freed, freedom meant the ability to cultivate their independent plots, without being forced to work on the properties of others, under the command of others, and for the profit of others. The political current advocating self-cultivation of own plots was represented by Moïse, one of the officers of Toussaint L'Ouverture, even before the independence. Although the constitution established large properties, Moïse, a proponent of small properties, demanded the division of large properties into small parcels and subsequent allocation to small farmers. Property was, in his view, the essential attribute of the newly conquered freedom (Saint-Louis, 1970, 44–46).

This rendered difficult the maintenance of plantation agriculture after the proclamation of independence. There was a clear distinction between the beneficiaries of colonial succession, who were preoccupied by the need to mobilize labor on their farms for the production of commercial crops, and the newly freed who sought access to small individual properties. For two decades, a struggle emerged between large landowners and the independent peasantry, between cultivation of a large portion of land by a hired group of peasants and the tendency of individual peasants to make good use of their own parcels. A divorce occurred between the necessity of large-scale production of commercial crops and the expansion of small family farms. The peasant saw no benefit in the maintenance of large properties, which symbolized for him servitude. The peasant refused to accept the plantation system.

At the end of the nineteenth century, small individual property prevailed. According to Moral (1961, 55), in spite of resistance, the small farmer conquered his or her autonomy and thus freedom. Beyond the plains, small property prevailed over large domains. In the end, the Haitian peasant conquered his right to ownership and peaceful enjoyment of family plots. Even export crops such as coffee are grown, in large measures, on small family farms. The ways of life of the emerging peasantry combined elements of African and indigenous past as well as European influences, in a new cultural setting. The mixing of African and European elements can be found in religious beliefs as well.

In an attempt to safeguard Haiti's territorial boundaries from foreign aggression and encroachment, Haiti's early ruler, Dessalines, virtually sealed the country off from outside contacts in the two years after independence. In a move to avert the reinstatement of slavery in the black nation of Haiti, Dessalines forbade whites from ever again owning property or land there. In his view, Haiti would be a nation of free landholders. The freedom contract signed at Arcahaie in 1791 with the creation of the flag with two colors called for free access to the land by both blacks and mulattoes. In some sense, the appropriation of the best lands of the country by powerful oligarchs in the aftermath of the independence represented a deviation from the premise of the revolt of 1791. The nascent republic posed a major threat to slave-owning nations, who worried about both the overthrow of slavery and the support of anticolonial struggles. Because Haiti had set a precedent in black self-governance, the country was isolated in the international arena. Latin American planters feared that their slaves would seek to replicate the success of the Haitian Revolution. Benedict Anderson (1991, 48) wrote, "In 1791, Toussaint L'Ouverture led an insurrection that produced in 1804 the second independent republic in the Western Hemisphere. This insurrection terrified the slave owning planters of Venezuela." This explains the early granting of independence to Nicaragua to preempt a revolution as occurred in Haiti.

The Haitian Revolution also provoked significant fear among slave-owning planters in the United States. The white planter class curtailed the level of autonomy achieved by black ministers and slave congregations by 1800 in response to the Haitian Revolution and Nat Turner's rebellion (Dubois, 1903, 22–26). Thomas Jefferson was among the Virginian planters who fiercely opposed the proclamation freeing slaves who broke with their seditious masters. The United States would not recognize Haiti's independence until 1860.

Haiti fought vigorously to effectively maintain its independence from foreign powers. The threat of re-colonization was evident. The Treaty of Paris, which was signed on May 30, 1814, and which was recognized by Britain, granted Louis XVIII the right to regain all his American properties, including Haiti.

THE LEGACY OF THE HAITIAN REVOLUTION

The Haitian Revolution marked the military defeat of France, which was one of the superpowers of the time. Although French forces lost their North American territories in the Seven Year war, they continued to harbor New World ambitions. They sought to control the Louisiana Territories not just for the sake of control per se but also to supply resources to the Caribbean colony. Therefore, both Saint-Domingue and Louisiana were part and parcel of a larger hegemonic plan under Napoleon. However, the lynchpin of Napoleon's North American expansion was Saint-Domingue in part because the road through Louisiana passed through Saint-Domingue. The defeat of French forces in Saint-Domingue resulted in the collapse of Napoleon's whole plan as the loss diminished Louisiana's strategic appeal. In this sense, the blacks of Haiti and their Revolution were instrumental to the Louisiana Purchase deal, which forever changed the American landscape.

In an attempt to safeguard Haiti's territorial boundaries from foreign aggression and encroachment, the Haitian constitutions of 1805, 1806, 1816, 1843, 1846, and 1849 prohibited "white" persons from owning real estate because of the association in Haitians' minds between "white landowner" and "slaveholder" (Adam, 1989, 50; Logan, 1941, 307). It was only during the first American occupation (1915–1934) that the property rights policy was changed to allow foreign land ownership.

The Dessalines administration sought to control foreign trade to protect local industries and diversify agricultural production. This explains the exclusion of foreigners from the retail trade. In its quest to "assure exclusivity to Haitian speculators the benefits resulting from the exploitation of salt" and… "desiring to favour the prosperity of this branch of internal commerce," the Haitian government forbade the importation of salt (*Gazette Politique et Commerciale d'Haïti*, December 19, 1805; Linstant de Pradines, 1851–65, 1:32–33).

By law, foreign trading houses could not purchase export crops except through Haitian intermediaries, and their activities were restricted to eight ports where they could engage only in wholesale trade (Lacerte, 1981, 500). Because they were prevented from owning land, foreign merchants established shops near the wharf of a few designated cities, including the capital, Port-au-Prince, where they engaged in haut commerce. The privileged access of foreign merchants to capital, technological knowledge, and markets in their homelands also made it easier for them to engage in "haut commerce." They purchased licenses that authorized them to import and distribute wholesale staple and luxury goods in Haiti and to export the country's main commodities: coffee, cacao, and a specialty wood called *bois de campèche* (Joachin, 1971, 1502; Turnier, 1955, 161). Most of the country's bois de campèche, one of Haiti's most prized natural resources in the first half of the nineteenth century, came from the Artibonite region. However, the importance of the foreign trading house in the Haitian import market contributed both to the perpetuation of the dependent nature of the Haitian economy and to state instability. An entirely new elite dominated by light-skinned Haitians arose to replace the French and to wield disproportionate political and economic power. Although the composition of the Haitian elite has changed over the years, the term "elite" still refers to families of exceptional wealth, status, or education. Though differing in emphasis on unity and harmony within the Haitian elite, Simpson (1940, 499) and Wingfield and Parenton (1965, 345–347) shared the view that its members have absolute dominance in Haitian political and economic affairs. Leyburn (1941) took Simpson's concept of the Haitian elite further in his division of Haitian society into two clearly separate castes. The first caste was urban, Catholic, educated, and culturally oriented toward France. The second was largely rural and illiterate and practiced voodoo. In Leyburn's view, the peasant caste was bound to the land almost exactly the way Jean-Jacques Dessalines and Henry Christophe managed labor relations. On February 17, 1807, Christophe returned to the Cape to organize, according to his political vision, the state of Haiti in the North, which ruled over the North, the Northwest, and the Artibonite regions of Haiti. In 1811, when Aléxandre Pétion is reelected president, Christophe, losing all hopes of governing the whole island, proclaimed himself king of the northern kingdom of Haiti on March 26th, under the name of Henri the First. The labor relations policies of Christophe closely resembled the practices of Dessalines.

S. and J. Comhaire-Sylvain refuted Leyburn's simplistic class model by advocating the existence of four classes in urban Haiti. The first class contained foreign immigrants such as Jews from Curacao. The second class contained members of the rural aristocracy whose economic means did not allow them to join the ranks of the commercial and professional aristocracy of Port-au-Prince. The third class, the working class, referred to Haitians who had distinguished themselves by the high value they placed on education of their children, which explained the presence of these children in the capital city of Port-au-Prince, where secondary and higher education could be obtained. The fourth and last class was composed of elements of the "sub-proletariat," who were most native inhabitants of Port-au-Prince and who often lived in the slums of the capital. Although the Comhaire-Sylvains' work correctly emphasized social differentiation, it did not emphasize the fluidity of the Haitian class system, which is the best means of refuting the caste model proposed by Leyburn. Evidence of fluidity can be found in the way human and financial capital that was accumulated during migration abroad translated to improved social standing upon return to Haiti. Remittances and influence can raise an individual's class status, especially if acquisition of consumer goods is part of the conception of class standing. The remittances of Haitians living abroad have a positive influence on Haiti (1) Remittances enable satisfaction of basic consumption needs, the payment of debt, and the construction and renovation of a house; (2) they increase the foreign exchange value of the Haitian currency; (3) they alleviate balance-of-payment difficulties in Haiti. A portion of remittances is brought back personally by the migrants or their friends and converted into domestic currency. Remittances benefit not just the immediate recipients but also suppliers of goods and services on which the money is spent. The effect is increased national spending and small business development.

The immediate post-independence era was an important phase in Haitian class formation. Many members of the current elite of Haiti are descendants of the free mulatto class of the colonial period and the civil and military officials of the revolutionary, imperial, and early republican eras, from 1791 to 1843 (Wingfield and Parenton, 1965, 340; Plummer, 1984, 123). The new state was quickly captured by the ascending elite seeking to consolidate its domination. This group kept for itself the most fertile plots in the plains and coffee-producing land in the mountains. Generally, they are absentee landlords who prefer living in large cities.

Agricultural production was assumed by the peasantry. The small peasantry emerged in Haiti in the period between 1804 and 1850. In short, a rural society was established after independence and consolidated in the nineteenth century. The distribution of plantations to military personnel and personalities of the new regime after independence did not prevent the collapse of the plantation economy. In spite of various measures taken to maintain the former slaves on the plantations, situated on the more fertile land in the plains, the newly formed peasants elected to establish family properties in the mountains. The parceling of large colonial domains spread. The commodities of the plains, especially sugar, disappeared while the vitality of mountain systems with their forest resources fed the progress of the small peasantry.

Most peasants cultivate parcels that are far from one another and that belong to different ecological systems as a means to produce different crops, to spread the time required for agricultural work, and to benefit from harvests throughout the year. This strategy also permits them to minimize risks on plots that are exploited under various legal arrangements. Peasants also mix cereals, leguminous plants, and tubercles. This strategy permits them to spread food availability and lengthen financial benefits across time.

The settlement in coastal towns of mostly foreign merchants created a new class of intermediaries who exported Haitian products (coffee, dye wood, and cotton). These new intermediaries typically buy from peasants to resell to exporters. Rather than investing initial capital or profits to maximize agricultural production, they engage in commercial or speculative activities. The rural elite use control over exchange circuits to exploit the local peasantry. In spite of command of financial resources, a significant segment of the Haitian elite depends on agricultural production for its survival. In this sense, the peasantry and the export-oriented commercial elite are bound together in unequal but interdependent relationships. This gave birth to a new trading economy, which served not only to perpetuate the dependence of the Haitian economy but also to weaken the new state. The repression of peasant revolts, which demanded better prices for export crops but also access to land; state imposition of taxes on export crops, which reduced peasant earnings; and political crises served to widen the gap between the centralized state based in Port-au-Prince and the rural peasantry. A gap also emerged between the coastal towns and the rural interior of the country.

The Haitian state quickly confined itself to a predatory function. This increased the mistrust of the population toward the state and fostered the development of self-regulation mechanisms to escape state authority.

The tendency to bypass the state is also reflective of the high value that Haitians place on freedom. In fact, the war of independence was driven largely by the thirst for the freedom associated with land ownership. If slavery meant exclusion from ownership of the principal means of production, or land, then freedom from oppression would have to be associated with land ownership. For the average peasant, a piece of land represented the basis upon which his existence and autonomy depended as well as his standing and influence in society (Métraux et al., 1951, 30). The bulk of coffee is produced on small coffee gardens near the dwellings of coffee growers. The autonomy associated with land ownership explains the virtual domination of small farms in the Haitian coffee market.

Increasing coffee exports led to the creation of several towns in Haiti. Because of its growing commercial importance in the import-export trade, the town of Les Cayes secured judiciary and administrative functions in 1779 with the establishment of a court of jurisdiction of a *sénéchal* and an admiralty. In the French colonial system, the term *sénéchal* referred to a public official in charge of justice and the administration in a town or province.

Les Cayes became the county-town *(chef-lieu)* of a district composed of the parishes of Cayes, Torbeck, Côteaux, and Port Salut. In the nineteenth century, the port of Les Cayes was integrated in the circuit of the regular shipping lines that linked Europe to North America. Moreover, in 1891 three steamers that transported passengers and mail offered their services to Les Cayes. Far from being an isolated backwater cut off from the rest of the world, Les Cayes was integral to international transportation networks. Traveling from the United States (New York) to Europe (Amsterdam), one of the five boats of the Royal Dutch West India Mail Service Company made a stop in Les Cayes every three weeks. To these regular crossings, one must add the tramps that came irregularly in search of passengers and cargo (Girault, 1981, 255–266). This implies constant contact with a wide range of countries and cultures. In 1887–1888, the port of Les Cayes exported significant quantities of coffee and *bois de Campeche* as well as cacao, leather, and shells. Total exports surpassed the size of imports (Rouzier, 1983).

The convenient location of the southern town of Jacmel made possible an intercourse between the Spanish ports of the island and South America. Jacmel also served as a communication point with Jamaica (Franklin, 1970, 301). It served as a center where mail and passengers gathered from throughout the Caribbean for Britain-bound steamships in the middle of the eighteenth century. Jacmel, the regional capital of the southeast, remains one of the cultural centers of the country. The Alcibiade Pomeyrac Center, the only French-speaking secondary school operating in Haiti, provides quality education from Jacmel.

In the post-independence era, the Haitian state distributed or rented estates to high-ranking officials, state functionaries, and military officers according to their rank (Mackenzie, 1830, 145). These land grants *(don de leta)* generally were made because, in the early nineteenth century, the state lacked revenues to pay its army. Eventually, payments in land were made on a large-scale basis. The domain of Aléxandre Pétion, for instance, extended without interruption from the Plain of Léogane to the locality of Cul-de-Sac, an area of nearly 6,000 acres (Simpson, 1940, 503–504). Officers of the indigenous army soon became members of the rural elite through control of state land. (For clarity of discussion, I use the term "rural elite" to refer to powerful social and economic actors—for example, planters, influential moneylenders, grain vendors, and exporters—in the provinces.)

Progressively, as the state neglected to enforce its rights, state-owned estates became private properties. Because of the focus on agriculture, land ownership became the main source of wealth. Class differentiation began with the establishment of the social class of large property owners.

Having a majority of African people has been important to the foundation of Haitian society. This distinguishes Haiti from other Latin American countries, where African people and their descendents are a minority. Dessalines's view that the riches of the country should be shared among all of the sons and daughters of the Haitian nation brought him to scrutinize land and labor contracts. This penchant eventually cost him his life. Dessalines is attributed the following statement "and those children whose fathers are in Africa, they would have nothing" This statement came amid conflicts between the planter class and the peasants. The slaves liberated by the Haitian Revolution—known as *nouveaux libres* (newly freed)—were for the most part without properties, often squatting on vacant land left idle. In contrast, the *affranchis* (free people of color) not only possessed land from before the revolution but also acquired properties from their fathers and departing whites. They also seized vacant properties. As Dessalines sought fairness in land distribution, he lost the support of mulatto landowners and a new group of black generals who secured land grants from the state.

The deviation from the revolution of 1791, in the aftermath of independence, which resulted in the appropriation of the best land by oligarchs in power broke the contract of liberty of Arcahaie. The conquest of the real liberty still remains a social project.

In the end, Dessalines sided with the Creole planter class, which strove for the reinforcement of the plantation economy. In an effort to secure the rebirth of agriculture and to arrest the desertion of rural areas, Dessalines enacted and enforced coerced labor as the rule for the peasantry. At the same time, the barons of the Dessalines administration enjoyed their large domains and their servile labor force. In contrast, the peasants were harnessed to serfdom on the big plantations, where they were deprived of true freedom and closely watched.

Ultimately, sugar production declined because of its huge demand for labor and the labor scarcity associated with newly discovered enjoyment of personal freedom. Sugar was increasingly replaced by less labor-intensive food crops such as coffee. This occurred partly because many of the sugar plantations were ruined or subdivided. Coffee also grew in importance largely because it was cultivated on the hills and did not require large tracts of land. Moreover, in Haiti, less labor is expended on coffee per acre than any other crop. Because coffee could be transformed through the use of implements no more elaborate than the beetle, it has become the main source of income for cultivators who are also engaged in subsistence agriculture. Since the late nineteenth century, then, coffee has been the country's main export crop. Even in the middle of the twentieth century, when many plantations were constituted to produce crops of either strategic or commercial importance, coffee was never produced on plantations.

A presidential decree enacted on September 1, 1806 that sought to establish efficient rules, threatened the higher payoffs that flowed to members of the rural elite. For instance, the decree established rules for rental contracts between large landowners and tenants, which made it difficult for landlords to overcharge their tenants and keep them in conditions of dependency. Government dispossession of numerous planters in the south added fuel to the fire.

In others cases, strict sanctions were imposed. In the end, Dessalines lost the support of both the planter class and the peasantry.

The planter mobilization against Dessalines demonstrates the high political costs associated with government intervention in the agricultural sector. In August 1806, Dessalines provoked hatred and fear among the rural elite, particularly in southern Haiti, and on October 18, 1806, the south exploded. Dessalines tried to subdue the rebellion, which erupted from Port Salut and inflamed the south and the whole department of the west. Led by Mécerou, a proprietor, rural leaders in Port Salut ambushed Moreau Coco Herne, Dessalines's lieutenant (Heinl and Heinl, 1978, 137). When he left his palace, a furious Dessalines expressed his intention to crush the sedition. The planter class combined forces with disgruntled generals of the Haitian army to assassinate Jean-Jacques Dessalines. Several army generals, including Henry Christophe, Gérin, Yayou, and Vaval, and their troops plotted against and ambushed Dessalines at Pont Rouge ("Red Bridge").

At dusk, General Pétion ordered a squad of soldiers to recover the emperor's remains and to give him a burial. The traitors who plotted against Dessalines included both blacks and mulattoes. The assassination of Dessalines can be seen as the expression of private appropriation of the wealth of the country. The main beneficiaries of his assassination included generals Aléxandre Pétion and Henri Christophe, who were allies of the planter class of the south of Haiti. Although Dessalines was both a military genius and a staunch defender of the integrity of the Haitian national territory, he failed to orchestrate a negotiated solution to conflicts between divergent segments of the Haitian population. The emperor's acts of aggression against the planters of the south were an inauspicious decision that, from the birth of the nation, initiated a climate of division between Haitians instead of promoting the unity necessary to the construction of the new state.

For many years after the assassination of Dessalines, his name was disgraced. It took several decades before the memory of the principal founder of the Haitian nation was recuperated. It was only under the first American occupation that the national anthem was renamed after Dessalines.

The army, which played the central role in the struggle for independence, asserted itself as the only source of political legitimacy and assumed control of the state. Increasingly, the state moved farther and farther from the execution of the task of consolidation of the nation. More and more the state became militarized and repressive.

A succession of officers of the independence army followed each other as heads of state. Upon Dessalines's death, Haiti split into two rival states from 1806 until 1820: a western republic under the leadership of Aléxandre Pétion and a northern kingdom under the leadership of King Henri Christophe. In the end, the competition between the two clans, the dark-skinned affranchis and the mulattoes who were also affranchis, resulted in the split of the countries into two competing states. The national alliance that had culminated in the conquest of national independence was definitely broken.

In this battle between the two elites, neither will emerge as the winner. They will be constrained to political cohabitation generation after generation. This serves as a basic logic of the functioning of the Haitian political system. There is a confrontation between the black and mulatto elite and between the people and the Haitian elite as a whole. Let us now examine the administration of the two fiefdoms that emerged in Haiti after the death of Dessalines.

THE REPUBLICAN ADMINISTRATION OF ALÉXANDRE PÉTION

A mulatto general, Aléxandre Pétion governed the republic, which contained the southern peninsula and the western department of Haiti. The powers of the president were expected to be counterbalanced by those of the Senate and Chamber of Deputies. From 1816 until 1918, the country experienced bicameralism with the creation of the second Chamber that subsisted under various appellations: House of Representatives of the Communes (1816); House of Representatives (1846, 1849, 1874, 1888); House of Communes (1843, 1867, 1879, 1889); and Chamber of the Deputies from 1918. The Senate kept its original identity and was sometimes referred to as the "High Chamber."

Pétion ruled by decrees, which were considered as laws and published in *Le Télégraphe* (The Telegraph), which passed for the official newspaper until the creation of *Le Moniteur* (The Monitor) on February 8, 1845. Pétion recognized the strength of position for individual farm ownership and accepted the division of some properties to benefit the new independent peasantry. The republic of Pétion contained eight precincts known as *arrondissements*, which were established for administrative purposes.

In search of political legitimacy, President Pétion distributed or sold over 70658.07 acres to more than 10,000 officers, war veterans, and others (Moral, 1961, 31), thereby enabling small landowners to have access to land ownership. The government of Pétion sold most large properties in whole or in part. The 1809 land distribution was later dubbed the first agrarian reform in Latin America. For Pétion, the growth in the number of proprietors strengthened the state (Linstant de Pradines, 2:245). Sugar plantations such as Bérard and Petit Delmas and the Gobé coffee plantation were slated for sale under the law of March 10, 1814, in an effort to increase the numbers of proprietors and to give a new impetus to agriculture. Army officers and soldiers, who formed with their families an important segment of the south and the west, received a parcel of land. In spite of land distribution, the period lasting from 1807 to 1820–1821 was characterized by an economic depression, with the downfall of large production of sugarcane, cotton, and indigo on a large portion of the national territory. This period also witnessed significant gains in coffee production, which occurred on small family farms.

In 1826, Pétion also promulgated the Rural Code, a piece of legislation that sought to curtail black mobility and to force the return of former slaves to plantations. It is also interesting to note that the Rural Code prohibited any experience in land cultivation by a collective of farmers. It stated clearly that "no meeting or association of stationary farmers on a same agricultural dwelling will be able to secure rental of the totality of the land assets where they live to manage it by themselves in society."

The Rural Code was applied by both Pétion and Christophe, although more harshly by Christophe. In spite of the aim of the Rural Code to return to the plantation economy, in the western state, the small family garden continued to coexist with large plantations.

Several strategies of land concentration were, however, applied, notably through the game of sale and purchase. Wealthier beneficiaries purchased land grants received by poorer beneficiaries, a process that enabled them to control larger properties. Therefore, a process of privatization took place with important plantations formerly owned by the Haitian state.

THE ADMINISTRATION OF HENRY CHRISTOPHE

Contrary to Pétion, Christophe maintained the plantation economy in the north. The northern state became a kingdom in March 1811. The trend of national governance as a kingdom marked a shift away from the French republican model. The kingdom remained ready for the defense of its independence, with its resources expended in the construction of forts to prevent a possible offensive from French forces or other colonial powers. King Christophe built numerous castles both as symbols of long-lasting rule and to protect the country against possible foreign re-occupation.

The kingdom of Christophe comprised three large territorial divisions, the first headquartered at Sans-Souci, the second headquartered at Plaisance, and the third headquartered at Saint-Marc.

King Christophe encouraged the naturalization of the foreigners in his kingdom, notably, black immigrants from America. A large number of American blacks left the continent for Haiti (Vergniaud, 1931, 325).

Christophe developed an authoritarian governance system, with strong compulsory methods, as exemplified by his adoption of the code of Toussaint. He strictly enforced order and discipline even at the cost of arbitrary measures and decreed laws known as Code Henry, which introduced elements of moralization of social life (e.g., marriage obligation, law on natural creatures).

Christophe's kingdom was keen on maintaining good relations with Britain in search of diplomatic support and even military assistance in case of conflict with France. The kingdom developed a modern education system based on the English methods known as Lancaster, named after Joseph Lancaster (1778–1838). It was a popular education system (introduced in England in 1798) that gave easy and fast access to instruction while extolling the virtue of education for all, financed and controlled by the state.

The agricultural establishments enjoyed a rebirth in northern Haiti's kingdom of Christophe, under military authority and to the benefit of a new class of planters. Export taxes were lifted, and foreign trade resumed. Merchants were, however, restricted to specific ports and were forbidden to operate in the interior. These measures resonated with antislavery activist Thomas Clarkson (Griggs and Prator, 1968, 146), who warned King Henry Christophe against foreign penetration of the country, suggesting that the right of foreigners to own property should be restricted to the trading cities of the coast.

Prince Saunders noted that the former revolutionary leader Christophe succeeded in creating an era of peace and prosperity unknown beforehand. Under Christophe, the people of Haiti proved themselves a tribute to the greatness of their race. Saunders noted, "Among the troops, good order and discipline prevail[ed]"; "the republic's finances [were] in a satisfactory state," even with all the destruction and expenses of civil war; the laws [were] regularly executed; the magistrates fulfilled their duties; justice [was] exercised with scrupulous exactness; the people daily acquire[d] knowledge of their rights and of their duties; their public spirit [was] excellent"; and public education and the arts was being established to guide the state into greatness (Saunders, 1818, 126, 142–145).

One of Christophe's main achievements, the Citadelle Laferriere, remains the largest fort in the Caribbean. In 1982 the Citadelle was declared a World Heritage site for humanity by the United Nations Educational, Scientific and Cultural Organization (UNESCO). This fortress remains a privileged site for domestic and international tourism. In the south, separatist movements were not as successful as in the north. André Rigaud returned to Haiti in 1810 to lead a short-lived government in the south (1810–1812). Although the act of separation of the south under the leadership of Rigaud was published on November 2, 1810, oddly the Departmental Assembly recognized Pétion as President of Haiti. This fragile state didn't survive the death of Rigaud in the night of the September 17–18, 1811. Three days later, General Borgella was chosen to succeed him, but it was too late. As a result, on March 22, 1812, the south united with the republic of the west. The Constituent Assembly designated General Pétion, who had protected the region from public condemnation by Christophe, President of the Republic.

The division of the country between the north and the west and south persisted until the administration of Jean Pierre Boyer, himself also a general (1818–1843). Boyer ordered a *cadastre* and a census of the population. The term *cadastre* refers to a process for recording and, in some countries, guaranteeing information about land ownership. The *cadastre* typically makes a distinction between individualized rights governing control of farming land and communally-owned residential holdings.

It is important to note that class standing was more important than skin color. King Christophe's land and labor policies included forced labor, rigid work discipline, and restrictions on labor mobility. The stated purpose of Code Henry was to rebuild the economy shattered by the war of independence and achieve the desired increase in export crop production. In this sense, black oligarchs undermined sharecroppers' rights just as much as their mulatto counterparts. But in Christophe's kingdom, every laborer was expected to perform a full day of labor as required by article 22 of the law regulating the culture of the soil, which was included in Code Henry. Every noncompliant farmer was harshly published.

The rebellion of Goman in the region of the Grande-Anse crystallized the discontent of the farmers. The rebellion succeeded in organizing a zone that, for the dozen years between 1807 and 1819 escaped the control of the western and southern states alike. Other peasant revolts exploded in the north (Gros-Morne), in the mountains of the Hotte, and in the south (Cayes), widening the space of social struggles in the countryside. These peasant struggles and the persistence of resistance to agro-industrial plantations in favor of small family farms impeded the maintenance of large plantations for export as the mainstay of the economy in the post-independence era.

During the administration of Pétion, Haiti developed strong ties with the pro-independence movement in Latin America. Many of the region's revolutionary leaders found that Haiti could be a powerful ally and contributor to their own independence. For instance, it is telling that it was from Haiti that Venezuelan hero Francisco de Miranda made his first appeal for independence from Spain on March 12, 1806.

In spite of his many accomplishments, King Henry Christophe could not win the sympathy of his subjects because he ruled with an iron fist. He was disowned by all sectors, including his close collaborators. In the face of rising popular discontent and mutiny in his army, Christophe decided to end his own life on October 19, 1820. His kingdom collapsed and fell under Boyer's republic. After the downfall of the northern kingdom of Christophe, the country engaged in small-scale production for export of coffee, cacao, cotton, specialty wood, leather, sugar, honey, rum, molasses, spices, and orange peels, in descending order.

THE ADMINISTRATION OF JEAN-PIERRE BOYER (1818–1843)

Upon the death of Pétion in 1818, Jean-Pierre Boyer became president-for-life and continued the practice of land distribution to secure legitimacy among the peasantry. Boyer found a staunch supporter in the person of French intellectual Henri Grégoire, who in turn found in Haiti a new space full of promise of realizations. In his *Considérations sur le mariage et le divorce, adressées aux Citoyens d'Haïti*, published in 1823, Grégoire wrote, "What's more, indubitable relations attest that there is progress in Haiti, which once again enjoys liberty, a sensible amelioration in everything that has to do with education, decency, good customs, and work activities which are the guardians of good customs. Here is a happy foresight that Haiti, once considered as the metropolis of the Antilles, could retake, with even more bursts and glory, a title which will be conferred upon it by means of virtue" (1823, 56–57).

A grateful Boyer addressed a letter to Henri Grégoire dated May 7, 1820 in these terms: "I thank you for the great services that you rendered to the Haitian nation by advocating the cause of the Africans and their descendants, at a time when a barbaric prejudice and a Machiavellian government conspired their extinction. Your talents, your private virtues have traversed with us the storms of our political revolution and are engraved in our grateful hearts."

Under Boyer's administration, the Rural Code was enacted by the Chamber of the Communes on April 21, 1826, favorably voted on in the Senate on May 1, 1826. The Rural Code received the president's seal of approval on May 6 of the same month (Franklin, 1970, 335). The Rural Code of Boyer included these essential points: interdictions of the associations of farmers managing properties themselves (article 30); obligation to have a permit to leave the agricultural unit during the week (article 71); a requirement placed upon farmers to be respectful toward the owners, leaseholders, and managers (articles 69 and 160); permission for rural police to repress wandering and idleness (articles 136, 143, 174, 180); reduction to half-hour the lunchtime at noon; and worse, article 178, which clarifies that the children of farmers will follow in the same conditions as their parents (Code Rural d'Haïti, 1826).

Upon Christophe's death in 1820, President Boyer unified the country under one government. With sweeping powers, President Boyer implemented an aggressive Haitian foreign policy. First, Boyer invaded the Spanish portion of the island in 1822 and ruled over the whole of Hispaniola until he was removed from office by the revolution of 1843.

Achieving control of the island meant for the Haitian government the ability to abolish slavery on the eastern part of the island, but it also afforded Boyer a privileged position to thwart any French attempt to regain the lost territory by means of an invasion through the Dominican Republic. It bears reminding that successive Haitian administrations held the fear that the French army would attempt to repossess its former colony.

Upon the reunification of the island in 1822, Boyer divided the territory into six departments, subdivided into administrative districts *(arrondissements)* and then communes. Departments established in the west were the north, the south, the west, and the Artibonite. The east was divided into l'Ozama and the Cibao. The frontiers of the departments of l'Ozama and the Cibao were well established.

After the formal abolition of slavery on the eastern part of the island in 1822, President Boyer distributed land to the peasantry as a means of securing political legitimacy. However, the implementation of the Rural Code of Boyer did not bode well with the citizens of the east as it implied discipline in agricultural work on large plantations as a means to increase agricultural production, export revenues, and therefore Boyer's capacity to repay the debt of independence. In the face of opposition from entrenched landowners specialized in rearing of cattle and horses, the full implementation of the Boyer Rural Code was postponed.

THE CAUSES OF THE SCHISM OF THE EASTERN PART OF THE ISLAND

Dr. J. C. Dorsainville (1934, 200) examined the main causes of the schism of the east in his book on Haitian history. In his view, the Boyer administration "subjected to a population, of which one quarter was white, the articles of the Haitian constitution touching upon real estate property. These restrictions were maintained and even aggravated in 1843." A major scandal exploded because many churches, convents, and abbeys had been dispossessed of their pensions. In the end, Boyer wanted to raise revenues in the eastern as in the western part of the country to pay the debt of independence. The independence of Dominican Republic in 1844 nullified previously established borders.

Several bilateral treaties were established to settle the borders between Haiti and the Dominican Republic. These included the Treaty of Ryswick (1697); the Treaty of Aranjuez (1776); the Treaty of July 2, 1867; the Treaty of November 9, 1874; the Convention of 1895; and the Treaty of Haitian-Dominican Borders of January 21, 1929. Technical difficulties in the execution of these treaties would later lead to a revision protocol signed on March 9, 1936, which foresaw the creation of an international road (Victor, 1944, 72).

The reunification of the island in 1822 complicated Boyer's efforts to secure recognition of Haiti's independence. This act was interpreted as the prelude to Boyer's imperialistic aims, which were said to include the entire Caribbean

Basin. Rayford Logan (1941, 201) reported that a newspaper published in the south "warned the American government against the supposed aims of Boyer towards Cuba and Puerto Rico." There was, at that time, a true psychosis about black expansion, which compelled the concerted action of France, the United States, and Great Britain.

An official request for the recognition of Haiti was addressed to the United States government in 1822. The request was quickly declined. The refusal was largely founded on the absurd apprehension of the supposed project of Boyer to conquer Cuba and Puerto Rico and to transform them into black independent republics. This forced Boyer to seriously pursue negotiations with France.

Haiti obtained France's recognition of its independence in 1825. However, France made Haiti pay dearly for the humiliation inflicted to Napoléon Bonaparte. The newly independent nation was forced to dole out to France an indemnity of 150 million gold francs to dispossessed planters. Moreover, although Haitian ports were open to vessels of all nations, customs duties on French ships were placed at half those paid by ships of other nations.

To eliminate foreign threats to the independence of Haiti, the country that had defeated Napoléon Bonaparte's glorious army accepted to pay reparations to defeated France, which enjoyed the support of slave-owning states. Although the first black republic of Haiti had secured recognition of its political independence through this agreement, it faced significant limitations because of this burden on its economic independence. The payment of the previously mentioned indemnity beginning in 1825 was a contributing factor to the country's financial strangulation. Writers of the indigenous orientation assailed Boyer for not adopting policies to limit Haiti's dependence on foreigners. The country took more than a century to repay the debt, as interests accrued. In 1938, the national debt to France was finally paid, but by then the country was financially dependent on American banks.

The early Haitian administrations welcomed and supported the immigration of free people of color to Haiti. An article of the Constitution of the Republic allowed for assumption of Haitian nationality after a residence of 12 months by all Africans, Indians, and their descendants. In fact, President Jean-Pierre Boyer provided travel stipends to African Americans seeking to relocate to Haiti. African Americans formed branches of the Haytian Emigration Society in Philadelphia, Boston, New York, Baltimore, and Cincinnati in the 1820s. The Haytian Emigration Society expressed a sense of kinship with Haiti (Berry and Blassingame, 1982, 401). The nineteenth century witnessed a high level of circulation of ideas and practices in the revolutionary current spearheaded by the Haitian Revolution. This renders necessary a discussion of patterns of global interconnectedness and citizenship. Key African American leaders, for instance, expressed a strong sense of racial kinship and global citizenship. These leaders reimagined the relationship between themselves and the African world. They came to believe that the state of black America in the United States was linked to global standing such as the independence of the Haitian state and the African nations. Black antislavery militants viewed Haiti as a source of racial pride and achievement as well as an example of the universal liberty and equality. That understanding of kinship networks led African American leaders to express moral concerns beyond their locales to humanity in general.

Recent works have challenged the binding notions of citizenship and national borders in the study of North American and Atlantic history. For instance, April Lee Hatfield (2004, 3) challenged the unspoken assumption that each colony operated as a self-contained entity. She emphasizes instead the "impact of boundaries' permeability on the spread of ideas and information [and peoples] that affected Virginia's political, social, cultural and economic development."

Both migrants and travelers carried news and information on cultural practices and ideas. In the United States, the planter class curtailed the level of autonomy achieved by black ministers and slave congregations by 1800 in response to the Haitian Revolution and Nat Turner's rebellion (Du Bois, 1903). Therefore, the meaning of the Haitian Revolution was adapted by a variety of actors.

Between 1790 and 1825, a revolutionary current was evident in the Atlantic world. African Americans traversed the Atlantic world seeking emancipation and autonomy. African Americans found in the Haitian Revolution a source of inspiration and a symbol of freedom and equality.

The emigration of African Americans to Haiti provided an outlet through which people subjected to discrimination in the United States manifested their discontent. Inspired by the possibility of freedom and prosperity in the Caribbean, a new generation of African Americans chose migration over racial oppression in their native country. They responded to political exclusion in the United States with migration and resettlement in other parts of the black world that offered freedom and opportunity, notably Haiti. Their actions reflect aspiration for life beyond racial prejudice and a yearning for property ownership. In this sense, the establishment of the black Republic of Haiti spurred the expansion of freedom, autonomy, and citizenship beyond racial barriers. Haiti offered free people of color both opportunity for political equality and legal rights to landed wealth in a country where black people were in charge. In this sense, the Republic of Haiti represented a perfect fit for their notion of black Jacobinism. In his *Appeal to the Coloured Citizens of the World*, David Walker encouraged the American slaves to actively emulate and promote black Jacobinism in order to bring about their own freedom and equality, as the rebels of Saint-Domingue had done (2000, 19).

My approach is partly inspired by the work of Paul Gilroy (1993). If Gilroy writes of a transhistorical, global, and diasporic black culture rooted in and anti-imperialist protest, this chapter situates the historical patterns of black emigration within the context of collective protest of discrimination in the United States.

For many free people of color, the choice was between fleeing the United States and living in constant fear of the slave catcher. Because racial prejudice made black advancement impossible in the United States, immigration to the Caribbean and Africa was widely considered. A major proponent of emigration was the clergyman James T. Holly.

On October 3, 1829, James T. Holly was born in Washington, DC. Holly later became a religious leader, missionary, and black separatist. He saw in Haiti the best location for black progress. The idea of creating a model black republic in Haiti appealed to many African Americans because Haiti had achieved its independence through a successful slave insurrection. It was not a negotiated agreement as occurred in many countries. The Haitian slaves militarily defeated the local whites, the soldiers of the French monarchy, and the soldiers of the Spanish crown as well as a British expedition of 6,000 soldiers. The defeat of well-armed French, Spanish, and British armies is eloquent testimony to the deep aversion of freed slaves to a return to their former condition. This is reflected in Frederick Douglass's (1893) view of Haiti as the "only self-made Black Republic in the world." In 1857 James Holly described Haiti "as the vanguard of the Black race." Holly called upon African Americans to "contribute to the continued advancement of this Negro nationality of the New World," and he finally made Haiti his home. Like Holly, some 6,000 African Americans relocated to Haiti in the first quarter of the nineteenth century. This pattern continued throughout the nineteenth century. In 1859, for instance, the *Daily Picayune*, dated June 22, 1859, noted that a vessel of some 200 people had left for the island.

In order to facilitate the settlement of African Americans, Haiti eased foreign ownership rules for this group. People of African descent and Indian indentured laborers would become citizens after a year's residence. President Geffrard created immigration offices in the major ports of the country by decree on April 24, 1860.

Haiti was also revered in Latin America. For free blacks and mulattos in Cartagena, Colombia, Haiti was a vision of what their movement could accomplish, as well as an image of a virtuous, benevolent republic forged through revolutionary action against slavery (Lasso, 2001, 176–192).

The nineteenth century witnessed crossings in both directions. While African Americans resettled in Haiti to take advantage of freedom and opportunities, many refugee planters, with their slave retinues, sought haven in Philadelphia and New York. But planters feared that their slaves would seek to replicate the success of the Haitian Revolution. Robin Blackburn (2004) writes that the belated phasing out of slavery in New York (1799) and New Jersey (1804), expressed in the freeing of children born to slave mothers when they reached adulthood, served to discourage such unwelcome guests in those states.

The same way that African Americans reimagined their relationship with the rest of the black world, white planters often saw commonalities in their class interests. For Hatfield (2004, 139), planters who acquired slaves and created slave codes were members of a highly mobile group of English Atlantic elites. Provincial officials, who also displayed mobility across borders, often perceived their condition as shared and their interests as linked.

DOMESTIC POLICY

The evolution of domestic policy was shaped by an increasing emphasis on regionalism with the strength of regional movements counterbalancing centralized authority based in Port-au-Prince. Several social groups acquired control of trade circuits. They strengthened their financial controls and became dominant factions while controlling the import-export activities in their regions. The transmission of political power between the dominant factions occurred through various backstage political maneuvers. For instance, the Boyer administration was overthrown by the convergence of two separate regional social movements. The first originated in the liberal fraction of the southern elite. The second movement rode the waves of a popular uprising that also originated in the south. Peasant leaders Jean-Baptiste Goman and Jean-Jacques Acaau led heroic struggles for the fundamental rights of the Haitian peasantry. Their movement brought increased freedom to the peasantry. These leaders served as role models for future generations of peasant leaders. Their rhetoric was later used to demand agrarian reform. For instance, in 1844 a southern-based peasant movement called for an effective agrarian reform. The Piquets, who were so named after the pikes they carried, sought the implementation of an effective agrarian reform starting with state land.

The Praslin Manifesto of 1843 expressed the demands of the insurgents, which included the adoption of a rational plan for public education and national development. Development refers to the process through which the real per capita income (output) of a political unit (country, region, or locality) rises, with the understanding that the majority of the population can reap the benefits associated with this increase. This conception of development includes notions of individual freedoms that are conducive to personal fulfillment and participation in local affairs.

The constitution of 1843 reflected the predominance of liberals in the insurgent movement, which ultimately paved the way for the coming-to-power of a civilian government. Between 1843 and 1957, most governments sought a majority in the two chambers of parliament as a means to prevent the formation of an opposition there. Candidates were given a choice between inclusion in the presidential majority, which came with the hope of securing a ministerial post, and the opposition with its many perils. Needless to say, few individuals chose to remain independent of established regimes.

A consensus emerged with a group of mulatto politicians' selection of the black general Faustin Soulouque. It was believed that a black man should govern Haiti as a figurehead, while mulattoes ruled the country. This practice became known as *la politique de doublure*. Soulouque was self-proclaimed emperor in 1849.

Writer Edmond Paul (1882, 228) advocated governance by experts instead of politicians. "Power for the most competent" was the slogan of the future. This slogan was later adopted by the Liberal Party. The views of Edmond Paul were similar to that of Venezuelan writer Andrés Bello, who had written in 1836, "it is not enough to turn out men skilled in the learned professions; it is necessary to form useful citizens" (1881, 220).

Foreigners became predominant in commerce and industry very early in Haiti's history. By the end of the nineteenth century and the beginning of the twentieth century, German nationals were dominant in commerce and import-export activities in Haiti (Martinez, 1973, 3). The presence of foreign traders undermined the growth of the indigenous merchant class. Writing in the mid-nineteenth century, Louis Joseph Janvier observed that small industry and commerce in Haiti were "killed" by foreign competition (cited in Martinez, 7).

Most Haitian traders engaged mostly in middleman occupations, the retail trade in imports and the purchase of crops for export. The more resourceful indigenous traders did engage in "haut commerce" in the first half of the nineteenth century. Many invested in forestry, especially in the Artibonite (Joachin, 1972 146). Haitian traders exported large quantities of specialty woods, one of Haiti's most prized natural resources, to Europe and the United States. Adding trading housing, wholesale outlets, and commercial houses specialized in the export of coffee, Haitian-owned commercial houses represented more than half (70 out of 125) of all trading houses in Haiti in 1853–1856 (Joachin, 1971, 56–69).

Martinez (1973, 7) and Joachin ascribe the economic decline of the Haitian commercial elite to three main factors: (1) the inability of Haitian commerce and industry to withstand competition from imported goods; (2) the failure of the Haitian government to take steps to encourage domestic production and trade; and (3) civil strife that progressively destroyed the indigenous commercial infrastructure (Martinez, 1973, 7; Joachin, 1971, 146–147). One may add to this list the indigenous class' deprivation of foreign traders' resources. By the end of the nineteenth century and the beginning of the twentieth century,

German nationals were dominant in commerce and import-export activities in Haiti (Martinez, 1973, 3).

REFERENCES

Adam, André Georges. *Une Crise Haïtienne, 1867–1869 (Sylvain Salnave)*. Port-au-Prince, Haiti: Imprimerie Henri Deschamps, 1989.

Anderson, Benedict. *Imagined Communities: Reflections on the Origins and Spread of Nationalism*, rev. ed. New York and London: Verso, 1991.

Bello, Andrés. *Obras Completas*. Vol. 8. Chile: Imp. de Pedro G. Ramírez, 1881.

Berry, Mary Francis, and John Blassingame. *Long Memory: The Black Experience in America*. Oxford: Oxford University Press, 1982.

Blackburn, Robin. "Of Human Bondage: A Review." *The Nation*, September 16, 2004.

Boyer, Jean Pierre. Lettre de Boyer à Henri Grégoire du 7 Mai 1820. Paris, Bibliothèque de l'Arsenal, Mss. Fr. 6339, s.p. 3 pages.

Code Rural d'Haïti. Port-au-Prince, Haiti, 1826.

Comhaire-Sylvain, S. and J. "Urban Stratification in Haiti." *Social and Economic Studies* 8, no. 2 (1959): 179–189.

Dorsainville, J. C. *Histoire d'Haïti*. Port-au-Prince, Haïti: Henri Deschamps, 1943.

Douglass, Frederick. *Lecture on Haiti Delivered at Quinn Chapel Church* (January 1893).

Du Bois, W.E.B. *The Negro Church: Report of a Social Study Made under the Direction of Atlanta University; Together with the Proceedings of the Eighth Conference for the Study of the Negro Problems, Held at Atlanta University, May 26th, 1903*. Reprint of the 1903 edition. Walnut Creek, CA: Alta Mira Press, 2003.

Franklin, James. *The Present State of Hayti (Saint Domingo) Remarks on Its Agriculture, Commerce, Laws, Religion, Finances and Population*. Westport: Negro University Press, 1970. (Originally published in 1828 by John Murray.)

Franklin, John Hope, and Alfred A. Moss. *From Slavery to Freedom: A History of African Americans*. 2 volumes. New York: McGraw Hill, 2000.

Gazette Politique et Commerciale d'Haïti, December 19,1805.

Gilroy, Paul. *The Black Atlantic: Modernity and Double Consciousness*. Cambridge, MA: Harvard University Press, 1993.

Girault, Christian A. *Le Commerce du café en Haïti: habitants, spéculateurs et exportateurs*. Mémoire du Centre d'Études de Géographie Tropicale, (CEGET)-Bordeaux. Paris: Editions du Centre National de la Recherche Scientifique, 1981.

Grégoire, Henri. *Considérations sur le mariage et le divorce, adressées aux Citoyens d'Haïti*. Paris: Baudoin frères, 1823.

Griggs, Earl Leslie, and Clifford H. Prator. *Henry Christophe and Thomas Clark-son: A Correspondence.* Berkeley: University of California Press, 1952. Reprinted in 1968.

Hatfield, April Lee. *Atlantic Virginia: Inter-colonial Relations in the Seventeenth Century.* Philadelphia: University of Philadelphia Press, 2004.

Heinl, Robert D. and Nancy G. Heinl. *Written in Blood: The Story of the Haitian People, 1492–1971.* Boston: Houghton Mifflin Company, 1978.

Joachin, Benoit Brennus. "Commerce et Décolonisation: L'Expérience Franco-Haïtiennes au XIXe Siècle," Annales: Economie, Société, Civilisations 27 (1972): 1502.

———. "La Bourgeoisie d'Affaires en Haïti de L'Indépendence à L'Occupation Américaine." *Nouvelle Optique* 1, no. 4 (October–December 1971).

Lacerte, Robert K. "Xenophobia and Economic Decline: The Haitian Case, 1820–1843." *The Americas* 37 (April 1981): 499–515.

Lasso, Marixa. "Haiti as an Image of Popular Republicanism in Caribbean Colombia: Cartagena Province (1811–1828)." In David Patrick Geggus, ed., *The Impact of the Haitian Revolution in the Atlantic World.* Columbia: University of South Carolina Press, 2001.

Leyburn, James. *The Haitian People.* New Haven: Yale University Press, 1941.

Logan, Rayford Whittingham. *The Diplomatic Relations of the United States with Haiti, 1776–1891.* Chapel Hill: University of North Carolina Press, 1941.

Linstant de Pradines, S. *Recueil général des lois et actes du Gouvernement d'Haïti.* 5 vols. Paris: Par l'auteur, 1851–1865.

Mackenzie, Charles. *Notes on Haiti, Made During a Residence in that Republic,* v. 2. London: Henry Colburn and Richard Bentley, 1830.

Martinez, Gil. "De l'ambiguïté du nationalisme bourgeois en Haïti." *Nouvelle Optique* 9 (January–March 1973): 1–32.

Métraux, Alfred. "Making a Living in the Marbial Valley (Haiti)." Paris: UNESCO, Occasional Papers in Education, 1951.

Moral, Paul. *Le paysan Haïtien.* Paris: Maisonneuve et Larose, 1961.

Paul, Edmond. *Les causes de nos malheurs: Appel au Peuple.* Kingston, Jamaica: Geo. Anderson & Co.: 1882. 1882.

———. *Questions politico-économiques: II, Formation de la Richesse Nationale.* 1837–1863. Paris: Imprimerie de P. A. Bourdier, 1863.

Plummer, Brenda Gayle. "The Metropolitan Connection: Foreign and Semi-foreign Elites in Haiti, 1900–1915." *Latin American Research Review* 19, no. 2 (1984): 119–142.

Rouzier, Sémextant. *Dictionnaire Géographique et Administratif d'Haïti.* Port-au-Prince, Haïti: Imprimerie AUG A. HERAUX, 1983.

Saint-Louis, René A. *La présociologie haïtienne; ou, Haïti et sa vocation nationale,* Préf. de Roland Lamontagne. Québec: Leméac,1970.

Saint-Rémy, Lepelletier de. *Saint-Domingue: Etude et Solution de la question haï-tienne*. 2 Volumes, Paris: Arthur Bertrand, 1846;.

Saunders, Prince. *Haytian Papers, A Collection of the Very Interesting Proclamations and Other Official Documents, Together with Some Account of the Rise, Progress, and Present State of the Kingdom of Hayti. An Address, Delivered at the Bethel Church, Philadelphia, on the 30th of September, 1818, Before the Pennsylvania Augustine Society, for the Education of People of Color*. Memoir, Presented to the American Convention for Promoting the Abolition of Slavery and Improving the Condition of the African Race. Boston: Caleb Bingham, 1818; Philadelphia: Rhistoric Publications, 1969.

Simpson, George E. "Haitian Peasant Economy." *The Journal of Negro History* 25, no. 4 (October 1940): 498–519.

Le Télégraphe, June 10, 1819: 1.

Turnier, Alain. *Les États-Unis et le Marché Haïtien*. Montréal: L'Imprimerie de Saint-Joseph, 1955.

Vergniaud, Leconte. *Henri Christophe dans l'Histoire d'Haïti*. Paris: Editions Berger-Levraut, 1931.

Victor, René. *Recensement et Démographie*. Port-au-Prince, Haiti: Imprimerie de l'Etat, 1944.

Walker, David. *Walker's Appeal, in Four Article, Together with a Preamble, to the Coloured Citizens of the World, But in Particular, and Very Expressly, to Those of the United States of America, Written in Boston, State of Massachusetts, September 28, 1829*. Edited, annotated, and with an introduction by Peter Hinks. University Park: Pennsylvania State University Press, 2000.

Wingfield, Roland, and Vernon J. Parenton. "Class Structure and Class Conflict in Haitian Society." *Social Forces* 43, no. 3 (March 1965): 338–347.

4

The Pre-Occupation Era
(1843–1915)

The period between 1843 and 1915 was marked by significant state instability, particularly toward the end of the nineteenth century and the beginning of the twentieth century. During this period, the predatory state reached its maturity in Haiti. The political process degenerated into a simple competition to grab public assets. Most of the presidents concentrated on their personal revenues at the expense of their security. The outcome was that they did not last long in power. Some 22 heads of state succeeded one another from 1843 to 1915. Only 11 of them lasted for more than one year. Generally, the administrations were too weak to prevent their downfall by opponents in search of power.

Foreign merchants of different nationalities manipulated the political process to their benefit, which further destabilized the country. To fully understand this process, it is important to fully grasp the historical relationship between the government of Haiti and foreign traders.

The late nineteenth-century Haiti faced limited access to credit. From 1804 to 1880, Haiti did not possess any banking institutions. Efforts by successive governments to establish a state-owned bank repeatedly failed because they lacked the required initial capital. As a result, in 1880 the Haitian government signed a concession agreement with a French limited company, the National

Bank of Haiti, which authorized that company to issue currency and to serve as the country's only commercial bank (Thoby, 1955, 16). By this means, the Haitian government hoped for a rejuvenation of national production and commerce. Instead, using its position as the only bank in the country, the National Bank made a fortune, largely through financial speculation, the provision of high-interest loans to the Haitian government, and the collection of important commissions for issuing paper money and managing the Haitian treasury department (Châtelain, 1954, 37; Thoby, 1955, 92). Edmond Paul and Boyer Bazelais, the leader of the Liberal Party, attacked the Salomon government on the issue of the founding of the bank in these terms: Salomon had handed the country to the whites (Bazelais, 1883). This warning was justified. American interests in the reformed National Bank of Haiti were part of the rationale for the American invasion of 1915 and 19 years of American military occupation.

The National Bank of Haiti profited from the political instability of the country. For instance, in the absence of income taxes, import and export duties were the country's most important source of recurrent revenue. These duties financed the majority of the Haitian budget in 1880–1881. In times of civil wars, the ports usually open to foreign trade were either closed or operating under capacity. Revenue collection was also severely undermined. This deprived the central government of an important share of its revenues. Because Haiti's international credit standing was conditioned on its stability and repayment capabilities, the recurrent political instability of the country created credit shortages. The central government needed between 150,000 to 180,000 gourdes every month to balance its budget (Marcelin, 1909, 64). It also needed advances to pay its internal and foreign debts. Successive governments did not raise taxes in fear that this would fuel support for their opponents. As a result, they contracted loans at usurious rates from the National Bank and merchant-bankers (Joachin, 1979, 151). Some 71 percent of short-term and statutory loans made by the bank went to the Haitian government. The Haitian government signed another trade agreement with France on July 31, 1900, which further opened the Haitian market to goods of French manufacture. The signing of a trade agreement between Haiti and France occurred after Haiti was allowed to borrow a substantial loan on the French credit market in 1898 (Joachin, 1971, 56, 69). If anything, this trade agreement testifies to France's influence on political development in Haiti throughout that period.

THE SIGNING OF THE CONCORDAT OF 1860

For many observers, the signing of the Concordat of 1860 between the Haitian government and the Vatican augured poorly for Haiti. In particular, Louis Joseph Janvier (1884) wrote, "This religious treaty of 28 March 1860 was bad. The treaty instituted another source of power. The church will quickly become unmanageable and overly proud as it finds itself unchangeable, always increasing its power on the side of the temporary, ephemeral and decreasing political power."

STATE INSTABILITY

The second half of the nineteenth century witnessed constant political strife as various political factions vied for power. This exacerbated instability with increased frequency of political scandals, constitutional crises, coups d'état, and successions of provisional governments. Frequent regime change meant constant changes of political appointees and thus instability of state policy. In turn, unstable policy decisions increased investor uncertainty and subsequently decreased investments in the country.

Black-led regional armies constantly challenged centralized mulatto rule. Rebellions ousted successive administrations. The instability associated with the fight for control over the central government crippled the economy, which remained dependent on export crops and subsistence agriculture. The country witnessed unstable authoritarian rule. Outbreak of civil violence in Haiti undermined policy continuity and stability. National commerce constantly suffered important losses as a result of power struggles between incumbents and presidential aspirants. Few presidents remained in office for the entire term for which they were elected, and even fewer were reelected. Most were prematurely forced from office through outbursts of civil violence. In this regard, the Commission of Inquiry of the United States Occupation of Haiti concluded that "until the basis of political structure is broadened by education, the Haitian government must necessarily be more or less unstable and in constant danger of political upheavals" (Moore, 1972, 58).

Disputes between foreign merchants and Haitian nationals led various foreign merchants to call in their respective gunboats. One of the most revealing episodes of this period was the Lüders Affair. In 1897 a German citizen who had assaulted a police officer was condemned to a prison term. Under the pressure of the cannons of the Kaiser Guillaume II, Lüders was freed and compensated by the Haitian state, which he later left. This is often referred to as Gunboat Diplomacy. In this context, between 1849 and 1913, U.S. warships anchored in Haitian waters on 26 occasions to protect Americans in the context of civil wars, coups, and insurrections.

This long spate of political instability (civil violence, wars, coups d'état, and politically motivated fire) invited the first American intervention in Haiti. Aside from consolidating the position of American merchants, the American intervention aimed to suppress the black-led regional armies, which posed a major threat to national and international elite interests.

In the period between 1850 and 1915, demographic pressures and erosion of natural resources led to the establishment by the peasantry of a production system in which coffee occupied an important place beside subsistence foodstuffs. The Haitian peasantry also emerged as a political force. Two major peasant rebellions emerged in the period between 1844 and 1922: by the Piquets in the south and the Cacos in the north. In 1844 a southern-based peasant movement called for open revolt against mulatto rule. The Piquets, who, as noted in the previous chapter, were so named after the pikes they carried, aimed to "dispossess the rich, implement an effective agrarian reform starting with state land and suppress the dominance of the mulatto bourgeoisie by installing a 'black'[person] in the presidency" (Dorsainville, 1943, 199). Although the Piquets were subsequently forced into submission, the power elite adopted a policy of rule through black presidents as a means to secure the acquiescence of the population that came to be known as the *politique de doublure*. They facilitated the coming to power of black emperor Faustin Soulouque. Soulouque proved very efficient in calming demands for black representation in governance.

Rival groups used arson and pillage to gain or maintain power. For instance, a politically motivated arson destroyed the commercial infrastructure at Port-de-Paix in 1895. All trading establishments and foreign residences disappeared in the fire of January 17, 1895. With this nefarious act, some 2.5 million francs in tariffs that were collected annually by the Haitian government also vanished (*Le Peuple*, March 23, 1895, 3).

The Haitian military forces carried out coups on a regular basis, either on their own behalf or for politicians. In some cases, one rival group preferred inviting foreign intervention rather than sharing power with its enemy. These disreputable practices, at worst, destroyed the commercial infrastructure of an entire city.

The opening of the country to foreign investments at the end of the nineteenth century and the beginning of the twentieth century reinforced the position of foreign merchants. First, they received much of the commercial credit allocated the National Bank. Second, for fear of arousing foreign hostility, the Haitian government compensated foreign merchants for losses incurred during civil strife. Many foreign merchants made a fortune sowing civil discord and collecting grossly exaggerated indemnities from the government of Haiti. Some merchants collected indemnities that represented many times the market value of the original asset. Many foreign merchants entrenched themselves in the Haitian political arena. The Syrians were blamed for the arson that took the palace and the life of Haitian president Leconte (*Le Matin*, August 28, 1912).

Third, many foreign merchants financed presidential aspirants whenever incumbents refused to comply with their demands. This practice triggered sociopolitical strife and further destabilized the political process. For instance, during 1959–1910, nine Haitian presidents succeeded each other: (1) Fabre Nicholas Geffrard (1859–1867); (2) Sylvain Salnave (1867–1869); (3) Nissage Saget (1870–1874); (4) Michel Domingue (1874–1876); (5) Boisrond Canal (1876–1879); (6) Lysius Félicité Salomon (1879–1888); (7) François Denis Légitime (1888–1889); (8) Florville Hyppolite (1889–1902); and (9) Nord Alexis (1902–1908). Successive compensations for civil unrest, which were supplemented with pillage, murders, and arson, bankrupted government finance and impeded investments in development, as Haiti suffered continuing net losses of capital.

Continuing instability undermined American exports and depressed the American share of the Haitian import market. By the middle of the 1880s, American imports were limited to the trade in provisions and lumber. The

President Hyppolite distinguished himself from others by erecting the Iron Market of Haiti. Photographs and Prints Division, Schomburg Center for Research in Black Culture, The New York Public Library, Astor, Lenox and Tilden Foundations.

American flag was disappearing from Haitian ports in part because of the prominence of German traders. In the 1880s, the Germans quickly became the most numerous and active element in the commercial sector. German merchants owned almost half of the large commercial houses in Port-au-Prince and other trading cities. The bulk of imported manufactured goods increasingly came from Germany (Nicholls, 1974, 19). An influential Haitian newspaper of the epoch, *L'Impartial*, wrote, "The protest of Germans Jews established in Haiti will remain an ensemble of absurd pretensions that will never be achieved. The Germans made their fortune by means of our civil discord" (October 22, 1897, 1).

One of the most identifiable goals of American foreign policy toward Haiti during that period was to eliminate German competition in the Haitian import market in order to increase investment opportunities for American businesses. When the Kaiser indicated his intention to increase Germany's investments in Haiti in the late 1914, the United States responded negatively (Lafeber, 1984, 51).

As a result, industries in North America began pressuring the State Department for aggressive foreign policies toward the other great powers. In particular, they sought specific export advantages through trade agreements with Latin American and Caribbean countries (Ferguson, 1984, 63). Then U.S. Secretary of State, William Henry Seward, forced the French out of Mexico and signed, on August 27, 1860, a reciprocity treaty with Venezuela, which was to serve as a model for the Haitian agreement (Logan, 1941, 293–304). Four years later, the United States concluded a bilateral commercial treaty with Haiti. The treaty granted American citizens the same treatment as Haitians in terms of taxes, patents, and licenses.

Several American firms secured contracts with the Haitian government. Under contract with the Boirond Canal administration in 1878, an American firm erected a bridge over the Artibonite River at Pont-Sondé. Except for the wooden roadway, the whole bridge was made of iron works, solid and elegant and measuring 300 feet long and 30 feet wide, a significant accomplishment in late nineteenth-century Haiti (Chauvet and Prophète, 1874, 90; Aubin, 1910, 280). This market attracted both local and regional commerce.

In spite of the 1864 treaty, American imports were still limited to trade in provisions and lumber. The Germans quickly became the most numerous and active element in the commercial sector, supplanting French, British, and American merchants. In 1890, the bulk of imported manufactured goods increasingly came from Germany (Nicholls, 1974, 19; Montague, 1940, 164). German merchants quickly developed friendly ties with Haitians of all social classes and married into elite families, thus becoming very conversant in Haitian ways of life. They carefully examined the tastes and habits of their clients, to which they catered even in the smallest details. They also managed to sell their goods at low prices—in some cases, 30 percent cheaper than comparable goods from other European countries. The United States was unable to compete with Germany in the Haitian import market largely because of the small size of its commercial community. The expiration of the Haitian-American Reciprocity Treaty in 1905 further undermined the commercial presence of the United States.

Rivalry between merchants' communities of various countries combined with the weakness of the Haitian state impeded the development of self-reliant policies. For instance, in 1903 President Nord Alexis enacted an exclusion law that restricted the Arabs' commercial activities to wholesale trade, made naturalization more difficult, and prohibited migration from the Levant (*Le Moniteur*, 1904, 1). The Arab community responded by threatening to use the military power of the United States to settle their disputes with the government.

In 1891 the first group of Levantine immigrants had landed in Haiti with little capital and market connections. In succeeding decades, they used thrift, ethnic solidarity, and commercial credit to establish import, wholesale, and retail businesses in Haiti. Although some Levantine immigrants secured Haitian nationality, most opted for French or American citizenship because this status was related to protection and commercial connections. American citizenship was particularly prized because, again, American citizens had been granted equality with natives in terms of taxes, patents, and licenses.

Levantine merchants used their foreign citizenship as leverage in their relations with the Haitian government. Under pressures from indigenous traders, the "Law on the Syrians" was voted by the Haitian legislature on August 13, 1903, with the aim to "protect Haitian commerce from the invasion of Levantine traders" (*L'Aurore*, April 1, 1909, 1). This law was subsequently published in the Official Bulletin of the Department of Justice in 1912.

In response, Levantine traders urged their commercial partners in the United States to lobby the State Department on their behalf. American manufacturers valued the Arabs as purchasers and distributors of American goods in Haiti and were determined to use the diplomatic and military influences of their country to assist them. Under pressure from the National Association of Manufacturers, the U.S. Minister to Haiti, William F. Powell, insisted that the Haitian government postpone the execution of the exclusion law under the guise that American manufacturers would incur major losses if their partners in Haiti were forced to leave the country without some months of notice (Plummer, 1981, 533). Under American pressures, the government of Haiti postponed implementation of the exclusion law for a full year. As a result, the Levantine community was characterized in the media as a small but powerful state within the Haitian state (Le Matin, 1911, 2). From 1909 to 1915, seven presidents succeeded each other, and all were overthrown by uprisings.

The last president, Vilbrun Guillaume Sam, remained in power only four months, at the end which and under threats from armed factions, he instituted a regime of terror that culminated, just before his fall, in the assassination of dozens of political prisoners. The political crisis then reached its paroxysm. The people of Port-au-Prince, in one moment of anger, hunted down the demised president and the prison chief, Charles Oscar Etienne, to the embassy of France and the Dominican consulate where they had sought refuge and executed them in the open air on July 28, 1915. These events gave the U.S. State Department the opportunity and rationale to intervene in Haiti.

The occupation occurred in the context of the application of the Monroe doctrine. Needless to say, under the American occupation of Haiti, American businesses thrived as never before, and German competition was eliminated.

REFERENCES

Aubin, Eugene. *En Haiti: Planteurs d'autrefois, negres d'aujourd'hui.* Paris: Librairie Armand Colin, 1910.

L'Aurore. "La Question Syrienne." April 1, 1909: 1.

Bazelais, Boyer. "La Banque Nationale" *L'avant-garde.* April 12, 1883.

Bulletin Officiel du Département de la Justice. Loi sur les Syriens. Votée par le Sénat le 23 Juillet; par la Chambre le 10 Août 1903. Promulguée le 13 Août 1903. Moniteur du 8 Juin 1904. Port-au-Prince, Haïti: Imprimerie Edmond Chenet, Numéro 1, 6ième année, Janvier-Février 1912.

Châtelain, Joseph. *La Banque Nationale: Son histoire, Ses problèmes.* Lausanne, France: Imprimerie Held, 1954.

Chauvet, Henri and Raoul Prophete. *A Travers la Republique d'Haiti: Relations de la Tournee Presidentielle dans le Nord* (Premiere Serie). Paris: Imprimerie Vve Victor Goupy, 1874.

Dorsainville, J. C. *Histoire d'Haïti.* Port-au-Prince, Haïti: Henri Deschamps, 1943.

Ferguson, James. *Far From Paradise: An Introduction to Caribbean Development.* London, UK: The Latin American Research Bureau, 1990.

L'Impartial. "Les Allemands et leur protestation." October 22, 1897: 1.

Janvier, Louis Joseph. *Les antinationaux, actes et principes.* Paris: G. Rougier, 1884.

Joachin, Benoît. *Les Racines du Sous-Développement en Haïti.* Port-au-Prince, Haiti: Imprimerie Henri Deschamps, 1979.

Lacerte, Robert K. "Xenophobia and Economic Decline: The Haitian Case, 1820–1843." *The Americas* 37 (April 1981): 499–515.

Lafeber, Walter. *Inevitable Revolutions: The United States in Central America.* New York: W. W. Norton and Co., 1984.

Logan, Rayford Whittingham. *The Diplomatic Relations of the United States with Haiti, 1776–1891*. Chapel Hill: University of North Carolina Press, 1941.

Le Matin. "La Catastrophe du Palais National: l'Enquête du Matin. Interview de Monsieur John Laroche. " August 28, 1912.

———. "Encore la Question Syrienne." November 21, 1911: 2.

Marcelin, Frédéric. *Le Général Nord Alexis*. Paris: Société Anonyme de L'imprimerie Kugelmann, 1909.

Martinez, Gil. "De l'ambiguïté du nationalisme bourgeois en Haïti." *Nouvelle Optique* 9 (January–March 1971): 1–32.

Le Moniteur. "Liste des Syriens et Levantins qui se sont inscrit au Bureau Central de la Police Administrative de la Capitale." no. 52 (29 Juin 1904): 1.

Montague, Ludwell Lee. *Haiti and the United States, 1714–1938*. Durham: Duke University Press, 1940.

Moore, Ernest O. *Haiti: Its Stagnant Society and Shackled Economy*. New York: Exposition Press, 1972.

Nicholls, David. *Economic Dependency and Political Economy: The Haitian Experience*. Montreal: McGill University Centre for Developing-Area Studies, 1974.

Le Peuple. "Un Sinistre a Haïti." March 23, 1895: 3.

Plummer, Brenda Gayle. "Black and White in the Caribbean: Haitian-American Relations, 1902–1934." PhD thesis, Cornell University, 1981. Includes bibliographical references. Ann Arbor, MI: University Microfilms International, 1997, 751–773.

Thoby, Perceval. *Nos Crises Economiques et Financières: Nos Contrats de Banque, Nos Emissions de Monnaie, Nos Emprunts, et la Réforme Monétaire, 1880 à 1888*. Clamart: Imprimerie Habauzit, 1955.

Turnier, Alain. *Les Etats Unis et le Marché Haïtien*. Montréal: Imprimerie Saint-Joseph, 1955.

5

The American Occupation of Haiti and Its Aftermath (1915–1957)

After the demise of President Guillaume Sam, American troops invaded Haiti and started an occupation to prevent Rosalvo Bobo, an anti-American but popular Haitian leader, from taking power. American forces intervened under the command of Admiral William B. Caperton of the U.S. Navy. Every so often, American-backed Haitian presidents succeeded each other.

The landing of American troops took place in the afternoon of July 28, 1915. The Washington warship arrived in the roadstead of Port-au-Prince. That evening, some 400 Marines disembark at Bizoton. They quickly took over the main control stations of Port-Au-Prince. The United States then handpicked Philippe-Sudre Dartiguenave, a pro-American mulatto politician, to become president for seven years on August 12, 1915. As an elite representative, Dartiguenave received the occupants with open arms. By convention, the United States committed to maintain order in the country, to restore the national finances, and to lead a police force called *Gendarmerie d'Haïti*, public hygiene service, and public works. For 12 years, from 1918 to 1930, the Council of State fulfilled the function of parliament, marking the return of the unicameral parliamentary system. On June 12, 1918, the American forces secured the ratification of a constitution written by then Assistant Secretary of the Navy Franklin D. Roosevelt. This new constitution reversed all previous barriers to the penetration of foreign capital. It revoked the clause of prohibition of foreign land ownership that had been present in the previous 18 Haitian constitutions.

The occupying force instituted a system of strict financial control, and American firms came to dominate the Haitian economy. Two major beneficiaries were National Citibank and the American Manufacturers' Association. Roger L. Farnham was then vice president of the National Citibank of New York, a shareholder in the two largest American companies in Haiti in the early twentieth century, the National Bank of Haiti and the Railroad Company. Farnham was a personal friend of Boaz Long, then division chief in the Latin American Bureau of the State Department. In 1914, Woodrow Wilson himself asked Farnham to negotiate with the Haitian government an agreement that would grant the United States control over Haitian customs (Castor, 1971, 28).

The census of the population in the period of the American occupation reflected a stunning increase in demographic growth. From a population of 500,000 in 1804, the country had a population of 2.1 million in 1920. In the absence of major migratory movement to Haiti, this growth has to be attributed to natural factors. Official census estimates show a constant pattern of growth from 780,000 in 1850 to 1.6 million in 1900 to 2.1 million in 1920.

The African American reaction to the U.S. occupation of Haiti reflected a particular worldview in which Haiti was regarded as the symbolic center of Pan-Africanism (Guterl, 1999, 345). W.E.B. Du Bois drew powerful connections between the fate of African Americans in the negrophobic United States and the fate of Haiti's own "darker people" (Plummer, 1982, 127). Prominent African American writers such as Herbert Seligman, James Weldon Johnson, and W.E.B. Dubois all viewed the Haitian expedition by the United States as having nothing to do with benevolence. Dubois stated, "the United States is at war with Haiti."

In the middle of the twentieth century, the Haitian government imposed monopolies on four products: bananas, sugar, tobacco, and cement. Aside from these four monopolies, the exploitation of topsoil resources was subject to concession from the Government of Haiti. The Haitian government then granted land and market concessions to more than a dozen of companies, which received vast tracts of land in the fertile plains of northern and Artibonite sections of Haiti. These companies were the Haitian American Sugar Company, the Haiti Product Company, the United West Indies Corporation, the Société Commerciale d'Haïti, the North American Sugar Company, the Haitian Pineapple Company, the Haitian American Development Corporation, the Haitian Agricultural Corporation, the Société Haitïano-Américaine de Développement Agricole, the Caldos Sugar Company, and the Standard Fruit and Steamship Company. Among these, two main American companies, the W. Rosenberg and the HASCO, received land concessions amounting to 1,461, 875.43 acres.

Under the banana monopoly, the government of Haiti granted concessions for purchase of bananas in given areas and fixed the price at which the concessionaire could buy the product from growers. In 1935 the government of Haiti granted a concession to the New Orleans–based Standard Fruit and Steamship Company to grow and purchase bananas for export. When Standard Fruit began to penetrate the Artibonite Valley, it did not occupy virgin lands. These lands were already being planted in sorghum, corn, sugarcane, potato, and beans.

The Standard Fruit and Steamship Company developed plantations both in Les Cayes, the regional capital of the south, and the Artibonite provincial division in northern Haiti (Simpson, 1940, 507). For instance, the locality of Verrettes in the Artibonite department witnessed the establishment of many American-owned export-oriented corporate plantations in the first half of the twentieth century. Verrettes was fully integrated in transatlantic trade during the U.S. occupation of Haiti (1915–1934). The National Railroad Company linked the ports of Port-au-Prince to Verrettes by way of the Artibonite Valley.

American investments in the Artibonite department can be understood in light of the preponderance of flat plains and availability of water. Verrettes, in the Artibonite region, enjoys a flat surface. It is located between two mountain chains (the Montagnes Noires and the Chaînes des Matheux) and the Gulf of Gonâve. The plain has been formed by the accumulation of sediments carried by inundation waters. The U.S. occupation directly impacted agricultural production in the Artibonite region. Occupation forces rehabilitated irrigation networks, many of which were abandoned in the post-independence era. Some 99.41 miles or 160 square kilometers were rehabilitated, and several new dams were constructed in that region.

The Artibonite Valley, where Verrettes is located, reaches to a height between 54.68 yards and 109.36 yards and measures 2,936.60 miles. The valley derives its name from the Artibonite River (91.86 yards), the longest watercourse in the Republic of Haiti (200 miles in length). The Artibonite River rises in the Dominican Republic southeast of the town of Restauracíon and flows first southwest and then northwest before passing through the Grand-Saline, or salt plain, to a muddy outlet on the Gulf of Gônave (Dorsainville, 1932, 189).

Many historical events occurred in the Artibonite, leading political observers to view that region as the entrails of the country. The region witnessed the rebellion against the Colonial Assembly of Saint Marc on the Ducasse de Plassac Estate in 1789, the erection of a monument against French rule at the Crête-à-Pierrot fort, and the proclamation of the independence of Haiti in Gonaïves in 1804.

American companies were also active in other parts of the country. Several American companies established large plantations devoted to the production of sisal, rubber, sugarcane, and banana for export. Overall, the land controlled by eight foreign companies amounted to 81544.77 acres in 1946, including land leased from the state and private entities (Dartigue and Baker, 1946, 323). The Haitian state rented 2,500 hectares to the Caldos Sugar Company in northern Haiti by the middle of the twentieth century (Zuvekas, 1979, 6). The Haitian-American Sugar Company and the Société Haitïano-Américaine de Développement Agricole by themselves exploited 30,000 hectares in the Cul-de Sac Plain (Mazoyer, 1985, 10). The constitution of the Haitian American Sugar Company in 1918 reinstated the export of sugar from Haiti. Large sugar plantations in the Léogane and Cul de Sac Plains produced virtually all sugar production for export from 1918 to 1950.

The commercial production of sugarcane on large estates was reintro-duced in Haiti during the American occupation. The production of sugar-cane took place principally in the plains. Except for the sugarcane used by small private mills throughout the country for local consumption, the bulk of sugarcane was processed by the Haitian American Sugar Company (HASCO) to produce molasses and sugar for export. Rum of fine quality was produced by several private Haitian companies, using syrup or cane juice in the mash, rather than molasses for domestic consumption (United Nations Mission of Technical Assistance to Haiti, 1949, 97). In addition to the sugarcane produced on its own plantations, HASCO purchased sugarcane from peasants in sur-rounding localities. Twenty producers furnished HASCO some 46 percent of the cane that the company purchased from the Léogane Plain.

The Société Haitïano-Américaine de Développement Agricole also made substantial investments in sisal production (U.N. Mission, 1949, 96). For in-stance, the production of sisal took place almost entirely on large plantations owned in part by private concerns, including the Dauphin Plantation and the Haitian Agricultural Corporation, both operating in northern Haiti. The Dauphin Plantation in the northeast of Haiti occupied 49421.07 acres much of which was planted in sisal (Mazoyer, 1984, 10).

The plantations were established to promote the production of agricul-tural products of strategic importance to the United States during World War II. Briefly advantaged by the disappearance of the supply of rubber in the southeastern Asiatic area, the Société Haitïano-Américaine de Développe-ment Agricole successfully engaged in the production of hevea rubber, sisal, and lumber. The company benefited from the high price accorded to sisal in international markets in the late 1940s. It also invested roughly $700,000 in the establishment and maintenance of large rubber plantation at Bayeux, in the northern provincial division. Roughly 1,600 acres of flat land and some 300 acres of steep slopes were planted in rubber there. At Bourdon, in the Sources Chaudes section of the southern provincial division, about 2,250 acres of land were prepared, but only 250 were planted. An additional 1,970 acres or rub-ber were planted at Sources Chaudes proper by the same corporation (U.N.

Mission, 1949, 135). The United States Rubber Development Corporation also invested large sums in a program for the production of rubber from cryptostegia, which proved to be a failure despite support from the government of Haiti (U.N. Mission, 226).

Many members of American troops humiliated members of the traditional elite. But the true challenge to the occupation came from Charlemagne Péralte, the leader of the Caco War. Born in 1886, Péralte was the descendent of a prestigious family of the Central Plateau of Haiti. He was born in town of Hinche, a city founded in 1503, where still stands one of the oldest cathedrals in the Americas. He was a member of the educated Haitian elite. When the American forces landed, he was the military commander of the Place de Léogane, and in a rebellious act, he refused to cede to the marines. He was demoted, arrested, and humiliated. He reappeared a few years later with the title of defender of national sovereignty.

The Cacos resistance was, however, confined to the northern and Artibonite sections of Haiti, where Péralte succeeded in mobilizing dozens of thousands of men. Using guerrilla tactics, the Cacos posed a military threat to the American forces in spite of primitive armament. But this resistance movement failed to mobilize the populations of the west and the south of Haiti, and this enabled the marines to concentrate all of their firepower on the rebellious areas.

Popular discontent with the Americans was widespread. The institution of coerced labor (or *corvée* in French) forced peasants to work six days per year in road maintenance. The imposition of coerced labor for public works put fire to the powders. Several thousand peasants rose up to the word of order of Charlemagne Péralte.

The relative opening of the country to foreign investments at the end of the nineteenth century and the beginning of the twentieth century had reinforced the preeminence of the capital city of Port-au-Prince as the location of foreign enterprises. It was in this context that 1911 in the north of the country, a peasant revolt exploded. The political instability that followed the insurrection was manifest in the short presidential administrations (five between August 1911 and July 1915) and the assassination of the Haitian president in 1915 that provoked the American occupation.

The bilateral convention remained in effect until 1935. The American occupation responded to the social crisis through institutional means such as modernization of the bureaucratic sector, enhancement of technical capabilities of the army, urbanism, and establishment of new rules in the competition for power.

The leader of the Cacos insurrection, Charlemagne Péralte, perished in an ambush on November 1, 1919. His body was then nailed on a door in the posture of a cross at Petite Rivière of the Artibonite and exhibited in a public place as punishment. His cadaver was buried in a secret location to prevent his tomb from becoming a revered place for Haitian national-ism. After Péralte's death, the Cacos reorganized themselves and fought the American occupation for two years under the leadership of Benoît Batraville. The assassination Batraville culminated in the end of the Cacos revolt in the summer 1920.

The pro-American policies of Louis Borno, who became president of Haiti in 1922, broadened public support for the end of the occupation. Some promi-nent elite intellectuals, who had previously supported the occupation, began to change their positions because their dignity was hurt by the manners of the American soldiers and the exclusivity of privileges accorded to the Americans.

In the late 1920s and early 1930s, a pro-indigene current emerged in Latin America that influenced Haiti. The indigenous person was revalorized in the literature. In Haiti, the focus was placed on African traditions. Several writers initiated archeological research, and the first works on the island before the arrival of Christopher Columbus were published by Edmond Mangones and Jacques Roumain.

In particular, Haitian writer Jacques Roumain articulated a nationalist posi-tion and agitated for an end to the American occupation. Roumain was one of the founders of *La Revue Indigène,* a magazine that sought to articulate an authentically nationalist voice in the face of the U.S. occupation of the country. Haitian nationalism was born out of the resistance against American occupation.

Jacques Roumain was born on June 4, 1907, in Port-au-Prince (Haiti). High-ly politically involved, he was first imprisoned in 1929, under the American occupation. He published successively three major works: *La proie et l'ombre* (1930) (The Prey and the Shade), *La montagne ensorcelée* (1972) *(The Enchanted Mountain)*, and *Les fantoches* (1977) (The Ghosts). Upon leaving his govern-mental functions, he was again arrested in 1933 and 1934, right after found-ing the Haitian Communist Party, which he served as Secretary General. He traveled a lot and stayed nearly a year by the side of poet Nicolás Guillén in Havana, Cuba. The election of President Lescot, in 1941, allowed him to return to Haiti.

Upon his return, he founded the Bureau of Ethnology of Republic of Haiti and served as its director. He also published *Contribution à l'étude de l'ethnobotanique précolombienne des Grandes Antilles* (Contribution to the Study of the Pre-Columbian Ethno-Botanical of the Greater Antilles) in 1942 and, then, in 1943, *Le Sacrifice du Tambour-Assoto* (The Sacrifice of the Assoto Drum). Roumain quickly took the defense of voodoo, particularly during the occu-pation. From the standpoint of religious orthodoxy, voodoo was considered a superstition, but actually, the mixing of Catholicism and voodoo expresses a conception of the world.

Roumain's *Master of the Dew* is a posthumous novel that crossed national borders to become a heritage of the humanity. It is true that this book, which has been reissued repeatedly, expresses creative writing, so much in form and in depth. The language is refined as characters express themselves in a Creole replete with images and double meanings. In this cosmopolitan novel, Manuel returns to Haiti from Cuba and settles in Fond Rouge, where he uncovered an untapped source of water. The author is as cosmopolitan as his writings. Jacques Roumain accepted the position of chargé d'affaires at the Haitian embassy in Mexico, and Lescot took this opportunity to send him to a golden exile. It was in Mexico that Roumain wrote *Master of the Dew*.

An election supervised by the marines in November 1930 led to the ascent to power of Sténio Vincent (1930–1941). Vincent had a reputation as a nationalist. At the same time, a chamber of deputies full of Haitian nationalists took office. Haiti reintegrated its national life in the presence of American forces. Several bilateral agreements permitted the removal of occupation forces in public services and the increasing Haitian presence in the Garde d'Haïti. The Haitian military academy was created in 1930 as a replica of the naval academy of the United States. Vincent witnessed the departure of American troops from Haiti on August 21, 1934.

After the departure of American troops, the Haitian army exercised functions of interior security in the tradition instituted by the American occupants in 1915. Committed since its creation to operations of pacification of the cities and countries, notably against the Cacos, this institution remained prepared against all attacks. Set in motion was a national defense strategy to repress demonstrations and save the nation against the internal threat of democratization.

Haitian military expenditures captured an important proportion of the country's national budget. This trend persists in the contemporary period. In the 1990s, defense expenditures represented some 30 percent of the Haitian national budget. This allocation drained away crucial revenues that could have been used for economic development.

With the establishment of the Institute and the Bureau of Ethnology emerged several studies on the African origins of the Haitian nation. Roumain's work influenced many Haitian writers, including Jacques Stephen Alexis, who authored the novels *Compère Général Soleil* (General Sun, My Brother) and *L'espace d'un cillement* (In the Flicker of an Eyelid). Alexis was assassinated by the thugs of Haitian dictator François Duvalier in 1961.

THE AFTERMATH OF THE AMERICAN OCCUPATION

There are significant differences in the interpretations of the outcomes of the U.S. occupation of Haiti. Some authors claimed that the occupation performed a positive role in the democratization process in Haiti (Allison and Beschel, 1992; Smith, 1994). Their critics have emphasized that U.S. interventionism in Haiti in the early twentieth century aimed at excluding European merchants from the Haitian market, not at promoting democracy (Castor, 1971, 28; Lafeber, 1984, 51; Kehoe, 1994, 2581). One other critic went as far as stating that the democratic instruments and practices that developed during the occupation forces were neither participatory nor competitive (Archer, 1973, 57–58). This view is shared by Plummer, who argued, "The Haitian protectorate was unprecedented in its duration, the racism that characterized U.S. behavior in the black republic and the brutality associated with the pacification efforts" (1992, 101). Plummer went further in stating, "The United States neither changed nor reformed Haitian politics but inadvertently strengthened and assured the survival of many of its worst features" (1992, 120). This statement finds support from Haitian scholar Michel-Rolph Trouillot, who wrote, "In the end, the U.S. occupation worsened all of Haiti's structural ills. In our view, it is simply unfortunate that America's military and political interventions in Haiti have never been backed by sufficiently sustained or vigorous efforts to ease the country's crippling poverty" (1990, 107).

Despite differences over the effects of the prewar U.S. occupation, these authors are in agreement that the American occupation had a lasting impact on Haiti.

Levels of mortality receded beginning in the 1920s. It has been estimated that life expectancy at birth rose from 30 years at the beginnings of the 1920s to 38 years between 1950 and 1955 and to 53 years between 1980 and 1985 (United Nations, 1985). This major progress, which cannot be ignored, has been attributed to improvements in sanitary conditions as manifested by the amelioration of public health and hygiene, the establishment of health centers, and campaigns against large epidemics.

FIRST MAJOR OUTCOME OF THE OCCUPATION: DOMINATION OF AMERICAN CAPITAL

Even after the departure of American troops, Haiti remained a strategic location for the United States. The American occupation consecrated the domination of American capital over the emerging Haitian economy. At the end of World War II, the only important industries in Haiti were a sugar refinery and a sisal-processing plant, both American-owned (Moore, 1972, 7).

As noted previously, in 1935 the government of Haiti granted a concession to the New Orleans–based Standard Fruit and Steamship Company to grow and purchase bananas for export. The market concessions stimulated banana production in the Artibonite region. The Standard Fruit and Steamship Company established centralized plantation systems and promoted banana production. Large banana plantations measuring more than 1,2355.26 acres existed in many localities in the Artibonite. Larose (1976, 9) reported that 29 proprietors possessed altogether 5,268.28 acres in the Léogane Plain in the early 1930s.

Although the Standard Fruit and Steamship Company purchased bananas produced on individual small peasant holdings, it also maintained its own plantation on 1,500 hectares in the Artibonite region rented from the government of Haiti. The Standard Fruit Company possessed large banana plantations in Canneau, Verrettes (Knappen Tippetts Abbett Engineering Company, 1950, 31). From 1937 to 1947, it developed its plantations by tapping the open banks at Daquin (Head Gate Canal) and installing irrigation pumps in the left and right banks of the Artibonite River. In 1947 the Inter-American Service for Agricultural Production installed new pumps for further irrigation of the Artibonite Valley. The irrigation system resulted from a contract between the government of Haiti and the Export-Import Bank of the United States.

When the Standard Fruit Corporation was operating in Désarmes, a tap of the Artibonite River and the Canal of the Maury River irrigated the locality. The capture of water at Moreau, on the Artibonite River, permitted the cultivation of 2,000 hectares. The Standard Fruit Company exported 2,000,000 stems of bananas grown in Haiti in 1938–1939, primarily to the United States (Simpson, 1940, 508). Difficulties in enforcement of quality control and the retraction in 1946 of monopoly rights previously accorded to the Standard Fruit and Steamship Company caused the abandonment of the Haitian market by that company and the related downfall of national banana production. The decline of Standard Fruit led to a transition to other agricultural systems, notably the culture of rice, to take advantage of the irrigation system established by Standard Fruit.

Although Haitian banana exports declined in the 1940s, coffee production and export increased in the same period. Coffee exports increased significantly starting in late 1938. The growth of coffee exports was linked to producer organization in this sector. In the 1940s, loose associations of producers acquired more structures. The Conseil National des Coopératives was established in 1953. It launched a series of fiscal incentives that permitted the growth of cooperatives throughout the country. Unfortunately, in the period between 1950 and the 1960, considerable damage was inflicted to the coffee and cacao plantations by various hurricanes.

SECOND OUTCOME: TRANSFER OF LARGE DOMAINS TO HAITIAN STATE

Another major impact has been the transfer of large domains to the Haitian state and subsequent sale of such properties. Both Barthélemy (1990, 133) and (Girault, 1981, 93) reported the existence of former corporate plantations in Cul-de-Sac and Léogane Many large estates were transferred to private entities because the state was unable to maintain its ownership rights. What occurred was private appropriation of state land by real operators of these lands. In cases where new occupants lacked full-fledged titles, they subleased these domains in small plots on insecure terms. But many large estates were suddenly subject to dissolution. As stated by Simpson (1940, 504), many bourgeois Haitians were compelled to divide and sell their last reserves of land. According to Métraux et al. (1951, 53), the splitting up of properties reached an advanced stage in the late 1930s and the beginning of the 1940s. An increase in land conflict led to the enactment of the law of September 7, 1949, as amplified by the decree of August 18 1950, which established the official land Register (Office National du Cadastre) as a means to determine and matriculate all parcels constituting the Haitian land domain.

Haitian land-succession practices are largely inspired by the Napoleonic Code. On the one side, the land tenure system rests on the equality of children at the time of dividing the familial inheritance. On the other, there is no obligation to engage in joint ownership. It is entirely possible for heirs to engage in joint ownership of the inheritance. The customary law favors, however, some heirs at the expense of others. Land succession practices can be employed to exclude young females from the land inheritance. They can also lead to inequalities in the sharing of inheritance by children of different forebears. Overall, small peasant property dominates the fundamental land systems in Haiti. Large properties are rare and in general are circumscribed around the big cities. Most properties are not legally divided. Legal splits of inherited properties do not keep up with the rhythm of inheritance. Joint ownership within a family is managed by the attribution of specific benefits to individuals or groups of individuals.

Peasant property is established as individual in spite of joint ownership. The rights of each inheritor can be identified or alienated at all times. The management of joint ownership is often achieved through individualization of parcels, with defined limits, farmed by specific individuals. There is no collective property as can be found in Africa.

THIRD OUTCOME: LABOR EXPORTATION

The third outcome of the U.S. occupation is an important pattern of labor exportation toward Caribbean islands and Latin American countries. Migration is prevalent among all social classes in Haiti. Before the American occupation, migration was an option for the middle and upper classes of Haiti. With the labor exportation policy, all social classes became involved in emigration. Some 300,000 Haitians left for sugarcane harvests in the Dominican Republic and Cuba until 1929. This explains the presence of Haitian descendents in both Cuba and the Dominican Republic. Several large waves of organized Haitian labor-oriented migrations to other Caribbean territories took place during this period as well. The strong growth of emigration in the 1920s and again in the 1960s reduced natural birth growth, but Haitian families in Haiti remained connected to their kin abroad. The maintenance of these links is crucial for family survival and national development.

Haitian Labor Migration to Cuba

The migration to Cuba and the Dominican Republic exerted a significant influence on population levels. Haitian emigration was connected to structural crises, which affected the sugar industry. A weak Haitian emigration wave to Cuba was observed at the end of the nineteenth century due to the emergence of an anti-immigration movement. In response, a Cuban ordinance of 1902 sought to curb the entry into Cuba of "Haitians, Jamaicans and Chinese laborers." In spite of these restrictions, Haitian labor migration to Cuba continued until 1930. There was an important flow of peasants from southern Haiti to Cuba, where they worked in the sugarcane fields and sugar mills. Several peasants returned from Cuba with enough capital to purchase land in the south of Haiti, which explains the significant occurrence of peasants with a legal ownership deed called a *manman pyès*. This is a legal document issued by a notary that testifies to the legitimacy of ownership of actual occupants of parcels.

However, it was truly in the second decade of the twentieth century that Cuba and the Dominican Republic were forced to hire the abundant cheap labor of neighboring countries to work in sugar plantations then in high growth. Records show the immigration to Cuba of 280,000 Haitians, Jamaicans, and Puerto Ricans from 1909 to 1934 (Centro de Estudios Demográficos, 1974). Taking into account the respective populations of these countries in this era, Haitian workers would have represented more than half of the total.

Ethnographic research reveals the trajectory of Rodier, a young peasant from the south of Haiti who migrated to Cuba in search of a better life. In June of 1927, Rodier decided to leave for Cuba along with other family members. Like other peasants from the south of Haiti, they took the boat in Cayes, the location of established recruitment agents for Cuban sugar companies. Upon arrival in Cuba, Rodier was a domestic servant in Camaguey for a few months before being hired by a sugar company. According to data furnished by the Cuban Bureau of Immigration, the number of Haitians residing in Cuba totaled approximately 54,429 for the provinces of Camaguey and Oriente in

1930. This figure likely under-represents the actual Haitian presence because many Haitian laborers did not have an identity card. Haitians living in the Cuban province of Santa Clara went unreported.

After eight years in Cuba, Rodier returned to southern Haiti with Spanish fluency and memories of bateys (sugarcane plantations). While in Cuba, Rodier met Rosina Clerval, a native of Gandou in southern Haiti. Rosina traveled to Cuba in 1925 in the company of a *viejo*, a person who had sojourned in Cuba or Dominican Republic and who had returned to Haiti. At first, Rosina was a domestic servant. Later, she engaged jointly with a female friend in itinerant petty trade in different bateys in Cuba. Upon meeting Rodier, Rosina abandoned these activities to settle down with Rodier, who had the fortune of winning 10,000 pesos in the Cuban lottery. In 1935 both Rosina and Rodier had a triumphal return to southern Haiti, where they married a year later.

Upon their return to Haiti, the couple moved to Les Cayes, the regional capital of the south, where they cultivated relations with middle-class individuals of the town. The stories of Rodier and Rosina were widely shared in town and stimulated further migrations of southern Haitians to Cuba.

Haitian Labor Migration to the Dominican Republic

Labor exports to Dominican Republic started during the American occupation of both countries, beginning with Haiti in 1915 and the Dominican Republic in 1916. The Dominican census of 1920 revealed the presence of 28,000 Haitians, and that of 1935 indicated the presence of 53,000 Haitians (Veras, 1983). It is worth noting that these numbers reflected only regular Haitian migration. Clandestine migration to the Dominican Republic was significant but unreported in these figures.

The international economic crisis of the 1930s, which severely affected the sugar economies of the region, considerably reduced these patterns and even produced return migrations. In 1937 the presence of numerous Haitians in the Dominican Republic, in a context of crisis, was at the origin of troubles that resulted in the massacre of more than 30,000 Haitians. The massacre of 1937 poisoned relations between the two countries. It fomented greater mistrust between the two governments and between the Haitian people and their own government.

In 1937, Dominican dictator Rafael Leonidas Trujillo ordered the Dominican military to kill any Haitian living on the Dominican side of the border in order to arrest the invasion of the country. In an effort to justify the massacre, Dominican diplomats also presented the Haitian presence as a menace to public safety. In 1942, according to Bernardo Vega (2007), Dominican chancellor Arturo Despradel stated in a correspondence addressed to the American ambassador that the Haitians brought illnesses to the country. Thousands of innocent Haitians and Dominicans of Haitian descent lost their lives as Trujillo sought to cleanse the border with Haiti. In early October 1937, the Dominican military, accompanied by armed civilians, entered the areas of Manzanillo Bay, Tierra Sucia, Capotillo, El Aguacate, La Penita, El Cajuil, and Santiago de la Cruz and killed thousands of Haitians, Dominicans of Haitian descent, and Dominicans of dark complexion. This genocide was an act of terror directed at Haitians and black and poor Dominicans, but also against peons, journeymen. The Cut, as the massacre became known, had a political and class connotation, because it articulated both racism and anti-Haitianism. That the Massacre of 1937 occurred within days of the Day of the Race (Día de la Raza) was not by chance. The Day of the Race celebrates the existence of Hispanic identity and community in the Dominican Republic and rejects African heritage, which is often relegated to Haiti. There is a mental structure that posits that "Hispanic" identity is associated with development whereas blackness is associated with the ignorance and underdevelopment. Haiti is associated with savagery and devil worship due to the connection with voodoo, and to poverty and economic backwardness. These processes can be traced back to political manipulation by the Trujillo regime.

Haitians blamed Vincent for settling for an indemnity of $550,000 from Trujillo. In 1938 the Haitian government engaged in an enterprise of internal colonization with the Haitian agricultural workers who had escaped from the Dominican Republic. Five colonies measuring a total of 10892.40 acres were established with the first installment of the indemnity that was presumed to be paid by the Dominican government for massacred Haitians on its territory. Some 6,000 individuals were settled in these colonies (Dartigue and Baker, 1946, 315).

In order to consolidate his power, Trujillo suppressed dissent both in the Dominican Republic and abroad. It is in this context that repression of the right of expression of Haitian dissident Jacques Roumain can be best understood. In the middle of April 1938, the legation of the Dominican Republic filed a complaint with Quai d'Orsay, which is often used as a synonym for the Ministry of Foreign Affairs of France. In response to this complaint, Jacques Roumain and Pierre Saint-Dizier, manager of the magazine *Regards,* were arrested and charged of defamation against a foreign head of state. The arrest came on the heel of *Regards'* publication of an article by Roumain titled "The Haitian Tragedy," in the November 18, 1937, issue of the magazine (in other words, five months before the arrest). The article accused the Dominican dictator, Rafael Trujillo, of genocide. It also accused Haitian president Sténio Vincent of complicity in this case. This was the first time that a French newspaper was pursued for "defamation of a foreign head of state."

With widespread popular discontent, Vincent's administration ultimately succumbed in 1941. His successor, Elie Lescot, came from the ranks of the mulatto elite. The administration of Haitian president Elie Lescot (1941–1946) distributed state land at derisory prices to partisans in the Artibonite provincial division in search of regime stability. Like his predecessor, Lescot's reputation was tarnished by rumors that he too received a gift of $35,000 from Dominican dictator Trujillo. Haiti signed a Haitian-Dominican Commercial Convention on August 26, 1942, which stated that the number of Haitians residing in Dominican Republic was 16,000 (Victor, 1944, 45).

The period between 1915 and 1946 marked the ascension to power of several mulatto politicians, including Sudre Dartiguenave, Louis Borno, Eugène Roy, Sténio Vincent, and Elie Lescot. The year 1946 marked the departure of the mulattoes from power. A populist movement emerged that demanded power in the name of a black majority and the formation of a black bourgeoisie.

The uprising against Lescot in 1946 was led by numerous intellectuals. In the years that immediately preceded 1946, Haiti witnessed the emergence of eminent men who contributed to creating in Port-Au-Prince a climate full of intellectual effervescence that quickly reflected itself in the columns of a newspaper titled *La Ruche* (The Hive). These intellectuals included Jacques Roumain, Pierre Thoby-Marcelin, Jean F. Brière, Félix Morisseau-Leroy, and Carl Brouard. The poetic works of many intellectuals sparked the explosion called the "Five Glorious of 1946" (Les Cinq Glorieuses de 1946), which referred to the revolutionary days of January 7–11, 1946. It started with Jacques Roumain's *Master of the Dew*. There was also the magazine *Tropics* by Aimé Césaire, which was avidly read in Haiti., René Depestre published his compilation of poems in 1945. In the end, the revolution of 1946 was the result of an exploding fusion between poetry and insurrection.

In the 1950s, Haiti was a prime Caribbean tourist destination, which was visited by then vice president Richard Nixon. In the 1960s and 1970s, the place attracted figures from famous author Graham Greene to performer Mick Jagger. Plush resorts dotted the white sand beaches between Port-au-Prince and St. Marc. Philanthropist Albert Schweitzer came to Haiti and founded one of the best medical facilities in the country, the Albert Schweitzer Hospital. The hospital first opened its doors to patients on June 26, 1956, in the Artibonite region of Haiti. It serves more than a quarter of a million patients per annum and has gone beyond its original structure to become an integrated system of health care that emphasizes health prevention and education, public health, and community development.

FOURTH OUTCOME: CENTRALIZATION

The fourth outcome of the American occupation was the continuance of centralization, which bore negative consequences. André-Marcel D'Ans (1987, 221) wrote, "The American occupation ended tipping up the scale of hegemony in favor of Port-au-Prince" (formerly called the Western Department). A new bifurcation occurred between the Port-au-Prince and the hinterland.

Centralization undermined institutional development in the provinces. The extent of administrative centralization is gauged by applying available measures of the weight of national and local administrations, including the proportion of public revenues raised and expended by these units of governments, and the concentration of authority, responsibility, and resources. Most public employees work in Port-au-Prince's metropolitan area. Commercial houses engaged in the export of coffee also base their operations in the port cities of Haiti and principally in the capital city of Port-au-Prince.

Centralization also makes it difficult to harness local resources for the purpose of influencing national and local legislation, policy, and practice. This translates into reduced absorptive capacity. Although the central government repeatedly asserts its commitment to reduce interregional disparities, the concentration of powers and resources in the capital city remains a factor. The localization of economic and political institutions in or around the capital city of Port-au-Prince and related perceptions of career advantages and privileges stemming from placement at the center reinforce the centripetal bias of development and cause major disparities in resources and salaries between Port-au-Prince and rural areas. Shortage of technical expertise causes significant economic loss. Centralization contributes additionally to a centripetal bias of development. The concentration of most administrative, commercial, and educational facilities there has served to reinforce the position of the capital city as the most vibrant center of the country. In particular, the concentration of government, banking, import and export functions, manufacturing, and other functions in of Port-au-Prince has served to attract the more dynamic elements from the rural areas to the capital city. Internal migration continues unabated from the provincial towns and the countryside toward Port-au-Prince. As a result of limited education facilities in rural areas, the great majority of the population is illiterate and, as such, bound by ancient traditions and inadequate cultivation techniques.

Generally, urban areas grew four times faster than rural zones and three times faster than the overall population between 1950 and 1982 (Maingot, 1986–1987, 79). The rural population currently represents roughly 70 percent of the total population, in comparison with 88 percent in 1950 (Nations Unies, 1990, 10). Because of the instability associated with rural–urban migration, it takes time for rural migrants to become fully active in urban political systems. Moreover, many rural migrants are women who were sent to the city as domestic servants, or *restavèk* in Haitian Creole.

As alluded to previously, the centralization of educational facilities in the capital city of Port-au-Prince and limited investments in rural education undermine educational attainment and participation in the provinces. The contribution of educational attainment to democratic participation has been widely acknowledged (Moore, 1972; Cook, 1948). The high rate of illiteracy renders difficult the definition, articulation, and defense of the collective interests of rural dwellers. It also hinders adoptions of effective public services.

FIFTH OUTCOME: POLITICAL EMERGENCE OF THE HAITIAN ARMY

The fifth and last major outcome of the U.S. occupation was the emergence of the Haitian army as a political force. The American occupants abolished the traditional army. One year into the occupation, they trained and maintained an indigenous police force to guarantee stability, which took the successive names of "Gendarmerie d'Haïti" and "Garde d'Haïti." This force was trusted with the monopoly of organized violence, which it used to assert itself as a major political force in the post-occupation era. This institution used its monopoly over violence to eliminate social and political movements. The Garde d'Haïti helped the American military crack down on an internal insurgency that threatened the U.S.-backed regime during the American occupation.

During the occupation, the country was divided into military districts with a unified military command. Section chiefs controlled rural areas at the local level but ultimately reported to Port-au-Prince commanders. The Garde d'Haïti was renamed "Armée d'Haïti" in 1947 and "Forces Armées d'Haïti" in 1958. The organization and institutional capacity were largely superior to that of any sectors in Haitian society. Benefiting from American assistance and influence in the context of the cold war, the Haitian army managed to acquire considerable social control and political power. Operating in virtual autonomy from civil control, the army consistently imposed on contending factions the means and conditions for access to power. Prospective candidates for elective offices at all levels regularly courted the army hierarchy.

With privileged access to American assistance and influence, the Haitian army acquired considerable social control. Operating with virtual autonomy from civil society, the army imposed on contending factions the means and conditions for access to power. Because of its social control, the Haitian military had historically enjoyed impunity. Impunity is the absence of investigation, trial, and punishment of serious human rights violations.

The armed forces dominated the political life of the country until the arrival to power of François Duvalier in 1957. The "Five Glorious" revolutionary days of January 7–11, 1946, contributed to the Dictator Élie Lescot's departure for exile. The pro-mulatto regime of President Lescot was widely criticized by the Black Power Collective in Haiti, which sought to install a black-oriented government. In the logic of the collective, any Haitian government should distribute important posts in the public administration according to the ethnic composition of the population. Because blacks formed the majority of the population, they should occupy a majority of posts in the public administration. According to this view, the collective adopted the former slogan of the National Party of Lysius Salomon: "The power to those in biggest numbers!" Indeed, a historical controversy opposed the National Party (founded in 1874), which proposed governance on the basis of numbers, and the Liberal Party (founded in 1870) by the honorable Anténor Firmin, Boyer Bazelais, and Edmond Paul, which sought to bring Haiti to a new era of modernity.

The Haitian army consistently imposed its terms and conditions on contending factions seeking power. The threat of use of sheer violence by the army consistently prevented the emergence of coalition-building practices because support from the army gave the ruling faction leverage to implement unilateral state actions. The imposing stature of the army was reflected in the country's national budget: military expenditures captured an important share of resources. Frédéric Marcelin (1910, 13) expressed a dissenting note with the statement that "as long as the army is what it is in our home country, the only national institution, the only one institution before which all bend and all fold, the one institution that absorbs all, finances and men, the one that levels everybody under its domination, nothing good, nothing right, nothing useful could be done." Using its exclusive access to tools of coercion, privileged access to American assistance, and influence, the Haitian army acquired considerable social and political power. The most powerful actor on the ground was the Military Executive Committee (C.E.M., the French initials for Comité Exécutif Militaire), which was composed of army majors Paul E. Magloire and Antoine Levelt and Colonel Franck Lavaud. Fully aware of the power of the army, Dumarsais Estimé successfully courted the army hierarchy to secure elective offices at various levels. He first secured the support of Astrel Roland, the former army commander of the Artibonite region, to become deputy. He was later able to leverage the allegiance of two of the most powerful officers of the Haitian army to become president.

A political deal between Army Major Paul E. Magloire and Dumarsais Estimé would culminate in the election of Deputy Dumarsais Estimé by his peers to the presidency. Estimé was a powerful black intellectual with significant landholding in his native town of Verrettes in the Artibonite region of Haiti. During his tenure, Estimé purchased support for his government by reserving official positions for his benefactors, including those in the legislature. Estimé was deposed in 1950 by a military coup d'état led by Magloire himself.

Magloire began his rule with the solemn promise that neither mulattoes nor blacks would dominate Haiti at the expense of the other. With the backing of the 6,000-man army, Magloire's rule seemed entrenched. Tourism flourished, and relations with the United States improved. The period between 1950 and 1957 was relatively stable because of the effects of the boom of the 1950s and the stability of the price of coffee in the international market. Postwar coffee exports were at their highest during the early 1950s, when they exceeded 30,000 tons (500,000 bags) on several occasions. The boom of the postwar era in the United States resulted in signs of prosperity in Haiti during this period. However, neither Magoire's reign nor political stability lasted long. A major social crisis hit the country with the advent to power of François Duvalier.

In the period preceding the 1957 elections, François Duvalier was a relatively obscure candidate, particularly in the Artibonite region. Rather than presenting an electoral platform that identified and addressed the expectations of voters, Duvalier sought the favors of Dumarsais Estimé, who had still retained significant popular support in the Artibonite region. In campaigning for the presidential office, Duvalier identified with Estimé to secure the votes of his supporters in the Artibonite. Many voted for Duvalier there with the understanding that he would pursue Estimé's policy of promotion of the interests of the black middle class. This period was influenced by a pro-black ideology, which promoted both the numerical superiority of blacks over mulattoes and the predominance of African heritage in Haitian culture, which were taken as a basis of legitimacy of governance by the fraction that was closest to African.

Duvalier subsequently established a predominantly black militia force, the Tontons Macoutes, which engaged in heavy recruitment in the region. The Duvalier regime fully politicized land grants. It purchased the loyalty of the few and engaged in the repression of the many. On many occasions, the regime withdrew state land from one disgraced planter to allocate the land to a zealous follower. In this sense, group political action in Haiti exhibited clientelistic characteristics rather than fulfilling associational functions. As defined by Lemarchand and Legg, political clientelism refers to a "personalized, affective and reciprocal relationship between actors, or sets of actors, commanding unequal resources and involving mutually beneficial transactions that have political ramifications beyond the immediate sphere of dyadic relationship" (1972, 151–152). Land distribution created an atmosphere of messianic expectations from Duvalier, who was dubbed "Papa Doc."

REFERENCES

Allison, Graham T., and Robert P. Beschel. "Can the United States Promote Democracy?" *Political Science Quarterly*, 107, no. 1 (Spring 1992): 81–98.

Archer, Jules. *The Plot to Seize the White House.* New York: Hawthorn Books, 1973.

Barthélemy, Gérard. *L'Univers rural haïtien: Le pays en dehors.* Paris: Editions l'Harmattan, 1990.

Castor, Suzy. "L'Occupation Américaine d'Haïti." *Nouvelle Optique: Recherches Haïtiennes et Caribéennes* 1, no. 2 (1971). Centro de Estudios Demográficos. *Emigración hacia Cuba.* La Habana, Cuba: Centro de Estudios Demográficos, 1974.

Cook, Mercer. *Education in Haïti.* Washington, DC: Federal Security Agency, United States Office of Education, 1948.

D'Ans, André-Marcel. *Haïti: Paysage et Société.* Paris: Éditions Karthala, 1987.

Dartigue, Jehan, and Edouard Baker. "Quelques Données sur la Situation Agraire dans la République D'Haïti." Washington, DC: Caribbean Research Council, 1946, pp. 315–325.

Dorsainville, Luc. *The Rivers and Lakes of Haiti.* Washington, DC: Union of American Republics, 1932.

Douglas, Paul H. "The Political History of the Occupation." In Emily Greene Balch, ed., *Occupied Haiti* (pp. 15–36). New York: Writers Publishing Company, 1925.

Dubois, W.E.B., Herbert Seligman, and James Weldon Johnson. "Haiti." In David Levering Lewis, ed., *W.E.B. Dubois: A Reader.* New York: Henry Holt, 1995.

Dupuy, Alex. *Haiti in the World Economy, Class, Race, and Underdevelopment since 1700.* Boulder and London: Westview Press, 1989.

Girault, Christian A. "Le Commerce du Café en Haïti: Habitants, Spéculateurs et Exportateurs." *Mémoire du Centre d'Etudes de Géographie Tropicale,* (CEGET)-Bordeaux, Paris: Editions du Centre National de la Recherche Scientifique, 1981.

Guterl, Matthew Pratt. "The New Race Consciousness: Race, Nation, and Empire in American Culture, 1910–1925." *Journal of World History* 10, no. 2 (1999): 307–352.

Kehoe, Mark T. "A History of Hard Feelings." *Congressional Quarterly* (September 17, 1994): 2,581.

Knappen Tippetts Abbett Engineering Company. *République d'Haïti: Rapport Technique et Économiques Développement de la Vallée de l'Artibonite pour l'Irrigation, le Control des Crues, le Drainage et l'Énergie Hydroélectrique (traduit de l'Anglais).* New York and Port-au-Prince: Knappen Tippetts Abbett Engineering Company, 1950.

Lafeber, Walter. *Inevitable Revolutions: The United States in Central America.* New York: W. W. Norton and Co., 1984.

Larose, Serge. *L'Exploitation Agricole en Haïti.* Fonds-St-Jacques: Centre de Recherches Caraïbes, 1976.

Lemarchand, René, and Keith Legg. "Political Clientélisme and Development." *Comparative Politics* 4, no. 2 (January 1972): 149–178.

Maingot, Anthony P. "Haiti: Problems of a Transition to Democracy in an Authoritarian Soft State." *Journal of Interamerican Studies and World Affairs* 28, no. 4 (Winter 1986–1987): 75–102.

Marcelin, Frédéric. *Bric-à-brac.* Paris: Société anonyme de l'Imprimerie Kugelmann, 1910.

Mazoyer, Marcel. *Crise de l'Économie Paysanne haïtiennes et Conditions de Développement.* Paris: Institut national agronomique Paris-Grignon, Département des sciences économiques et sociales, 10 Juillet 1984.

Métraux, Alfred." Making a Living in the Marbial Valley, Haïti: Report Prepared by Alfred Métraux in Collaboration with E. Berrouet and Dr. and Mrs. Jean Comhaire-Sylvain." Paris: UNESCO, 1951.

Moore, Ernest O. *Haiti: Stagnant Society and Shackled Economy.* New York: Exposition Press, 1972.

Nations Unies. *Monographies sur les politiques de population: Haïti.* New York: Nations Unies, Département des affaires économiques et sociales internationales, Politique de population, document numéro 25, 1990.

Nicholls, David. *From Dessalines to Duvalier: Race, Colour and National Independence in Haiti.* Cambridge: Cambridge University Press, 1979.

Plummer, Brenda Gayle. "The Afro-American Response to the Occupation of Haiti, 1915–1934." *Phylon* 43 (June 1982): 125–143.

———. *Haiti and the United States: The Psychological Moment.* Athens: University of Georgia Press, 1992.

Roumain, Jacques. *Sur les superstitions.* Montréal: Mémoire d'Encrier, 2005.

———. *Les Fantoches.* Port-au-Prince, Haiti: Ateliers Fardin, 1977.

———. *La Montagne Ensorcelée.* Paris: Éditeurs français réunis, 1972.

———. *Le sacrifice du tambour—Assoto.* Port-au-Prince: Imprimerie de l'État, 1943.

———. *Contribution à l'étude de l'ethnobotanique précolombienne des Grandes Antilles.* Port-au-Prince: Imprimerie de l'État, 1942.

Simpson, George E. "Haitian Peasant Economy." *The Journal of Negro History*, 25, no. 4 (October 1940): 498–519.

Smith, Tony. *America's Mission: The United States and the World-Wide Struggle for Democracy in the Twentieth Century.* Princeton, NJ: Princeton University Press, 1994.

Trouillot, Michel-Rolph. *Haiti, State against Nation: The Origins and Legacy of Duvalierism.* New York: Monthly Review Press, 1990.

United Nations. *Haiti Sequel to Civil Unrest. UNDRO Situation 86/0812.* New York: United Nations, 1986.

United Nations Mission of Technical Assistance to Haiti. *Mission to Haiti.* New York: Lake Success, 1949.

Vega, Bernardo. *Trujillo y Haití, la agresión contra Lescot.* Santo Domingo: Fundación Cultural Dominicana, 2007.

Veras, R. A. *Inmigración, Haitianos, Esclavitud.* Santo Domingo: Edición Taller, 1983.

Victor, René. *Recensement et Démographie.* Port-au-Prince: Imprimerie de l'Etat, 1944.

Zuvekas, Clarence, Jr. "Land Tenure in Haiti and Its Policy Implications: A Survey of the Literature." *Social and Economic Studies* 28, no. 4 (December 1979): 1–24.

6

Political Culture
(1957–1986)

Although marginally representative, Haitian governments remained dominated by competing factions. Many Haitian scholars have emphasized the dichotomy between state and nation. The tension between these two elements is reflected in a dialectic tension between two different political cultures in Haiti: the culture of authoritarianism and the culture of peace. The first political culture promotes mistrust and exclusion. The second culture is driven by trust at interpersonal and community levels.

THE AUTHORITARIAN POLITICAL CULTURE

The authoritarian political culture is as old as Haiti itself. Since the establishment of the Republic of Haiti, authoritarian regimes have used brute force to impose themselves. Although the state has not formally imposed property and language requirements to impede popular voting, armed forces, whether regular or irregular, have created an environment of fear and intimidation to discourage voter participation. Irregular armed forces have varied in name from the Zenglen under Soulouque, to the Macoutes under the Duvaliers, to the zenglendos and attachés under the coup regime that misruled Haiti between 1991 and 1994 and the Chimères under Jean-Bertrand Aristide. They all served their purpose of depressing participation and intimidating potential civilian opposition.

Prior to the 1957 elections, François Duvalier was a relatively obscure candidate. In order to bolster his standing in predominantly black Haiti, the Duvalier regime developed a false sense of nationalism. He also appealed to base instincts of darker-skinned Haitians as a means to create a political base by advocating the power of those with pure African blood as a means to marginalize his lighter-skinned political rivals. For instance, Jérémie has always had a commercial class engaged in national production for export, which competed with the commercial class of the sea side of Port-au-Prince, which specialized in the importation of foreign goods to Haiti. The commercial class of Jérémie was also known for some anti-Duvalier sympathies. Duvalier eliminated the competition with the massacre of 1963. The discourse surrounding the massacre is replete with pro-African slogans to marginalize the predominantly light-skinned commercial class of Jérémie.

Duvalier aligned himself with better-known black politician Dumarsais Estimé, who earlier rewarded François Duvalier with the post of minister of public health for his early support and his professed adherence to indigenism. Estimé was himself deposed by a military coup d'état in 1950. At the downfall of Estimé, Duvalier refused to accept the coup and the government of Paul Eugene Magloire and instead joined the opposition. Upon the fall of Magloire on December 6, 1956, Duvalier declared his candidacy for the presidency. In the elections organized on September 22, 1957, he was declared a winner with 678,860 votes. The nearest competitor, Louis Déjoie, received 264,830 (*Le Nouvelliste*, September 28, 1957).

As previously noted, Duvalier did not construct an electoral platform identifying and addressing the expectations of voters. Instead, Duvalier leaned on the class of the landowners and managers of the Estimé administration. Both Duvalier and Estimé were fervent promoters of Haiti's 1946 revolutionary movement aimed at having the black middle class seize power. Duvalier's discourse was fraught with indigenous overtones. He succeeded in mobilizing the black lower middle class in a quest of social ascension. His main opponent in the presidential race was Louis Déjoie. Déjoie was one of the rare Haitian entrepreneurs capable of developing the local industry, but he was a mulatto. Many voted for Duvalier with the understanding that he would pursue Estimé's policy of promotion of the interests of the black middle class. For 31 years, Duvaliers ruled the Republic of Haiti as presidents-for-life—first François Duvalier and then his son, Jean-Claude. The Duvaliers used coercion to maintain power because of their narrow social base, which consisted of large proprietors and a small faction of the commercial bourgeoisie. Many profited from the rise of Duvalier, eliminating their competitors and reinforcing, consequently, their own political position.

The Duvaliers engaged in unprecedented repression of their opponents. Unable to find mechanisms to legitimate their rule, the Duvaliers relied excessively on the use of force to impose their priorities. The designation of the National Unity Party, the political party of François Duvalier, as the only legal party in the country signaled the beginning of a monopoly rule in Haiti. Political activities were outlawed except under the auspices of the official party, thereby eliminating possibilities for political opponents to seek and assume power through competitive elections.

The Duvaliers consolidated power by eliminating the faintest attempt at opposition. They claimed more than 40,000 human lives. They developed a coercion network made up of the Macoutes, the Haitian army, right-wing paramilitary groups, and rural magistrates to prevent civilian resistance to authoritarian rule and repress political opposition activity, while censoring or castigating any critique of the state.

The regime enjoyed impunity because during the Cold War, security interests overrode American concerns about human rights violations. For several decades, the U.S. government supported friendly dictators because such regimes were seen as bulwark against communism. This prevented strict enforcement of punitive measures against dictators such as Duvalier.

The main instrument of repression under Duvalier was the predominantly black militia force, the Tontons Macoutes, which was used to counter the mulatto-controlled official army. The Macoutes had a parallel operation from the army and had direct contacts with the president.

One of the most notorious henchmen of François Duvalier ("Papa Doc") was Luckner Cambronne. Cambronne was once the second most feared man in Haiti. Cambronne set up the National Renovation Movement, which was essentially a front for extortion. Funds would be collected from businessmen, presumably to rebuild a slum or pave a road, but most of the money would end up in the pockets of Duvalier and his notorious henchman. Cambronne was also known for ruthlessly rounding up known or suspected political opponents and letting them rot in the notorious Fort Dimanche prison.

As the successor to the infamous Clément Barbot, Cambronne was entrusted by the dictator to lead the process of revising the Haitian Constitution of 1964, which established the president-for-life system and enabled the young Jean-Claude to succeed his father on April 22, 1971. The transfer of power from the senior Duvalier to Jean-Claude Duvalier, after the death of the former, is testimony of the strength of the Duvalier regime.

Cambronne also played a key role in the elimination of the guerrilla movement that emerged in Cazale, Haiti, in 1969, under the leadership of peasants and intellectuals of the Parti Unifié des Communistes Haitien (PUCH, Unified Party of Haitian Communists) and the Parti de l'Entente Populaire (PEP, Parti for Popular Alliance). In other to attract the support of the United States, while eliminating any form of opposition, Cambronne brutally repressed both internal and external attempts to unseat Duvalier, which were presented as the work of Communists. In this sense, Cambronne was a major figure in the repressive apparatus of the Duvalier era, whose other members were Breton Claude, Luc Désir, Edner Day, Zacharie Delva, and Albert Pierre, alias Ti Boulé. With the support of mercenary André Labay, Cambronne established an infamous laboratory in the center of Port-au-Prince that bought one liter of blood plasma for US$3. The product was subsequently exported to the United States, Germany, and Sweden to be used in hospitals. The blood scandal and other nefarious activities contributed to the dismissal of Cambronne by Duvalier. Fallen in disgrace and forced to go into exile, his political career was forever tarnished.

In addition to political repression, participation was suppressed through everyday exclusion from social and economic opportunities. In authoritarian culture, citizens are excluded from all stages of development. The state siphons off economic resources from citizens. It has been characterized as predatory because of its historical tendency to draw resources without returning corresponding benefits.

The authoritarian regime of François Duvalier skillfully employed color issues to divide the Haitian population. Color was used as the basis of systematic orientation of money, gifts, jobs, contracts, and public services to a new group in society, the black middle class (Fass, 1984, 5). Rather than purporting to represent class-based groups such as the peasant and working classes, Duvalier presented himself as the defender of the black peasant and working masses.

Skillful usage of color issues legitimized a renewal of the political, military, and administrative personnel who were loyal to the repressive Duvalier regime and who conformed to its conception of power. This process legitimized claims of transformation of the body of politics to ensure social mobility of a few black individuals from lower middle class and popular origins.

Beginning with the 1950s, a small group of Haitian industrialists started investing in industry for national consumption, including oil and "saindoux" refineries and soap factories. During the same period, under the guise of import-substitution policy the Duvaliers and their close associates reserved for themselves some of the most lucrative state monopolies, particularly in consumer goods and utilities. The regime used import-substitution outlets to incorporate the black urban middle class into the structures of power. In this sense, the Duvalier regime was vested with interests entirely its own.

Moreover, by presenting himself as a voodoo spiritual leader, the senior Duvalier managed to secure the loyalty of voodoo priests. The word "voodoo" comes from the language spoken by the Fon communities of the Dahomey region of Africa. The religion was born in secrecy. Early in its development, it became the religion of the black slaves imported from Africa. Voodoo is known for its spectacular dimensions (convulsions by possessed practitioners) or magical dimensions as exemplified by zombies or lively dead persons. Revered Haitian writer Jacques Roumain strived to demonstrate the place of voodoo as religion in the popular imagination of the Haitian people the same way that others religions play a role in the imaginary of other nations.

François Duvalier survived countless coups by presenting himself as in touch with the aspirations of the country. In positioning himself with the heroes of the war of independence, François Duvalier managed to secure some legitimacy in the eyes of many Haitians. The legacy of this demagoguery has been to divide the country along color lines while failing to address the rampant poverty in the country.

Duvalier maintained tense relations with Rafael Trujillo, the dictator in the Dominican Republic from 1930 to 1961. However, the regime benefited from labor migration to the Dominican Republic. Every year, more than fifteen thousand Haitians expatriated in six months to the Dominican side of the border, during the period of the sugarcane harvest, *la zafra*. The seasonal work was profitable for the Haitian government, which received dividends from the Dominican state and North American sugar companies for every labor contingent. Recruitment agents, most of whom were Tontons Macoutes during Duvalier's time, look around the shantytowns. Promise of enrollment and the temptation of gains encouraged workers' departure. Heaped in trucks, the cane cutters go through Malpasse, at the border, where they are delivered to Dominican authorities. They were taken to different bateys, which are immense plantations of sugarcane spread out in Dominican territory. Then begin for these men the hell of the bateys.

They live sometimes six or seven persons to a single room, in camps of sheet metal and cardboard. Every morning, at dawn, they go to the fields to cut the cane. Under a heavy sun, with their machetes, the Haitian cane cutters make the harvest. The guards watch closely. It is like convict's work for a salary of misery. Duvalier received from Balaguer a proposal to send to the Dominican Republic 45,000 Haitian cane cutters for the sugar corporation of the Dominican Republic. In exchange, Duvalier would receive in his personal account US$20 for each Haitian laborer—that is, a total of US$900,000. Among the conditions of the deal was the requirement that Duvalier guarantee the return to Haiti of the Haitians. The overexploitation of the Haitian manual labor force has been the subject of various studies (Americas Watch, 1990; Plant 1987.

On May 30, 1961, the 30-year reign of Dominican dictator Trujillo ended, when as Trujillo was on his way to a meeting, a spurt of bullets transformed his vehicle into a strainer. The Dominican president collapsed and died instantaneously. After the news reached Port-au-Prince, François Duvalier began to see plots everywhere.

Duvalier oriented money, gifts, jobs, contracts, and public services to the black middle class, which could now claim membership in the political class (Fass, 1984, 5). He convinced the Haitian parliament to adopt a new constitution, declaring him president-for-life in 1963.

In 1963, the year that Francois Duvalier declared himself president-for-life, the United States discontinued its assistance programs for Haiti in an attempt to overthrow the Duvalier regime. Duvalier responded by declaring Thurston, the American ambassador in Haiti, "persona non grata." The cessation of diplomatic relations between Haiti and the United States also led to the departure of American technical experts and to the end of the "Pote Kole," the American "food for work" program in Haiti. Many armed expeditions into Haiti from the Dominican Republic sought to end the Duvalier dictatorship as well. In response, Duvalier massacred many families from the town of Jérémie, whose sons and daughters were said to be members of these expeditions. Jérémie, the native city of Thomas-Alexandre Dumas and the famous naturalist John James Audubon, was the theater of horrible reprisals. The massacre of the "Vespers of Jérémie" ended in horror. Entire families were executed, and children were stabbed in their mother's arms. The adults were the last ones to be assassinated. But no matter its human rights record, the Duvalier regime benefited from the resumption of military assistance by President Nixon in 1969.

The Duvaliers severely undermined the independence of the legislative and judicial branches of government. For instance, on April 7, 1961, François Duvalier passed a decree stipulating the expiration of the mandate of the deputies and the lapsing of the mandate of the senators elected on September 22, 1957. He subsequently reduced the parliament to approving roles by rigging elections in favor of regime supporters. In exchange, once elected, parliamentarians were expected to enact bills proposed by the executive in total absence of debate.

In return for their generous support of his election, Duvalier integrated members of the Syrian-Lebanese population, which can be said to have been the only ethnic minority in the country. The Syrian-Lebanese merchant community progressively replaced European traders, who reigned over Haitian commerce in the nineteenth century. Duvalier officially integrated them in the political life of the country by offering them cabinet positions and even the position of mayor of Port-au-Prince (D'Ans, 1987, 214).

The regime established land commissions and a land court to address land conflicts. Yet even when the mechanisms were erected, they consistently failed to deliver on their promises because of the broader political dynamics in which they operated. For instance, a land commission was established under the auspices of the Justice Ministry on September 6, 1971, with the stated intent to adjudicate land conflicts. A Permanent Presidential Land Commission was established on March 4, 1974, to "protect peasant properties, arrest the bloody conflicts and restore confidence in the legal system" (*Le Moniteur,* 1974, 1). These instruments failed to address both conflicts and inefficiencies in land markets. The normal operation of the justice being inefficient, some legitimate demands of small landowners were undermined in cases where bloody rural conflicts put them in opposition to large property owners.

In addition to reducing the legislature to approving roles with the absence of debates, the Duvaliers ruled by decree when the legislature was in recess. For instance, Jean-Claude Duvalier ruled by decree during the eight months that the legislature was in recess. The regime co-opted most judges while denying others independent operational powers and finance.

The Duvalier regime never delivered on its promise to devolve power to regional offices of government ministries and to enhance their financial autonomy. The administration of Jean-Claude Duvalier presented functional devolution as a means to enhance citizen participation, to increase coordination between the central and local administrations, and to diffuse economic and social development (Downs, 1988, 9). The regime promulgated the Regionalization and Regional Planning Legislation of September 19, 1982, which divided the Republic of Haiti into nine departments. A regional planning council to be composed of agency directors, prefects, and legislative delegates was established to express the views of business and private institutions on devolution of authority and resources to regional and local units.

A communal consultative council composed of local officials and their staff and community representatives was expected to express community views. At the national level, an inter-ministry commission with direct links to the cabinet was proposed to cap this structure (Downs, 1988, 11). All key decision-making functions remained firmly in the Capital City of Port-au-Prince. As a result, these administrative reforms were questioned and abandoned after the downfall of the dictatorial regime in 1986 (Downs, 1988, 1).

To compound the problem, the Duvaliers granted significant powers to prefects who were accountable exclusively to the executive. The post of the prefect stemmed from the French Civil Law. The Haitian prefect administered the prefecture and, within it, one to three *arrondissements,* or regions. The decision by the Duvalier regime to select prefects and assign added powers to the post carried centralizing assumption in the political arena. For instance, political patterns and practices were such that a designated prefect coordinated all governmental activities in a given region. Throughout the Duvalier era, the prefects instilled terror, making the emergence of grassroots organizations virtually impossible. They engaged in physical elimination of actual or suspected opponents, summary arrests and incarceration without trials, abduction, secret torture, and selective and random murders. The prefect was the highest civic functionary under the president, to whom he was accountable exclusively. The most loyal prefect wielded significant power, as was the case of Zachary Delva.

Local prefects relied on a network of section chiefs, numerous lieutenants, and an array of ubiquitous spies and informers to repress dissent. The section chief is the local authority figure of the Haitian State, which most closely aligned with the tasks of policing and administration in rural areas.

A legacy of the American occupation of Haiti, the section chief exerted broad political and legal powers over the lives of inhabitants of his jurisdiction. Relatively autonomous from the central government, section chiefs preserved conditions for the profitable accumulation of economic resources by elite groups in exchange for community status, maintenance in their positions, and rewards from local elites. Under the supervision of the commander of the local military district, section chiefs passed laws, arrested, adjudicated, and punished anyone they considered a wrongdoer. They also imposed and collected taxes and settled land and family disputes (Lundhal, 1983, 271).

There has been some controversy over the level of control that local populations exercised over section chiefs. Comhaire (1955, 620–624) contends that local peasants sometimes insist on democratic procedures in settling litigations and therefore protest penalties taken by the section chiefs that are inflicted in the absence of public judicial process. I share the skepticism of prominent writers such as Lahav (1973) and Mintz 1974 (273) regarding the leverage of local communities over local authorities.

As the repository of absolute local power, the section chief could accumulate wealth by extracting financial rewards from the local elite and money from candidates in exchange for votes. They also profited from illegal arrests and detention, the ransom of prisoners and confiscation of property, and extortion (Péralte, 1992, 7). If the section chief knew that a family was making some savings, he could puncture the savings rate by taxing them or by arbitrarily arresting them to force them to pay. Extortions and asset confiscation aimed to siphon off the savings of the poor, to strip the individual of all means to live, and to undermine the social status and humanity of the victim. This system of terror dislocated families and depressed saving rates, therefore undermining communal development projects and the prospects of collective improvement of the conditions for the majority of the population. In the end, this system of terror sought to destroy any possibility of progress in society.

The section chief reported to the local prefect. There were 27 prefects in the national territory. With the downfall of the Duvalier regime in February 1986, the linchpin of regional administration, the prefect, disappeared as well.

HAITIAN CREATIVITY

An interesting element of Haitian culture is its ability to borrow foreign concepts and use them for purposes other than originally intended. For instance, the Voodoo religion integrates elements of African belief systems with the culture of saints in the Catholic religion.

Voodoo practitioners believe in a supreme being, identified as God for the Christians, to whom they refer as Bondye in Creole. However, the Bondye of the Voodoo does not interfere in human affairs. The Bondye is rather a royal figure, who delegates its powers to holy entities, spirits, and "loas," entities akin to saints or angels in Western religions in that they are intermediaries between Bondye (good god) and human beings. Unlike saints or angels however, the loas require that followers serve them in addition to praying to them. Followers of particular loas have to attend to their preferences, distinct sacred rhythms, songs, dance rituals, symbols, and specific offerings. The holy entities and the spirits act as the plenipotentiaries of Bondye among the voodoo practitioners.

Voodoo played a primordial role in the organization of slave revolt against French colonization. The ceremony at Bois-Caiman in the night of the August 21–22, 1791, marked the beginning of the insurrection against slavery in Saint-Domingue. During the American occupation of Haiti and throughout the first half of the twentieth century, the voodoo religion was the victim of an open and official campaign against superstitions. Given the high conversion rates recorded in Haiti since the departure of Duvalier, the voodoo religion has been under attack. However, the religion found a new source of support in cultural expressions as folkloric dance companies and the roots music of Haiti. The Aristide government openly used it for political purposes. By presidential decree dated April 4, 2003, voodoo became an official religion of Haiti. The country now has two recognized religions: voodoo and Catholicism.

Another example of Haitian culture's borrowing of foreign concepts came during the colonial period, when the slaves borrowed from the colonizers' vocabulary but used the terms to convey different concepts. For instance, the classification of "saints" of the Catholic Church were retained in the voodoo religion but was broaden to includes deities of the voodoo religion as a mechanism to avoid repression of their African religion by the colonizers.

Further, in the post-slavery era, Haitians continued to pervert foreign agendas, while receiving targeted assistance from international donors. During the Cold War, the Duvalier regime used the anticommunist discourse of Washington as a means to curry favor with various administrations and avoid isolation because of its human rights violations. The regime called its opponents "communists" to isolate them, even when the Communist Party was weak during the reign of François Duvalier. For instance, at the urging of the United States, Haiti cast the decisive vote on the expulsion of Cuba from the Organization of American States at the OAS Eight Meeting of Consultation of Foreign Ministers at Punta Del Este in January 1962 (Loescher and Scanlan, 1984, 9).

A combination of extreme poverty and sheer violence directed at opponents of the regime created a volatile political situation. A new phenomenon of the massive emigration of boat people can be dated back to the arrival to power of Jean-Claude Duvalier, who succeeded his father in 1971. This new phenomenon reflected both the harsher economic realities and the political persecution of the Duvalier eras. Peasant incomes eroded as the national economy became even more dependent on international markets. In order to disengage domestic opposition in the late 1970s, the administration of Jean-Claude Duvalier imported tons of American rice. The administration claimed that this policy was intended to palliate droughts in parts of the country. The imported rice, also called Jean-Claude Rice, became widely used in Haiti, providing the dictator with some measures of popularity.

In the late 1970s, the presidency of Jimmy Carter, with its emphasis on human rights, served to strengthen domestic activists in Haiti who were struggling for the establishment of the rule of law. Given the dependence of Duvalier on American assistance and political support, the regime allowed greater freedom of the press and association until Ronald Reagan came to power. The election of Reagan reinforced the position of authoritarian figures and the same activists who had been emboldened under the reign of Jimmy Carter were exiled in 1980. Duvalier complied with the desiderata of the Reagan administration, including the signing of an agreement in 1981 that allowed the American Coast Guard to intercept in high seas the flimsy boats of refugees and summarily return them to Haiti.

This agreement came on the heels of a massive influx of boat people from Haiti and Cuba in 1980 because of political turmoil in those countries. That year alone, some 125,000 Cuban migrants came to the United States by boat from the port of Mariel. Some 20,000 Haitians arrived to Florida by sea simultaneously. The Carter administration responded by devising a new immigration status, the "Cuban-Haitian entrant," which enabled recipients to stay in the United States until the political crisis was solved. Ultimately, U.S. immigration officials granted preferential treatment to Cubans and signed a repatriation treaty with Haiti because the foreign policy significance of the two migration flows was different. Treating Haitians in the same manner as Cubans would be to acknowledge the atrocities of the Duvalier regime. Conversely, sending back Cuban refugees to the Castro regime would imply a rapprochement between the two governments. This policy decision brought the Reagan administration closer to the Duvalier regime in the name of curbing illegal immigration. President Reagan enacted executive orders 4865 and 12324 on September 29, 1981, promulgating the suspension of the entry of undocumented aliens from the high seas and the interdiction of vessels carrying such aliens (Department of State Bulletin, 1981). The moral and human rights implications of a policy favoring Cuban entry and deterring Haitian refugee flows escaped the Reagan administration. This administration paid little attention to the legal obligation to provide refuge to all fleeing persecution regardless of race, religion, nationality, and political belief.

The presidency of Ronald Reagan accorded security primacy over democracy. The Haitian government secured certification regardless of the severity of human rights violations. In 1982 the U.S. Congress passed the Mica Amendment, which conditioned economic aid to Haiti on Duvalier's efforts to restrain emigration and guarantee democratic development and civil liberties. The emphasis on security and repatriation of refugees undermined implementation of the terms of the Mica Amendment. On the ground in Haiti, an awareness movement spurred anti-Duvalier mobilizations.

With only 20 percent of its population considered urban, Haiti remained a large rural country in 1982. Some progress had been achieved. In the field of education, the percent of illiterate in the population of 15 years and over decreased from 90 percent to 65 percent between 1950 and 1982. These gains are too slow and unequally distributed to radically transform socioeconomic prospects.

Between 1980 and 1985, the gross domestic product dropped by .8 percent on average per year because of the fall of agricultural and manufacturing sectors. The peasant economy was hit the hardest. In its blind pursuit of American support, the Duvalier regime permitted the elimination of the Creole pig population by the United States Agency for International Development (USAID) as part of a USAID-run project that eliminated millions of Creole pigs because some were infected with African swine fever. The versatile and hardy pig was the backbone of the peasant economy at that time. This loss devastated the peasant economy for two reasons. First, the small livestock was integrated in the farming system and was often used for the purpose of savings and income generation. Second, the indigenous pigs were hearty animals that required limited maintenance. They survived by eating household garbage. They were replaced by American pigs, which needed shelter from the sun and would eat nothing but grain. When the price of grain rose sharply, the pigs ended up costing more than they were worth. People stopped breeding the pigs and started killing them off for meat, and by 2003 the project had collapsed.

Income disparity widened in the early 1980s when economic growth benefited only a small minority of urban entrepreneurs. In 1985, 90 percent of Haiti's estimated 6 million people earned less than $150 per annum. By way of contrast, 1 percent of the population received 44 percent of national income (Prince, 1985, 51). The dominance of Haiti's tiny elite over the rest of the country is attributed to "class solidarity" by Wingfield and Parenton (1965, 340). These authors found "class solidarity to be rooted in a strong family system, blood relationships and common heritage." The Haitian elite is often attributed a strong sentiment against social change. Fauntroy (1994, cited in Cox, 1997, 199) found that the "Haitian elites...are opposed to any changes in the patterns of land ownership and distribution in Haiti, in apprehension of losing profits to competitive enterprises. Surpluses are seldom reinvested inhibiting local capital accumulation and efficiency of operation."

Another attempted reform was regionalization and decentralization, which began in 1982. Although the central government repeatedly asserts its commitment to reducing interregional disparities, few steps have been taken to enhance the development of the regions (Kernel-Torres and Roca, 1993, 26). Because the reform process produced few positive outcomes, international donors and creditors began to work directly with Private Voluntary Organizations (PVOs) and the rural community council as alternative channels to government-to-government aid.

Most domestic and international organizations promoted rural community councils in Haiti from the middle of the 1950s to the downfall of the Duvalier regime in 1986. The government of Haiti allowed foreign organizations to work directly with the rural community councils, while it used these same structures for different purposes. The structures were employed to channel foreign funds even though they were politically co-opted by the Duvalier administrations. The multiplicity of agendas implemented by the Rural Community Councils also rendered them ineffectual at development.

A 1981 decree issued by the government of Haiti sought to regulate the activities of the rural community councils. This law granted them legal status as apolitical organizations operating in rural Haiti. The law tended to promote the non-elective rural community councils as a local governmental structure. Although rural community councils were presented as apolitical, they were used for partisan political ends and overtly supported the Duvalier regime. In spite of this rhetoric of self-reliance, the rural community councils were unrepresentative of their local constituency and communities (Maguire, 1979, 28; Smucker, 1986, 107). Unlike the *gwoupman*, rural community councils were ineffective instruments of participation (Kernel-Torres and Roca, 1993, 38). The *gwoupman* is a territorially-based grassroots structure established to explore and address the causes of persistent poverty in rural Haiti. The grassroots nature of the *gwoupman* distinguishes it from the rural community councils which were instigated and co-opted by the Duvalier regime. In the early 1980s, for instance, rural community councils were torn between the donor community using them as mechanisms of local-level development and as a base of support by the Duvalier regime.

THE DOWNFALL OF THE DUVALIER REGIME

The seed of the downfall of the Duvalier regime can be found in its incapacity to deliver economic prosperity and political freedom. In the 1970s, inflation became an acute problem after decades of stable prices causing a rise in government expenditures. Diminished foreign assistance, exports, and tourism generated severe balance of payment problems. As arrears developed in the debt service and import payments, the government of Haiti drew extensively on internal loans, international reserves, and standby credit of the International Monetary Fund.

The already-strained national budget showed a deep deficit as the world recession hit primary products hard in the early 1980s. The real exchange rate of the gourde vis-à-vis the U.S. dollar began depreciating. The Haitian government sought external financing to stem fiscal deficits. The International Monetary Fund, however, conditioned its stand-by loans of 1982 to commitment to significant reduction in fiscal and external deficits through financial accountability for aid, notable reduction in public expenditures, and tax reforms. In an atmosphere of public deficit, a significant percentage of public revenues were regularly diverted to private bank accounts of members and supporters of the regime. Overall, the Duvalier regime proved unable to reform public finances and deliver on the basic demands of the Haitian population.

The signs of the imminent fall of Duvalier succeeded each other. On March 10, 1983, pro-democracy groups were encouraged by the speech of Pope John Paul II upon his arrival in Port-au-Prince, in which the sovereign pontiff declared, "Some things have to change here." Another sign was the hunger riots of 1984. On May 23, 1984, the army intervened in Gonaives, which is less than 1,24.27 miles to the north of Port-au-Prince. The soldiers repressed hunger riots, which showed publicly that the basic needs of the population were unmet. Last, the aforementioned fever epidemic among porcine livestock and the associated necessity of forced slaughtering of more than a million pigs further reduced the meager sources of incomes of the peasants, provoking further incentives to revolt.

In the capital, the structuring of social movements to articulate the demands of the population reflected the expression of a national will for change. These movements added their voices to those of peasants' associations, women groups, religious communities, and the independent press, exerting strong pressures in favor of a more equal and inclusive society.

The radio stations, particularly that of the Catholic Church, played a major role in raising social awareness by offering critical information for democratic learning. This process is intimately connected to the emergence of Haitian Creole in social and political life. Programming in Haitian Creole served to stimulate social communication, political motivation, and participation.

Until late 1985, the Duvalier regime could count on the staunch support of the army, elements of the rural elite, and the rural community councils. Between late 1985 and early 1986, however, a substantial segment of the urban commercial elite, which had been losing profits because of the negative image of the country abroad, withdrew its support for Duvalier and began pressing for reforms. Government incapacity to foster a prosperous environment led to distortions in investment behavior as the Haitian commercial elite discounted risk factors including labor militancy and outbreaks of civil violence.

Civil society was gaining strength. By civil society, I mean the sphere between family units and the state in which citizens can freely develop intermediary structures of collective interests to pursue common objectives. The violent military police response to unarmed student demonstrations in November 1985 unified the anti-Duvalier movement with denunciations emanating from unlikely sectors of the nation such as the Haitian Association of Industrialists.

This movement in civil society was, however, a response to the growing popular discontent with the Duvalier regime. When it became clear that popular pressures for the departure of the regime were spreading and that the Duvalier regime could neither maintain stability nor promote economic growth, civil society, the commercial elite, and the U.S. government withdrew support for the dictator. On January 30, 1986, the United States officially raised the prospect of blocking $7 million to Duvalier to force the departure of the regime. One week later, the regime collapsed; Jean-Claude Duvalier fled the country on February 6, 1986.

In this case, the strength of the *gwoupman* and the emerging civil society, combined with the inability of the Duvalier regime to deliver reforms, sustainable development, and prosperity, led to a political realignment, which resulted in political change (Bonnardot and Danroc, 1986). The nation prevailed against the state.

THE BEGINNINGS OF DEMOCRATIC TRANSITION IN HAITI

There are two major models of democratic transition in developing countries. Whereas the first model concerns transitions by means of pact, the second considers the oppositional role of civil society against the state. Stepan (1997, 657) finds both models in need of revision before incorporation in a democratic theory of opposition. He argues that a useful role of democratic opposition in the process of democratic consolidation is to deepen democracy by engaging in issue creation and in the establishment of new mechanisms of participation, transparency, and accountability. The Haitian case is a fine example of the second model where the nation is in constant struggle against the state.

National Governing Council

The National Governing Council (CNG) replaced the Duvalier dynasty after Jean-Claude Duvalier fled to France in February 1986. In its first message to the nation, delivered on February 25, 1986, the council's president, General

Henri Namphy, expressed its intent to establish "all institutions constituting the basis and the framing of a liberal, democratic and just society." The council urged exiles to return to and invest in their homeland and requested greater international assistance to implement swift changes in political and economic structures.

The departure of Duvalier occasioned a brief political opening that empowered the emerging labor unions to articulate the demands of their members, which until then were repressed. The Autonomous Federation of Haitian Workers (CATH) called for general strikes to force the National Governing Council to remove Duvalierists from the public sector and to raise the national minimum wage, which had been stagnant since 1984. General Namphy strongly condemned these demands, prompting the Autonomous Federation to call for its resignation. Claiming that the federation had violated the constitution by conducting political activities, the National Governing Council abolished the Autonomous Federation of Haitian Workers (CATH) in 1987. This decision provoked an outcry at both national and international levels, leading the government to reinstate the labor union a few days later.

In the late 1980s, the lack of a common strategy among the labor unions handicapped their ability to deter union busting, plant closings, frequent changes in work rules and rate structures, and dismal working conditions. For instance, union effort to overturn a 1982 law prohibiting public employees from creating a union or engaging in strike remained unsuccessful.

The National Governing Council convened a Constituent Assembly to debate its proposal for a new constitution. The Constituent Assembly gained some legitimacy by rejecting drafts submitted by the National Governing Council. It elaborated a constitution that was favorable to semi-parliamentary democracy. The constitution, which was approved by a majority of voters on March 9, 1987, provided for fundamental liberties for all Haitians and for a strict separation of power between the three branches of government. After ratification, these social forces exerted pressures on the military to respect the electoral calendar, which called for elections in November 1987.

THE HAITIAN CONSTITUTION OF 1987

The Haitian Constitution of 1987 preserved the principle of the unitary state but recommended the devolution of authority and resources to elected bodies in the regions. Local governance systems as set forth in the Haitian Constitution of 1987 rest on territorial collectivities, which are essential instruments of political representation. However, the constitution defined only certain aspects of the composition and political organization of the territorial collectivities. In fact, it established only partially the conditions of eligibility, the nomination and election process, and the length of the mandates of local officials. There are two organs of representation in each territorial collectivity, one council and one assembly. The councils administer the territorial collectivity. The assemblies assist the councils in their tasks. Councils present regular reports to their respective assemblies. This implies collaboration in decision-making processes and respect of the respective mandates of each of these two bodies and their political organization. The Haitian Constitution has explicitly or implicitly granted legal standing and autonomy to the territorial collectivities. In this sense, no territorial collectivities can exert oversight over another. This means that the councils and the assemblies have contractual relationships with each other and must therefore cooperate. The emerging body of law on the local state represents a major step toward representation and the culture of peace.

THREE CATEGORIES OF TERRITORIAL COLLECTIVITIES

There are three categories of territorial collectivities in the civil system of administration. In size-descending order, these categories are the department, the commune, and the communal section. Legal and constitutional provisions mandate the existence of councils and assemblies at all three territorial divisions. The main tasks of the councils are to lead, administer, and manage the collectivity on a daily basis. In this sense, they are jointly responsible for all initiatives aimed at the development and management of the community. Only the council administers and deploys resources to the territorial collectivity. The council also facilitates the work of the assemblies and makes available the resources necessary for the proper functioning of the assemblies. The councils give periodic reports to the assemblies. Every year, the councils prepare and present to the assembly for deliberation and decision a program of interventions. The assemblies ensure the representation of the population on a territorial basis.

The Department

The department is the largest territorial division of the country. It comprises several communes, which are subdivided into various communal sections. A departmental council administers this unit. A departmental assembly assists in this task. The departmental assembly reports to the central administration. It also sends delegates to the nine-member interdepartment council. This body is the common instrument of representation of departmental collectivities in decisions of the executive branch through the Council of Government Ministers. In particular, the interdepartmental council provides its input in the elaboration of national development plans and the nomination of judges and the members of the provisional and permanent electoral council. Members of the council have the right to speak and vote at working sessions of councils of ministers on issues of regional development. The councils are meant to guide and influence the intervention of not just the central state but also external agencies. They also shape laws determining the percentage and nature of public resources allocated to local bodies in the context of decentralized financial systems. This level of participation gives the interdepartmental council some political and strategic competence, which goes beyond their territorial base. In this sense, the proper operation of the territorial collectivities fosters electoral legitimacy and reflects democratic learning. The rural vote for the empowerment of territorial collectivities is reflective of democratic learning as it seeks to further integrate the peasantry in the national community.

The Commune

The legislation governing the communal section stipulates that the commune dominate smaller administrative units such as the communal sections and urban districts located within their jurisdiction. The commune is administered by a three-member municipal council, of which the sitting mayor is the president. Members of the municipal council are elected for a four-year term. The municipal councils are mandated to collaborate with municipal assemblies, which are composed of one representative per communal section. Together, these two units administer public facilities including local markets, slaughterhouses, graveyards, public parks, public schools, shelters, and dormitories. The municipal assemblies send delegates to the nine departmental assemblies, one for each of the country's nine departments. They aim to foster the reinsertion of the peasantry into civil life and the participation of inhabitants of all communes, both urban and rural, in national decision-making processes.

The consolidation of democracy requires application of constitutional and legal mandates on decentralization. Mandated arrangements on the political organizations of the territorial collectivities are the prerequisite of the following: (1) the implementation of democracy at the local level; (2) the participation of the population in local public affairs; (3) democratic operation of institutions. The thrust of the constitution is that democracy requires equity in the representation of the population, political pluralism, and democratic alternation.

The Communal Section

The communal section represents the smallest territorial and administrative entity in Haiti. Pursuant to the 1987 Haitian Constitution, the council of the communal section and the assembly of the communal section manage this unit. Haitians elected 565 administrative councils of the communal section (CASEC) in 1995. Each administrative council has three members who are elected by simple majority of the votes cast for a term of four years. The administrative council of the communal section is responsible for all aspects of the administration of the communal section. It manages communal resources to the exclusive benefit of local citizenry and is accountable to the administrative assembly. The legislation governing the communal section as a local collectivity established the administrative councils of communal sections as autonomous administrative entities (*Le Moniteur*, April 4, 1996).

The administrative assembly of the communal section (ASEC) is a local body composed of members elected by simple majority of votes cast. The administrative assemblies deliberate on matters of concerns to the community and advise the administrative councils. They also must approve most transactions effectuated by the councils, including those concerning communal property (land, buildings, and infrastructure), for the transactions to acquire legality. The assemblies approve gifts received by the councils as well as local development plans and budgets elaborated by either the administrative council or central government institutions (articles 10, 11–1, and 11–3 of the April 4, 1996, legislation; article 73 and 83 of the Haitian Constitution). The assemblies assist the executive branch in the planning of national and local development activities (article 87–2 of the Haitian Constitution of 1987) and in the preparation of legislation setting the percentage and nature of public resources to be allocated to local bodies by interdepartmental councils. The assemblies also contribute to institutional reform by submitting to the executive branch lists of candidates for posts in the judicial system and the permanent electoral council (articles 175 and 192 of the Haitian Constitution of 1987). The administrative assemblies of the communal section report to the municipal assemblies. These institutions have not been fully functional in Haiti, given that inclination toward administrative centralization is deeply embedded in national customs. Because the exercise of local governance functions depends to a lesser degree on participation in local process and to a larger extent on political choices made by centralized political actors, decentralization has not been fully implemented in Haiti.

For the same reason, the legal framework in local state governance is still incomplete. The law of March 29, 1996, further clarified the structure of the territorial collectivity of the communal section. This law decreed a model of composition and organization of the territorial collectivity of the communal section. It contains some necessary arrangements for local elections and the establishment of assemblies as foreseen by the constitution. These arrangements are, however, presented in the context of temporary arrangements, while waiting the definition and adoption of definitive arrangements. Up to now, the composition and political organization of the territorial collectivities are only partially defined. The legal framework is still incomplete. A legal framework that clearly and fairly distributes the individual and mutual roles and responsibilities of each level of administration would go a long way toward dispute settlements between the various administrative units.

The Haitian Constitution adopted in March 1987 provided for a president directly elected to office for a nonrenewable five-year term. The president is also not eligible to serve more than two terms. His duties include enforcement of administrative stability and respect for the provisions of the constitution. He presides over the council of ministers and designates a prime minister from the majority party in the parliament who is then ratified by both chambers of the legislature. The prime minister is the chief of government. He oversees the activities of the cabinet and implements national laws and plans. The constitution also calls for the office of the prime minister to counterbalance presidential power.

THE NEW HAITIAN MILITARY

With the military's advent to power, a new structure was established, inspired by the Israeli army, to modernize the military by creating 18 positions for generals as well as the functions of commander in chief and adjunct commander in chief. U.S. Army–trained generals Namphy and Regala named themselves to these positions for a period of three years. Based on a strengthened position, the military sought to delay democratic aspirations.

In June 1986, the National Governing Council issued an electoral calendar that established a timetable for the election of a constituent assembly, the holding of a referendum on a new constitution, and the constitution of local administration and the election of a president. At first, the National Governing Council reneged on its own electoral calendar. It later failed to provide inadequate election security, causing the massacre of many voters and the postponement of the November 1987 vote.

Assistance from the United States and cordial relations between the American and Haitian militaries shaped relations between the two countries. It is interesting that General Regala made a trip to Santo Domingo, the Capital of the Dominican Republic, two weeks before the elections to engage in a secret meeting with high command of Southern Command of the U.S. army to discuss the upcoming elections. The outcomes of the discussion were never publicly revealed, but both sides viewed measures that would neutralize endemic popular discontent as a priority.

On election day, the Haitian military and police tolerated and abetted the violence perpetrated by thugs against defenseless voters and determined election officials. In response to election violence and postponement, the Permanent Council of the Organization of American States passed Resolution 489 in December 1987 deploring "acts of violence and disorder" that had taken place in Haiti. The Permanent Council also voiced its "conviction that it is necessary to resume the democratic process" and urged the "Government of Haiti to adopt all necessary measures so that the people of Haiti may express their will through free elections," The resolution was, however, criticized for not blaming the National Governing Council for its repressive actions. A report from the same year published by the Inter-American Commission on Human Rights called for new elections to be monitored by international observers (Pierce, 1996, 481).

Many political movements and parties emerged to compete in the 1990s. To this day, the Haitian party system is characterized by its fragmentation and limited capacity to articulate constituency-based interests. Most political parties lack defined programs and strong organizational presence at the national and local levels. They have been dubbed micro-parties because of their narrow social base. The overly fragmented character of interest representation is troublesome for political scientists who see a world of individuals displaying limited plurality voting and scant avenues of interest aggregation and expression. The personality-based nature of political parties combined with the limited capacity to articulate constituency-based interests impede capacity for structural changes. Several short-lived governments emerged in Haiti between 1987 and 1990, with some resulting from military coups. After the aborted elections of November 1987, a civilian government issued from questionable new elections was established in February 1988. That civilian administration was overthrown in June 1988. After that, two military governments succeeded themselves. Neither the Duvalier regime nor the interim governments that replaced it engaged in meaningful decentralization of authority and resources. The announcement in September 1989 of an electoral calendar that foresaw municipal, legislative, and presidential elections gave the population the hope of better governance until a democratically elected regime.

The First Aristide Administration (February–September 1991)

Father Jean Bertrand Aristide was the first president to ever be elected democratically and under international supervision in Haiti and was removed by a military coup on September 29, 1991. A long-time proponent of liberation theology, Father Aristide relentlessly preached against exploitation and the capitalist system; "Capitalism is a mortal sin," he often told his followers. In a country characterized by sharp class differences, Aristide's message found a large echo among the majority of Haiti's poor population. His five-year term, which was interrupted by three years in exile until he was restored to power under a U.S.-led military intervention in October 1994, expired on February 1995. This section breaks down Aristide's rule in several administrations, each with a specific time period. We refer to the coup regime that lasted three years as an extra-constitutional government.

Many populist movements have gained power in Latin America since 1990. Populism also won in Haiti in the first democratic election of December 16, 1990. Jean-Bertrand Aristide used the banner of the National Front for Change and Democracy (FNCD) to make a run at the office of president. He won the presidential race with 87 percent of the vote. His closest competitor, Marc Bazin of the National Alliance for Development and Progress (ANDP), received only 13 percent of the vote.

Jean-Bertrand Aristide was elected president on an electoral platform promising to oppose corruption in the public administration and to introduce participation, transparency, and accountability in state affairs. The strong anticapitalist overtone of the campaign strained relations between the United States and the Aristide government.

One element that captured the mood of the period was an exchange that took place between Aristide and Alvin Adams, then U.S. ambassador to Haiti, prior to the election. On November 12, 1990, Ambassador Adams stated to a news agency, "Les Haïtiens ont un important choix a faire dans l'élection présidentielle de cette année" ("Haitians have an important choice to make in the presidential election of that same year"). He urged Haitian voters to make "an informed choice" for president because, he said, quoting a Haitian Creole proverb, "*Apre dans lan, tanbou lou*" ("After the dance, the drum is heavy"). In a rebuttal to the U.S. Ambassador two days later, Jean-Bertrand Aristide, who was then a candidate for the post of the president, stated, "*Anpil men, chay pa lou*" ("With so many hands, the load is not heavy"). During his first seven months in power, Aristide grappled with the challenge of modernizing the economy according to the principles of sustainable development while attracting private direct investments. The government began to increase state revenue, deter corruption, and raise the confidence of foreign donors in its capacity to control public spending. On July 3, 1991, the Aristide government sent a letter to the managing director of the International Monetary Fund (IMF) expressing its willingness to comply with IMF guidance and requirements to secure a loan of $21 million. These negotiations represented a shift from Aristide's previous position on foreign aid. Before assuming office, Aristide often blamed international financial institutions for not addressing the country's poverty. Instead, Aristide favored self-reliance and policies that would promote local entrepreneurship. It soon became apparent that the Aristide government was limited in its ability to achieve systemic changes in power distribution in Haitian society because of Haiti's dependence on the capitalist world economy.

Tensions emerged between the executive and legislative branches. A demonstration by supporters of then Prime Minister René Garcia Préval on August 13, 1991, effectively scared the parliament out of proceeding with a nonconfidence vote that would have culminated in the dismissal of the Préval cabinet. This exemplifies an increasing use of the popular movement to consolidate the power of the Aristide administration.

This period was marked by increasing polarization. Organizations that were co-opted by the Aristide administration achieved political ascendancy whereas those who remained independent were undermined and at times were deemed as deserving a "Père Lebrun," which refers to the brutal practice of neck lacing or burning opponents to death with burning tires.

Tensions also arose between the executive branch and the corporate sector. In 1991 the Aristide government supported Senate-sponsored legislation introduced by Senator Clark Parent that sought to raise the daily minimum wage. In response, the major corporate organizations in Haiti orchestrated an effective lobby to limit the increase in the daily minimum wage. The Haitian Association of Industries (ADIH), an employer association, noted that "between October 1990 and July 1991, some 8,000 jobs were lost corresponding to 20 percent of the labor force" (Slavin, 1991).

In August 1991, after six months of strife between the corporate sector and the government, a daily minimum wage law was passed in parliament. In a interview on Radio Métropole, a spokesperson for the Association of Haitian Industries (ADIH), an employer association, commented that "by raising the national minimum wage, Haiti would lose its main attraction to international capital, a vast pool of workers at a cheap price." It is worth pointing out that the legislation established one minimum wage rate for work in the capital city of Port-au-Prince and another for the rest of the country. Many feared that the legislation would worsen rural–urban migration.

The agrarian elite were particularly adverse to the wage increase because it raised labor costs. Alongside its urban allies, it reacted to this threat to its control of the economy. It plotted with its urban allies a military coup that deposed the first Aristide administration. About this connection, Fatton stated, "It is clear that the military and the bourgeoisie felt increasingly threatened by Aristide's appeal for popular justice. They feared a social explosion that would end their domination. The coup symbolized . . . their determined resistance to fundamental change" (1997, 145). Entrenched elite groups accused Aristide of inciting mob violence. They relied on the coercive capabilities of the military to quell the threat posed by Aristide and the popular movement.

At his inauguration, President Aristide pledged to give voice to Haiti's impoverished masses. With limited resources, Haiti was forced to negotiate an agreement with the International Monetary Fund, a prerequisite for additional funding from other international lending institutions. To raise national revenues, the government tried to increase taxation on the rich by raising the income tax, the corporate tax, and the import taxes. These measures caused extreme resentment and hostility from members of the Haitian army. These tensions culminated in the coup d'état of September 29, 1991, led by Brigadier General Raoul Cédras, then the army interim commander-in-chief. The execution of the coup suggested that it was well planned with massive involvement of both career officers and enlisted soldiers. During the coup era, all of the concessions made by employers under the Aristide administration were rolled back.

The overthrow of the constitutional government of Aristide was assimilated to a "vacancy" of power. On this perverted basis, three civilian, extra-constitutional governments succeeded each other in cahoots with the military.

In search of legitimacy, on October 7, 1991, the Haitian military extracted a signed statement declaring the presidency vacant from 29 members of the Haitian parliament. Joseph Nérette, a Supreme Court judge, was named provisional president the following day. The Haitian parliament later approved the nomination of Jean Jacques Honorat as prime minister. A well-known detractor of the Aristide government, Honorat was welcomed by the Haitian elite.

During the three years of extra-constitutional misrule, the high command of the army, which enjoys superior means of organization in comparison with the rest of the public administration, maintained narrow ties with all components of the army. Overall, the army rather resembled an organ of social and political control of the nation that sought to slow down national development by blocking mechanisms of cohesion and political space to enhance interest representation.

It is believed that the Haitian democratic transitions have had many authoritarian drifts. Could it be the reverse? Could it be that authoritarian regime has been interrupted by a few episodes of democratic experience? If one believes that Haiti has had many authoritarian drifts, the military coup that brutally deposed the democratically constituted government of Jean-Bertrand Aristide in 1991 would certainly qualify. On October 3, 1991, the foreign ministers of the Organization of American States (OAS) adopted a resolution calling for the reinstatement of President Aristide in his functions, his return to Haiti, and the concomitant financial, economic, and diplomatic isolation of the illegitimate authorities. The United Nations committed to support efforts undertaken by the OAS for a return to the constitutional order.

The United States cut off its economic assistance to Haiti and made resumption of economic assistance conditional on the return to constitutional rule. A month later, President George H. W. Bush called for a total embargo on Haiti. Many other countries such as France also condemned the military coup and cut off foreign aid. In return, Aristide was pressured to renounce popular justice.

The Coup Period (1991–1994)

During the coup period, which lasted from 1991 to 1994, the public sector wage bill grew significant as the coup regime placed its supporters in the public administration. The rapid expansion of public sector employment strained the national budget. The deficit recorded by the treasury reached 450 million gourdes. In fiscal year 1992, this careless practice resulted in the largest annual deficit since the creation of Haiti's present monetary system in 1919. The usurper regime also printed money without approval by the legislature, causing a rise in inflation.

The military coup regime of Lieutenant General Raoul Cédras instituted its own repression network. In an effort to undermine civilian resistance to its authoritarian agenda, the usurper regime passed a decree prohibiting gatherings of more than three people without prior consent from local military personnel. The military dictatorship terrorized the Caribbean nation of Haiti for three years, killing an estimated 4,000 people (Marquez, 1995).

There were many indications that the Haitian elite sponsored the coup. Jean Claude Roy, a Haitian businessman and known opponent of Aristide, publicly welcomed the coup. Aristide's public discourse of a "marriage" between the army and the people demobilized his political supporters.

The coup regime supported the establishment of Revolutionary Armed Front for the Progress of Haiti. This neo-Duvalierist front was known as FRAPH in its French acronym (for the Front Armé pour l'Avancement et le Progrès d'Haïti). This paramilitary group was held responsible for thousands of deaths during the coup period. The FRAPH quickly emerged as a new category of repressive agents. Many individuals targeted by FRAPH headed toward the Dominican Republic. The most prominent among them secured the status of political refugees with the Office of the High Commissioner for refugees of the United Nations (HCR). The less prominent joined the ranks of illegal migrants in the neighboring Dominican Republic. Others headed toward the French Antilles and the Bahamas where they were considered clandestine workers. Still others were granted political refugee status in Canada and France. However, the most spectacular pattern was the resumption of the phenomenon of the boat people toward Florida, first initiated under the regime of Jean-Claude Duvalier.

A legal action introduced by a Miami-based Haitian community center against the practice of summary deportation forced the United States to temporarily suspend this practice and to open a refugee camp on their military base at Guantanamo. From November 1991 to May 1992, roughly one-third of those interviewed presented enough evidence to warrant political refugee status. These individuals were then brought to the United States for further examination of their cases. Those who did not receive political refugee status were then sent back to Haiti. Alarmed by the high rates of individuals securing refugee status, President George H. W. Bush issued an executive order in May 1992 that called for an alternative system: the opening of offices in Haiti capable of receiving the requests for asylum of persecuted Haitians.

The coming to power of President Clinton in the United States marked an important shift in American foreign policy. The United Nations chose former Argentine minister Dante Caputo as the Special Representative in Haiti of the United Nations Secretary General Boutros Boutros-Ghali. In January 1993, Mr. Caputo added to this title the position of Special Representative of the Secretary General of the OAS. In February 1993, a civilian mission formed jointly by the OAS and the United Nations replaced the mission previously sent by the OAS in 1992. The International Civilian Mission in Haiti (MICIVIH) had a larger mandate than the previous one and exerted a significant influence.

In March 1993, Lawrence Pezzullo was named Special Representative of President Bill Clinton for Haiti. Pezzullo visited the country with army general John Sheean. On June 4, 1992, President Clinton announced the freezing of the financial holdings in the United States of 83 individuals linked to the perpetrators of the coup d'état. On June 16, 1993, the Security Council of the United Nations adopted Resolution 841, imposing an embargo on gasoline and weapons as well as the freezing of the holdings of extra-constitutional authorities. On July 3, 1993, President Aristide and General Cédras signed in New York the Governor's Island Accord. Although the accord was presented as a major breakthrough, it contained numerous flaws. For instance, it contained no mechanisms for enforcement, no penalties for noncompliance, and dangerous concessions to the military (Doyle, 1994, 205).

On July 16, 1993, as a complement to the Governor's Island Agreement, the Pact of New York was signed by 39 members of Haitian civil societies as well as Haitian parliamentarians in the presence of Dante Caputo.

Foreign pressures culminated in the formation of a broad-based transitional government under the leadership of Prime Minister Robert Malval in August 1993. Two days after the Haitian parliament's approval of President's Aristide's choice of transition Prime Minister Malval on August 25, 1993, the United Nations, the Organization of American States, and the United States lifted economic sanctions against Haiti. But the assumption of office by Malval did not end human rights violations. On September 11, a prominent Aristide supporter, businessman Antoine Izméry, was dragged in broad daylight from a memorial mass at the Sacré-Coeur church in Port-au-Prince and shot in the head by armed civilian-dressed gunmen in the presence of international observers.

On October 11, 1993, a demonstration was organized to prevent the docking of the American ship named *Harlan County,* which left without unloading the first contingent of soldiers of the future Mission of the United Nations in Haiti (MINUHA). This reversal was a major setback to the Governor's Island goals. It also emboldened the Haitian armed forces and the FRAPH. United Nations envoy Dante Caputo condemned the killing of Antoine Izméry, as did the White House, on September 14, 1993.

As October 30, 1993 (the date planned for the return of President Aristide in the agreement of Governor's Island) neared, the country witnessed an upsurge of repression. A succession of terrorist acts hit famed supporters of Aristide, including the murder of the two brothers Georges and Antoine Izméry (prominent businessmen and backers of Aristide) and the murders of Guy Malary, Claudy Museau, and Father Jean Marie Vincent.

On September 23, 1993, the Security Council of the United Nations, with Resolution 867, authorized the immediate deployment of 1,300 police and military officers of the MINUHA. Sanctions, which were lifted after the Governor's Island Agreement, were restored by the United Nations on October 16, 1993. The extra-constitutional regime was further isolated. The Vatican was the only power to maintain diplomatic relations with the extra-constitutional regime

In the July 12, 1993 report of the secretary-general, the United Nations warned, however, that "the suspension of sanctions should be automatically terminated at any time if... the parties of the Governor's Island Agreement or any authorities in Haiti have failed to comply in good faith with the agreement." The secretary-general would "consider that the failure to comply with the undertaking of the agreement would include, inter alia, refusal by the high command of the armed forces to obey the decisions of the commander-in-chief who is to be appointed in accordance with Point 8 of the agreement and numerous violations of the human rights and fundamental freedoms set forth in the international instruments to which Haiti is a party and in the Constitution of Haiti."

The Raboteau district of Gonaives is renowned as a source of opposition to successive political regimes. It was the target of intimidation and sheer violence originating in both the regular armed forces and the paramilitary forces in 1994. As unarmed civilians sought to run away by the sea, armed men waiting in boats gunned them down. As many as two dozen people were killed in one massacre at Raboteau, which was the most notorious massacre carried out in 1994.

The sanctions imposed by the international community proved unsuccessful, however, in dislodging the usurper regime, possibly because of insufficient targeting and enforcement problems. This was further complicated by Haiti's weak economy and low trade rate, which were not particularly susceptible to sanctions (Pierce, 1996, 506), and the country's habituation with external isolation. In this sense, the social history of Haiti is different from that of Puerto Rico and Cuba because these islands were forcibly integrated in world economic systems.

In March 1994, the Congressional Black Caucus imposed a forceful line of negotiation, pleading for a total embargo (except for supplies and medicines), the freezing of the assets of coup leaders and supporters, the interdiction to validate or to deliver American visas to Haitian soldiers, and the deployment of a control force along the Dominican border to guarantee the application of embargo measures.

On March 23, 1994, the United Nations Security Council adopted, unanimously, a resolution prolonging the mandate of the MINUHA until June 30, 1994. Intense pressures emanating from the Congressional Black Caucus, the liberal wing of the Democratic Party, and human rights activists such as Randall Robinson, who went on a hunger strike, forced President Clinton to change the American policy on refugees on July 5, 1994. Haitians intercepted in high seas were placed in security zones in the Caribbean. The end of the refugee flows largely depended on a resolution of the Haitian crisis.

Human rights groups denounced the lack of firmness of American mediator Lawrence Pezzullo and called for his replacement by a person known for his engagement in the domain of human rights. Pezzullo resigned April 26, 1994, and was replaced by a former American parliamentarian and member of the Congressional Black Caucus, William H. Gray. Resolution 917 of the Security Council, which was adopted unanimously on May 6, 1994, amplified sanctions with regard to Haiti. It implied a complete trade embargo and the imposition of financial restrictions on the Haitian military. New sanctions on the delivery of visas to the military and to their civilian allies were added to these measures. Some Canadian, French, American, and Venezuelan boats began patrolling the coasts of Haiti to control the application of the embargo.

On September 15, 1994, in a broadcast speech, American president Bill Clinton officially asked Haitian military authorities to leave power. The violation of the Governor's Island Accord by the Haitian military constituted the principal element of reference in the justification of the designation of Haiti as threat to regional peace and security in the region. After emphasizing the alarming situation of human rights in Haiti, President Clinton announced the intention of the United States to use force, if necessary, to put an end to this situation. Two days later, a delegation of three American political personalities— ex-president Jimmy Carter, Senator Sam Nunn, and the former Inter-Army Chief of Staff Colin Powell—attempted a last-hour negotiation. An agreement was signed which included permissive entry, the negotiated departure of the military leadership, and the physical return of President Aristide.

In July 1994, the Security Council, acting under Title VII of the United Nations Charter, adopted Resolution 940, which authorized member states to form a multinational force under unified command and control and to employ all necessary means to facilitate the termination of extra-constitutional rule and the return of President Aristide. On September 19, 1994, the American-led multinational force intervened militarily in Haiti with the stated aim of restoring democracy. The force took possession of military facilities. On October 3, 1994, the American military police searched the headquarters of

FRAPH, conducted arrests, and seized their archives. On October 10, 1994, army general Raoul Cédras resigned. It was not until October 15, 1994, after a three-year exile, first in Caracas, Venezuela, and then in Washington, DC, that President Aristide returned to power. Although many supporters of Aristide regretted Aristide's return by means of an intervention of foreign troops, the Haitian population benefited from the end of military rule, which had brought threats, beatings, and extortions from regular and irregular armed forces to unprecedented levels.

In the fall of 1999, the Clinton administration announced the termination of its policy of permanently stationing troops in Haiti. This announcement came amid widespread confusion over American foreign policy as well as the suspicion that American intelligence and military forces maintained close ties with right-wing figures in Haitian society. The 480 U.S. military personnel attached to the U.S. support group left the country by the end of January 2000.

One of the important measures taken by Aristide was the abolition of the Haitian Armed Forces in 1994. This decision was undermined by Aristide government's decision to include 1,000 former soldiers in the new police force under the guise of enhancing the experience of the force. This decision provoked controversy in light of the army's long-standing record of human rights abuses. The army's abolition, which was first proposed by Costa Rican president Oscar Arias Sanchez, was eventually supported by the President Clinton. On the occasion of the visit of Oscar Arias to Port-au-Prince, Aristide declared that he was favorable to the complete dissolution of the army, following the example of Costa Rica. He also vowed to bring the emerging police force under the tutelage of the Ministry of Justice. This brought the nation closer to a state of peace.

The Culture of Peace

The second culture, the culture of peace, is characterized by consensus-building in collective action. It represents a vision of Haiti that is truly inclusive of differences, where social actors collectively engage in the search for solutions to common problems. The emergence of this culture of peace and cooperation can be traced back to the work of *gwoupman* in rural Haiti in the late 1960s and early 1970s.

The 1960s witnessed the emergence of Liberation Theology, a movement led by Augusto Boal, Paulo Freyre, and Som Helder Camara. This movement inspired the emergence in the early 1970s of democratically structured associations in rural Haiti called *gwoupman*. Indigenous Catholic clergy and laymen who were influenced by the Freirian concept of social awareness and the liberation theology led this social awareness movement. These structures reflect the beginning of the new social consciousness movement of that period. A distinctive feature of this movement is the understanding that participation is critical to transformation of social reality. The *gwoupman* sought to understand the structural causes of poverty and to reflect on means to combat such structural causes. The reorientation of the church's social mission toward the poor, which emerged from the 1968 conference of Catholic Bishops in Medellin, legitimized this effort, yielding a mobilization of efforts unparalleled in the countryside, including the creation of numerous grassroots groups (Maguire, 1990, 32). These base groups held regular discussion groups designed to analyze common problems and to raise local consciousness about the issues and concerns facing small farmers. A distinctive feature of this movement is the understanding that participation is critical to the transformation of social reality.

The transformation of the *gwoupman* from small base groups into dynamic agents of change is testimony to the hard work of animators in rural Haiti. The *gwoupman* were important not just because they operated efficiently but also because they fostered democratic learning. By democracy, I mean processes by which ordinary citizens exert a relatively high degree of control over leaders in accordance with the views on democracy put forth by Robert Dahl (1956, 3).

In the early 1970s, the *gwoupman* engendered significant mobilization of civil society at the local level. The emergence of *gwoupman* led to an observable surge in political participation as well as a deepening of social participation. They encouraged lively group discussion, group awareness, and group formation. Participation in *gwoupman* resulted in acquisition of leadership skills, values of bargaining, and interest articulation. Among the leadership training programs established in the early 1970s, two deserve particular attention: the Institut Diocésain des Adults (IDEA) in the Cap-Haitian area and the Centre Emmaus at Papaye in the Central Plateau of Haiti. Over a 14-year period starting in 1973, IDEA trained hundreds of animators *(animatè)* who, in turn, catalyzed the creation of some 1,500 small development groups, primarily in Haiti's north and northeast departments. The Centre Emmaus has been equally active in training community grassroots leaders, having worked with individuals from throughout the country who have also stimulated the creation of thousands of grassroots groups (Maguire, 1990, 32). Trained animators encouraged peasants to form community development groups in which individuals could pool resources, skills, and energies. Members learned new social and economic relationships, such as revolving credit and mutual support, that changed social relations in the countryside. With the *gwoupman*, a shift in political culture occurred. *Gwoupman* became a neutral site of political and policy discussions by previously marginalized groups. Peasants who were caught in a web of mutual mistrust learned that cooperation was possible and that it yields mutual benefits. This process thus promoted community trust and social capital at unprecedented levels in Haiti.

Because the Haitian state was unaccustomed to civic participation, it repressed the emerging civil society. This fomented unprecedented popular mobilization that culminated in the departure of Jean-Claude Duvalier on February 6, 1986.

In recent years, the *gwoupman* have expanded their roles beyond their original focus on pre-cooperative economic ventures. In addition to mutual aid service and rights protection (e.g., credit arrangements, provision of legal services to imprisoned peasants), the *gwoupman* have engaged in successful economic endeavors, either by themselves or in partnership with other organizations. In many rural communities, the *gwoupman* have also expanded their membership from neighborhood population segments to a community-wide constituency. In the Haitian context, the *gwoupman* represent the incarnation of the participatory democracy.

Civic and popular sectors seek to establish new relationships with the state based on awareness of the common good. The need for accountability of state officials to civil and popular sectors has been expressed consistently. Also, to attain the common good, public policy, laws, and public expenditures have to reflect the interests of the entire population. This view corresponds to the sentiment of the nation. In other words, the very process of power-sharing strengthens the concept of the nation.

The democratic transition that followed the downfall of the dictatorial regime of Jean-Claude Duvalier in 1986 suffered a major setback with the coup that deposed the democratically constituted government of Jean-Bertrand Aristide in September 1991. Thousands of members of civic groups lost their lives in the crackdown by the paramilitary group known as FRAPH.

Although the culture of peace is relatively new, the concept of the Haitian nation from which it derives has been constant since the founding of the country. The Haitian nation is before all a permanent fact whereas power is temporary.

The culture of peace is increasingly strengthened by active local participation. The consolidation of the culture of peace requires equity in the representation of local population in decision-making bodies. Democracy requires representation of the diverse interests of various segments of the Haitian population. This requires not just diversity of political views but also representation of all corners of the Haitian territories.

THE AUTHORITARIAN DRIFT OF 2001–2003

The Haitian process of democratic transition witnessed an authoritarian drift as of 2001, which consolidated into a repressive political power until 2002–2003. This period reflected a chaotic perversion of the democratic process, in which one self-proclaimed savior purported to represent the will of the

Haitian people. The political chessboard was thrown into disorder at the end of 2003 and the beginning of 2004. An overt conflict emerged between pro-Lavalas gangs (Lavalas refers to the governing party of Jean-Bertrand Aristide) and civilian opposition, notably student movements and civic groups. The most meaningful and decisive factor was the deployment of insurgent forces called the Armed Forces of the North under the command of former police commissioner Guy Philippe. Aristide was driven to depart in the night of February 28–29, 2004, because he faced a situation where his own physical survival was at stake. From this misadventure, the country emerged somewhat disoriented and worn out by constant political and institutional crises.

The lifesaving plan put in place by the Caribbean Common Market (CARICOM) came up against the reiterated refusal of the Democratic Platform to cohabitate with Aristide and renewed demands for his resignation. As in the case of previous foreign occupations, internal political instability opened the door to international interference. The international community conceived and concretized a plan of action with a speed of execution uncommon in public affairs, which included the choice of the interim president, the selection of a tripartite commission, and the establishment of a "Council of Sages." These constitutional, structural innovations testified to a solution of institutional continuity bound to the specificities of this transition. Prime Minister Latortue took the reins of the transition government under the leitmotif, "To the impossible we are held," hammered several times during his inaugural speech. Gérard Latortue served as the Prime Minister of Haiti from March 12, 2004 to June 9, 2006. Before assuming the position of Prime Minister, Latortue was an official in the United Nations for many years. In spite of the limitations of this U.S.-backed technocratic regime including many reports of human rights violations, one has to acknowledge its determination to succeed. It is no easy task to unify the country of Haiti, which is divided by deeply-rooted class and color divisions. It is becoming increasingly clear that democratic consolidation will not be complete in Haiti until the culture of peace is accepted as the modus operandi by the majority of actors. The values attached to the culture of peace work best when they emerge from and are embedded in political culture. The first black republic has aspired since its birth to a destiny of greatness. Achievement of that greatness requires that the nation finally own the state rather than constantly fighting the state.

CONCLUSION

This chapter has described the two competing types of political cultures in Haiti. The first political culture, the culture of peace, favors a new configuration of power based on cooperation and reciprocity. In contrast, the culture of authoritarianism is based on coercion and unilateral action.

The culture of peace, although endowed of legitimacy, is not prevailing for two main reasons. First, its base of support in society does not hold final, economic, and political powers. Second, it requires social cohesion, which necessitates acceptance of valid rules for all and functioning management of the conflicts inside the society. It requires the reconciliation of the Haitian state with its obligations to its citizens because Haitian history has traversed a constant struggle between state-controlled violence and popular resistance to this violence. The culture of peace prevails, however, only when the balance of power favors cooperation. If incentives for cooperation exist, outcomes can be rewarding for both state and the nation. This unity of nation is the best way to avoid foreign interference. It is the best guarantee of the progressive conquest of the autonomy of governmental action even as lasting accompaniment of international cooperation persists.

The political culture of authoritarianism benefits from a favorable balance of powers. It benefits from political community and entrenchments in national political customs. It prevails even though it is unable to occupy the whole scene because of to lack of legitimacy.

REFERENCES

Americas Watch. *Harvesting Oppression: Forced Haitian Labor in the Dominican Sugar Industry.* New York: Americas Watch, 1990.

Atwood, Brian J. "The United States Must Stop Playing Ostrich in Haiti: Toothless Diplomacy May Fuel Incipient Revolution." *Los Angeles Times,* February 15, 1988: 1.

Bernier, Barbara L. "Democratization and Economic Development in Haiti: A Review of the Caribbean Basin Initiative." *The International Lawyer* 27, no. 2 (Summer 1993): 455–469.

Bonnardot, Martin-Luc, and Gilles Danroc. *La chute de la maison Duvalier (28 novembre 1985–7 février 1986).* Paris: Éditions KARTALA, 1989.

Comhaire, Jean. "The Haitian Chef de Section." *American Anthropologist* 57 (1955): 620–623.

Cox, Ronald. "Private Interests and United States Foreign Policy in Haiti and the Caribbean Basin." In David Skidmore, ed., *Contested Social Orders and International Politics.* Nashville and London: Vanderbilt University Press, 1997.

Dahl, Robert. *A Preface to Democratic Theory.* Chicago: University of Chicago, 1956.

D'Ans, André-Marcel. *Haïti: Paysage et Société.* Paris: Éditions Karthala, 1987.

Downs, Charles. *Politics, Design and Results: Regionalization and Decentralization in Nicaragua and Haiti, 1982–86.* New York: Columbia University, Institute of Latin American and Iberian Studies, Papers on Latin America no. 7, September 1988.

Doyle, Kate. "Hollow Diplomacy in Haiti." *World Policy Journal*, 11, no. 1 (Spring 1994).

Fass, Simon M. *Political Economy in Haiti: The Drama of Survival.* New Brunswick, NJ: Transaction Books, 1984.

Fatton, Robert A. "The Rise, Fall and Resurrection of President Aristide." In Robert I. Rotberg, ed., *Haiti Renewed: Political and Economic Prospects.* Washington, DC: Brookings Institution Press; Cambridge: The World Peace Foundation, 1997.

Garber, Larry. "What Can Be Done to Rescue Haiti?" *Washington Times,* December 11, 1987: 1.

Garrity, Monique P. "The Assembly Industry in Haiti: Causes and Effects, 1967–1973." *The Review of Black Political Economy* 11 (1981): 203–215.

Hayes, Margaret D., and Gary F. Wheatley. *Interagency and Political-Military Dimensions of Peace Operations: Haiti: A Case Study.* Washington, DC: National Defense University, Institute for National Strategic Studies, 1996.

Kernel-Torres, Doryanne, and Roca Pierre-Jean. *Sécurité alimentaire: Les politiques alimentaires nationales et leur influence sur l'évolution des systèmes ruraux, une étude comparative menée en Haïti, en Inde (Karnataka) et en Thaïlande (Nord-est).* Paris: ASP ORSTOM-CNRS, 1993.

Lahav, Pnina. *The Chef de Section: Structure and Function of Haiti's Basic Administrative Unit.* New Haven, CT: Yale University Antilles Research Program, 1973.

Loescher, G. D., and John Scanlan. *United States Policy and Its Impact on Refugee Flow from Haiti.* New York: New York University, Occasional Papers Number 42, 1984.

Lundhal, Mats. *The Haitian Economy: Man, Land, and Markets.* New York: St. Martin Press, 1983.

Maguire, Robert E. *Bottom-Up Development in Haiti.* Washington, DC: The Inter-American Foundation, 1979.

———. "Haiti's Emerging Peasant Movement." *Cimarron: New Perspective on the Caribbean* 2, no. 3 (Winter 1990): 28–44.

Marquez, Sandra. "Haiti's Tiny Parties Reject Vote Results People Accept." *Washington Times,* July 24, 1995.

Mintz, Sydney W. *Caribbean Transformations.* New York: Columbia University Press, 1974.

Le Moniteur. "Loi Portant Sur L'Organisation de la Collectivité Territoriale de Section Communale." *151e Année,* Numéro 24 (4 April 1996), 1.

———. "Le Décret du 4 Mars 1974," *Numéro 21* (17 Mars, 1974): 1.

National Democratic Institute for International Affairs. *Haiti Presidential/ Legislative Elections: A Report of the NDI International Observer Delegation.* Washington, DC: National Democratic Institute for International Affairs, 1987.

Le Nouvelliste. "Bureau Central du Recensement: Résultats pour l'Election du Président de la République," September 28, 1957.

Pierce, John C. "The Haitian Crisis and the Future of Collective Enforcement of Democratic Governance." *Law and Policy in International Business* 27, no. 2 (1996): 477–512.

Plant, Roger. *Sugar and Modern Slavery: A Tale of Two Countries.* London: Zed Books Limited, 1987.

Prince, Rod. *Haiti: Family Business.* London: Latin America Books, 1985.

Radio Métropole. "Nouvelles: Position de l'Association des Industries d'Haïti," 15 Aout 1991.

Slavin, J. P. "Layoffs at Factories Add to Haiti's Woes." *Miami Herald,* July 15, 1991.

Smucker, Glenn R. "Peasant Councils and the Politics of Community." In Derick W. Brinkerhoff and Jean-Claude Zamor, eds., *Politics, Projects and People: Institutional Development in Haiti.* New York: Praeger, 1986.

Stepan, Alfred. "Democratic Opposition and Democratization Theory." *Government and Opposition* 32, no. 4 (1997): 657–673.

United States Department of State. "Interdiction of Illegal Aliens," excutive orders dated September 29, 1981, nos. 4865 and 12324 (Reprint) Washington, D.C.: Department of State Bulletin 81, no. 5057, December 1981.

Wingfield, Roland, and Vernon J. Parenton. "Class Structure and Class Conflict in Haitian Society." *Social Forces* 43, no. 3 (March 1965): 338–47.

7

Social and Economic Reality (1986–2006)

For the average Haitian, particularly the jobless man on the street, life has not been good, in part because of low levels of job creation and high levels of human insecurity. For foreign donors, an improved economic outlook depends on privatization and private sector development in Haiti. Privatization is broadly defined as the shifting of a function, either in whole or in part, from the public sector to the private sector. The emphasis on private sector development is best understood in a context in which the state sector has historically levied taxes without supporting national and local development in Haiti. At times, the state sector competed with the private sector for resources rather than providing an atmosphere conducive to domestic stability and private investments.

Foreign donors and creditors have insisted on the implementation of public enterprise divestiture, reduction in public expenditures, and financial liberalization. They have increasingly made assistance conditional on the implementation of public sector reform packages. These reforms are presented as privileged means to promote prudent use of foreign assistance. They aim to restrict the role of government to the provision of legal and physical infrastructures. At the insistence of international financial institutions, the Haitian private sector has acquired ownership of state-owned assets, notably the Haitian flour mill. Moreover, street cleaning and refuse collection have been partly privatized.

State-owned industrial corporations have been involved in sugar refining, sisal production, extraction of essential oils, and the production of cement, shoes, textiles, cigarettes, and soap. However, industrial development has been impeded by several factors, including Haiti's narrow domestic market, the absence of government subsidies, competition of cheap foreign imports, an inadequate infrastructure base, and raw material shortages.

Historically, the Haitian government has centered its economic development strategy on attracting and retaining export-oriented assembly operations. In the early 1980s, foreign donors and creditors pressured the administration of Jean-Claude Duvalier to engage in administrative reforms. As a result, the Duvalier regime pursued an ambitious program of inviting foreign investors to establish export assembly operations in Haiti. The administration established an industrial park and, in October 1981, created a public enterprise called Société Nationale Des Parcs Industriels (SONAPI) to manage it. SONAPI subsequently leased the facilities to export assembly firms on preferential terms. The bulk of products assembled in Haiti (clothing, sporting and athletic goods, electronic equipment, baseballs, handicrafts, and toys) are sold to the Unites States. Three additional privately owned free zones were established in Haiti in the 1980s with government assistance. The free zones' proximity to the country's only international airport facilitated assembly firms' access to international markets. By keeping the minimum wage low and hindering the growth of labor unions, the Duvalier regime sought to make Haiti a "paradise" for foreign investors.

During the Duvalier era, management exerted significant influence because existing labor laws and customs were structured around the protection of private property and the attraction and retention of foreign capital. Haiti's main institutional framework for labor relation, the Labor Code, was carefully crafted to discourage union organizing in violation of international labor standards. The 1961 labor code was revised in March 1984 to bring the code more closely in line with the International Labor Organization's conventions. But the new Labor Code still required government approval of any association of more than 20 persons, a clear violation of international labor standards, which empowered workers to organize themselves in labor union without prior authorization by the government.

The only labor union allowed to exist, the Federation of Union Workers (FOS), was a conservative labor federation founded on January 12, 1984, in Port-au-Prince with nine active labor unions. From its inception, FOS adopted a nonconfrontational approach to labor relations. As Compa (1989, 20) noted, "FOS espouses a moderate approach to trade union action, criticizes political demands and calls...for an emphasis on collective bargaining and cooperative relations with employers." FOS worked closely with the AFL-CIO; with the International Confederation of Free Trade Unions (ICFTU), headquartered in Brussels, Belgium; and with the latter's affiliate, the Inter-American Regional Organization of Workers (ORIT), headquartered in Mexico City.

The Haitian government also provided significant fiscal incentives to foreign firms, including free repatriation of profits and tax exemptions. Unfortunately, these measures did not transform Haiti into the "Taiwan of the Caribbean," as was expected. The Duvalier regime's reliance on the export assembly industry failed to alleviate poverty as the assembly industry exhibited few backward and forward linkages with the rest of the economy. Virtually all of the raw materials, investment capital, machinery, and administration of assembly operations were imported from the United States. Limited articulation with local industries hindered the production of locally added value.

The Duvalier regime banned imports in several categories under its policy of import-substitution. Several state-run agencies emerged that specialized in sugar refining, preparation of sisal, extraction of essential oils, and the production of cement, shoes, textiles, cigarettes, and soap. As a result of these financial incentives, manufacturing recorded strong growth in the late 1970s, averaging 11.9 percent growth a year between 1976 and 1980. By 1985, manufacturing for domestic consumption accounted for roughly 50 percent of industrial production.

Because agricultural output did not keep pace with population growth, Haiti became a net food importer in the 1970s. By 1981, the shrinkage of the market for export crops and the explosion of contraband had accelerated the process of pauperization in the rural sector. This was translated in unprecedented sale of livestock and land assets. The situation was aggravated by the policies of the National Government Council, the military-dominated government that replaced the Duvalier regime in 1986.

Within hours after learning of the departure for France of Dictator Jean-Claude Duvalier, workers at the state-owned electric and telephone companies conducted wildcat strikes demanding higher wages and the removal of Duvalierists from the public administration. In response, a group of well-known American companies that had enjoyed success in Haiti's assembly sector for decades, including GTE, United Technologies, TRW, and Bendix, moved some of their operations from Haiti (Ebert, 1987, 1).

ECONOMIC POLICY IN THE POST-DUVALIER ERA

In the post-Duvalier era, the Haitian state continued to allocate financial and tax incentives to promote and expand the assembly industry. As noted, the bulk of the products assembled in Haiti are exported to the United States.

Although the assembly industry produced much needed jobs, the number of jobs created in the assembly industrial sector is insignificant when measured against the number of entrants into the labor force every year. In 1987 assembly plants employed some 40,000 workers, and roughly 39,000 new workers enter the workforce every year (Hooper, 1987, 35).

Until the 1980s, donor agencies focused exclusively on channeling aid through the Haitian government. However, monopoly over foreign assistance fueled corruption, inefficiencies in the management of foreign aid, nonprofessionalism, and the domination of the public sphere by the executive branch. This led foreign donors to increase support to nongovernmental organizations.

THE NATIONAL GOVERNING COUNCIL

When the National Governing Council replaced the Duvalier dynasty in February 1986, it requested foreign assistance to implement swift changes in Haiti's political and economic structures. In order to assure foreign powers of its commitment to market-based policies, the National Governing Council ordered the National Bank of the Republic of Haiti, the country's central bank, to use high cash ratios in commercial banks as a mechanism to regulate the money supply. The central bank also maintained a ceiling on interest rates at 22 percent (Garrity, 1981, 288).

Haiti's economy remained dependent on foreign aid and investments. At the end of 1987, foreign investments totaled $128 million, of which $72 million came from the United States and $39 million from France. The National Governing Council negotiated a structural adjustment loan of $25 million with international financial institutions in 1987. The council committed itself to reforming the tax structure, instituting fiscal austerity, eliminating monopolies, and further opening the economy. As part of its commitment to market-based policies, the government of Haiti sharply decreased customs duties, subsidies, and price controls, with the notable exception of petroleum products. The flood of cheap imports undermined the livelihood of thousands of farmers and urban entrepreneurs.

These policies were implemented at a time when Haitian agriculture was confronted with the grave problem of sustaining an increasing population on shrinking land. The rise in population has had negative repercussions on rural–urban migration. Dramatic population increases have intensified pressures on scarce cultivable land, producing considerable urban migration. The fall from 84 percent to 65 percent of the population engaged in the agricultural sector observed between the censuses of 1950 and 1982 reflects rural–urban migration, with a focus on the capital city of Port-au-Prince. The remaining peasants have no choice but to cultivate increasingly smaller parcels spread through different ecological systems, often distant from each other, with the aim of growing a wide variety of crops, spreading out the maximum time for agricultural works, and benefiting from harvest throughout the year.

Large land areas are typically state-owned, often leased out at small rent to influential families who in turn sublet at considerably higher rates, often through sharecropping arrangements. State land is rented on a yearly basis. The leaseholder must pay the lease amount to the contributions office in the town. Upon rental payment, the leaseholder is given a receipt *(resu)*, and the transaction is recorded in the contributions office. As long as the leaseholder pays the annual rent, he retains possession of the lease. When the leaseholder dies, the lease is transferred to his heirs.

In some cases, owners of large properties often use their access to capital to invest in modern processes that ultimately increase the production per acre such as irrigation, fertilization, and use of pesticides. It is notable that these large properties often grow one or two crops, which favors mechanization. This plantation economy is often characterized by use of techniques and machinery that are very advanced. A measure of development would be a societal shift toward more efficient production to meet the growing national demand for food. The small-scale garden economy, which aims for survival, still predominates. The average income in the garden economy is too weak for investments in irrigation systems or purchase of fertilizers and pesticides. Moreover, the proximity of small parcels owned by different owners excludes possibilities of use of heavy agricultural machinery. As a result, agricultural tools remain primitive in the garden economy.

Moreover, farmers with mountain gardens rarely use modern agricultural techniques in farming. The slopes are generally too steep for animal-drawn plots. Soil preparation is typically performed with hand tools such as machetes, pickaxes, and hoes.

The growth rate of the cities has been three times superior to that of rural areas. The annual rate of growth of the metropolitan area of Port-au-Prince was 5.2 percent between 1950 and 1982. Unfortunately, these patterns reflect more an aggravation of disequilibrium that characterized the Haitian society and economy than a positive modification of economic and social structures deriving from a process of development. This is a consequence of the growing concentration of economic and administrative activities in the capital city of Port-au-Prince. In contrast, the growth rate for the same period for the second largest town of the country, Cap Haitian, was 3.1 percent. The growth rate of more than 10 towns with more than 10,000 inhabitants was 2.65 percent. It is also interesting to consider gender differentiation in migration patterns. Women are more likely than men to engage in rural–urban migration.

The plots of those who remain in the countryside are becoming increasingly smaller. The French tradition of equal inheritance has progressively reduced the average size of holdings and caused an intensification of land use. In 1987, 63 percent of farm establishments in the rice sector measured 2.47 acres or less (Institute for Agriculture and Trade Policy, 1996, 1). This pattern of plots becoming increasingly smaller because of population growth has created a situation where small farmers are unable to live from farming alone. High population density of 781 residents per square miles combined with limited arable land limits more and more every year the plot of each family member, which declined by 40 percent between 1950 and 1995. This reduction of arable land has led to the reclamation and cultivation of land previously allocated for pasture.

Because small rice growers could not compete with the relatively low prices of rice imported from the United States, many of them were driven out of agricultural production. In addition to causing economic displacement, imported rice altered eating habits, as an increasing number of Haitians came to replace locally produced crops with the higher-quality imported rice. Faced with competition of cheaper foreign products, many farmers abandoned agriculture and moved to cities, particularly the capital city of Port-au-Prince. As a result, the contribution of agriculture has been declining for years, but that sector is still estimated to represent some 30 percent of the economy. Coffee exports have suffered steep decline but still represent one of the largest sources of foreign exchange.

Faced with a chronic balance of payment deficits, the National Governing Council reformed the tariff and tax structures, abolished state monopolies on such commodities as flour and cement, and liberalized trade in 1986. These policies have had both positive and negative effects on the economy. On one hand, the reform measures served to lower the government's deficit. On the other hand, by removing the tight import controls imposed by the Duvalier regime, the National Governing Council opened up the vulnerable Haitian economy to a flood of cheap food imports and contraband, further undermining the livelihood of thousands of farmers and urban entrepreneurs. Formal and informal food imports have increased significantly, leading to a fall of the price of items of basic necessity. These processes culminated in huge loss of income in the national economy. The case of Haiti thus provides a vivid example of damages that can be done to an economy when supporting economic measures are not in place to ease the transition period. Five short-lived administrations misgoverned Haiti between 1987 and 1990.

THE FIRST ARISTIDE ADMINISTRATION (FEBRUARY 1991–SEPTEMBER 1991)

The Republic of Haiti's first open and democratic presidential race on December 16, 1990, resulted in a massive victory for Jean-Bertrand Aristide.

Aristide was elected on an electoral platform against inequality and with a strong anti-American overtone. This strained relations between the United States and the first Aristide administration.

Aristide was inaugurated as president on February 7, 1991. President Aristide unified the exchange rate and eliminated export retention requirements before negotiations with the International Monetary Fund for a standby agreement. The Haitian diaspora was a recurrent theme in the discourse of President Aristide. Aristide promised a diplomacy that would enhance the dignity of Haitians living abroad. His government eliminated the bracero program with the Dominican Republic, the terms of which were unfavorable to Haitian migrant workers. Aristide often referred to the diaspora as the "tenth department," added to the nine geographic departments that composed Haiti. The tenth department is often referred to as the pillar of the Haitian economy. Beyond this, some crucial issues remained unaddressed, such as the urgency to revise the 1986 constitution to examine possibilities of dual citizenship and the related empowerment of Haitians living abroad with the right to vote in national and local elections under absentee balloting.

However, Aristide's polarizing political positions angered so many local and foreign actors that the door was open to a coup d'état. Seven months after Aristide's inauguration as president, he was forced into exile by a military coup in September 1991. These events received worldwide attention and resulted in greater awareness of the fragile nature of democratization in Haiti.

The danger of dependency is multifaceted and ever present, particularly in countries with a limited resource base such as Haiti. The Haitian case is interesting because of its resistance to globalization in spite of the country's dependence on foreign aid. As the poorest country in the Western Hemisphere, Haiti depends on foreign loans and grants for general operational expenditures. More than two-thirds of Haiti's national budget is typically financed through foreign assistance funds. Yet in spite of its apparent weakness, Haiti has displayed significant resistance to globalization. For instance, economic restructuring policies often require the formation of coalitions of external actors and domestic political forces for passage and implementation. This makes for difficulty in Haiti, where constant shifts on the political scene and competing agendas tend to undermine policy consistency and capacity to deliver expected public benefits.

The usurper regime systematically used state-owned agencies as bases of support. As a result, the public sector wage bill grew rapidly, straining the national budget and causing further inefficiencies in state operations. The extra-constitutional regime was supported by a narrow portion of the political spectrum. Regular and irregular armed forces roamed the streets in pickup trucks with their automatic rifles, quickly scattering and repressing dissent. Coup supporters argued that the coup was a preemptive measure because

Aristide was mobilizing his own paramilitary force to undermine the Haitian armed forces just as Duvalier had established the Tontons Macoutes paramilitary force to keep in line the Haitian military.

During the three years of extra-constitutional rule, conditions in the already deprived nation of the Western Hemisphere worsened. Unemployment neared 80 percent. Deforestation and land overuse were rampant. In the face of internal dissent and international isolation, the extra-constitutional government actively encouraged importation of rice. In 1992 it signed a treaty with the American Rice Corporation, the largest American rice milling and marketing company, which permitted the importation of 60,000 tons of rice to Haiti. The Rice Corporation of Haiti sold the American Blue Ribbon, White Sail, and COMET brands throughout Haiti. After the milling process, the different types of rice are generally mixed together. The Rice Corporation of Haiti initially committed to significant investments in technical assistance to improve the quantity and quality of rice grown in Haiti for blending with imported rice at its facilities in Haiti. Although the end product is often sold under the generic label of either Madame Gougousse or Imported Rice, the milled and commercialized rice is often mixed. The Rice Corporation of Haiti promised to stimulate local rice production so as to continue mixing higher-quality imported rice with improved local rice varieties. The company did engage in the plantings of improved seeds. There is no evidence, however, that local rice production increased because of these investments.

After a military coup deposed him, Aristide maintained his nationalist positions. In an interview with author Barbara Bernier (1993, 461), Jean-Bertrand Aristide affirmed, "I cannot accept that Haiti should be whatever the United States wants it to be." The position that Aristide's stand is typical of Haitian resistance to external pressures receives considerable support. Maingot characterized Haitian political attitudes as "stubbornly resistant to third party involvement . . . in the elaboration of a desired course of event" (1994, 223). Nationalist political discourse is also impregnated with the notion of an American plan for Haiti. This plan is often said to involve American desires to acquire Cape Nicolas Mole because of its strategic importance. In his *The Present State of Haiti*, James Franklin, describes the Cape Nicolas Mole matter in these terms: "the harbor of Cape Nicolas Mole was the principal place for the safe anchorage of shipping in the western world, but it has gone into neglect" (1970, 202). There is little concrete evidence of such an American plan. National resistance to external intervention is not specific to Haiti. Shin (1994, 165) recognized that, in most cases, strong outside intervention to encourage domestic reforms tends to jeopardize the legitimacy of reforms because they are likely to create more resentment than acquiescence.

Aristide's anti-capitalistic discourse partly explains why he was twice ejected from the presidential armchair. In 1994 the U.S. Government briefly considered whether then Haitian president Jean-Bertrand Aristide should step aside in favor of a figure more acceptable to the Haitian elite and military (Hayes and Wheatley, 1996, 12).

U.S. support for the restoration of Aristide came with strong strings attached. The Clinton administration made support for Aristide conditional on his commitment to reconciliation, the constitution of a broad-based government, and the implementation of economic restructuring policies (Hayes and Wheatley, 1996, 12–13). An agreement with Aristide that he would leave office at the end of his term was also a condition of American support. In order to hasten his return, Aristide agreed in 1994 to implement the "Strategy of Social and Economic Reconstruction," which insisted on the need for conservative fiscal policies and privatization.

After Aristide agreed to implement market reforms, the international community responded positively to his request for restoration of constitutional democracy. The coup d'état that deposed Aristide's democratically constituted government was perceived as an international issue, not merely a domestic one. Nearly a year later, the United Nations Security Council approved a near-complete economic embargo of Haiti. This measure was taken with the hope that the worsening fuel crisis would help convince the coup regime that there was no alternative to negotiation with Aristide. A small OAS team led by former Colombian foreign minister Augusto Ramirez Ocampo oversaw negotiations between the Aristide camp and the extra-constitutional regime.

Doubts remain regarding the effectiveness of the embargo, and not just because of the significant number of enforcement problems and violations. The threat of sanctions did not dissuade the Haitian military from carrying out the coup d'état, nor did the subsequent embargo, by itself, bring it to an end. Negotiations for departure of military rulers and the subsequent peaceful deployment of the multinational force were major contributing factors. Haiti's relatively low trade rate weakened the impact of sanctions.

A major source of pressure on Washington was the global solidarity movement. TransAfrica, headed by activist Randal Robinson, worked with the Congressional Black Caucus to end Aristide's Washington exile. The diplomatic track produced the Governor's Island Agreement. Refusal of implementation by the regime of Raoul Cédras set in motion the U.S. invasion of 1994.

On July 31, 1994, the Security Council, acting under Title VII of the United Nations Charter, adopted Resolution 940, which authorized member states to form a multinational force under unified command and control and to employ all necessary means to facilitate the termination of extra-constitutional rule and the return of President Aristide. On September 19, 1994, a multinational force of 20,000 troops, mostly Americans, intervened militarily in Haiti to remove a military dictatorship and reinstate the country's first democratically elected president. The force was active in Haiti until 1999. In the fall of that year, the Clinton administration announced the termination of its policy of permanently stationing troops in Haiti. The last 480 U.S. military personnel attached to the U.S. support group left Haiti in early 2000. During these five years, troops remained there at an annual cost of $20 million, as part of an assistance package estimated at $2 billion. This makes the Republic of Haiti one of the top Latin American recipients of U.S. assistance in this era.

With the embargo and related interruption of official development assistance, international donors channeled most of their funds through private voluntary organizations. Even after the return to constitutional rule, the percentage of funds allocated to private organizations for aid delivery remained significant.

THE RESTORATION OF DEMOCRACY IN 1994 AND THE SECOND ARISTIDE ADMINISTRATION (1994–1996)

With the restoration of democracy in 1994, hopes for political stability and economic deliverance surged in the population, which had endured the burdens of political repression and a crushing global embargo. The top military leaders went into exile, and order was quickly restored by American troops. Aristide vowed to work with foreign donors and the Haitian elite, under the banner of national reconciliation. His administration reduced import tariffs in February 1995 to levels that were significantly lower than prevailing rates in neighboring Dominican Republic. The tariff reduction was intended to attract foreign investors, particularly in the small manufacture-for-export assembly sector. It also sought to comply with U.S. insistence on low Haitian tariffs as a condition for bilateral and multilateral loans and grants.

The Aristide administration later reversed its position on privatization. This occurred not so much because Aristide opposed privatization per se but because he disliked the idea of foreign acquisition of national assets. The Clinton administration and International Monetary Fund responded to this reversal by suspending foreign aid and loans. In the end, the restoration of democracy did not yield a significant change in the country's poverty rate because of a lack of jobs and slow progress in judicial reform. As a sign of lost hopes at home, Haitians began fleeing Haiti again by sea.

THE FIRST PRÉVAL ADMINISTRATION (1995–2000)

The 1995 elections were organized by the provisional electoral council (CEP), a nine-person council whose members were appointed by the three branches of the Haitian government: three by the executive, three by the parliament, and three by the judicial branches. In this case, the Haitian government and political parties agreed to form a provisional council instead of the permanent council envisioned by the constitution of 1987 because of lack of legislation laying out the functions of local authorities who would, constitutionally, propose names to the council. The CEP appointed personnel to departmental and communal bureaus. Both the constitution of 1987 and the 1995 electoral law prohibited known human rights violators or corrupt Duvalierists from competing in these elections. Controversies arose over a number of disqualifications on technical grounds. Affected candidates were from both the right and left. René Garcia Préval, a low-key politician who had served as prime minister under President Aristide in 1991, easily won the 1995 presidential race, receiving 87.9 percent of the nearly 931,000 valid votes in a race against 13 minor opponents in the December 17 elections. Haiti witnessed the first peaceful and democratic transfer of power in its history, when Préval assumed the presidency in February 1996.

PRIVATIZATION UNDER THE FIRST PRÉVAL ADMINISTRATION

The Préval administration took some steps to privatize state-owned agencies and enterprises. It also established a Presidential Commission for Economic Growth and Modernization. However, only a narrow set of actors openly supported privatization, including external donors and creditors, the majority parliamentary party, and the executive branch. The Organization of the People in Struggle, which changed its name from the Lavalas Political Organization in January 1997, joined President Préval in advocating economic restructuring policies. As the majority party in parliament, the Organization of the People in Struggle facilitated the coming to power in 1996 of a government of neo-liberal orientation led by one of its members, former prime minister Rosny Smarth. Smarth promised that his program of modernization would make state agencies more symbiotic, not competitive with each other. As it happened, rival factions within the government pursued separate agendas, yielding limited public benefits. Haiti remained polarized. The traditional political parties, including most opposition parties, did not represent Haiti's majority of poor, rural voters.

The thrust toward privatization accelerated in October 1996 as the government of Haiti agreed to implement a structural adjustment program with the assistance of the International Monetary Fund. After some stalling and interparty bickering, the Haitian legislature enacted the privatization framework law authorizing the privatization and modernization of state-owned enterprises.

The October 1996 law marked the first time that a law admitted formally the principle of privatization and defined the mechanisms of implementation, even though the term used was modernization instead of privatization.

Legislation governing civil service reform, which was approved late in 1996, provided the government legal authority to pursue voluntary termination and anticipated retirement of public employees.

The Lavalas Family was established in November 1996 by former president Jean-Bertrand Aristide as a result of conflicts within the Lavalas movement over economic policy. This political party proclaimed its opposition to reforms imposed by international financiers, causing a shift in government policy. Heated arguments about the outcomes of the April 1997 elections caused further rifts in the Lavalas movement and weakening of the administration of President René Garcia Préval. Prime Minister Rosny Smarth resigned in June 1997 in protest of a dearth of progress on public sector reforms, massive frauds in the April 1997 elections, and governmental incapacity to satisfy popular demands for enhanced living standards. The impasse created by Smarth's resignation and the ensuing political instability hampered the process of privatization, the passage of legislation on budget mechanisms, monetary policy, and financial sector regulation and investment protection.

Nine principal state-owned enterprises have been designated for some form of privatization by the Haitian government and international financial institutions, including the telephone and electric companies, the cement factory, the flour mill, the ports and airports, the edible oil plant, and two commercial banks. The first round of privatization of state-owned enterprises witnessed the modernization of the flourmill. In September 1997, some 70 percent of shares in the Haitian Flourmill were sold for $9 million to Haiti Agro Processors Holdings Ltd. The buyer was a consortium of Continental Grain and Seaboard Corporation of the United States and Unifinance of Haiti. Within the consortium, each private entity held 23.33 percent of the mixed company's shares. The Haitian state retained the remaining 30 percent of total shares. The Mills of Haiti, formerly known as the Haitian Flourmill, held its inauguration on December 22, 1998 at Laffiteau, 12.42 miles north of the capital city of Port-au-Prince.

The conditions of the sale of the flourmill irritated opponents of privatization who argued that the sale was not motivated by a strategy of development and was not characterized by transparency and consensus. The Haitian Flourmill was closed for months, and investors were reluctant to commit to repairs, rehabilitation, and acquisition of new equipment prior to the sale. In their view, these factors reduced considerably the asset value of the flourmill.

Because the Haitian government did not commit the funds needed to upgrade these structures, revenues raised by the divestiture of this enterprise have been found to be minimal by opposition sectors. Critics accused the government of Haiti of undervaluing public assets and pilfering scarce national resources. Former Haitian president Jean-Bertrand Aristide declared that the economic reform program is an attempt by foreign financiers to "pillage the country" (Economic Intelligence Unit, 1997, 44). In this sense, the Haitian experience with privatization seems to constitute a sort of dissidence. The overall lesson is that public appeal of divestiture of state enterprises depends heavily on the conditions of sales. The Haitian case thus offers some lessons that could be usefully considered by countries in comparable economic conditions that still face a broad range of privatization options.

The challenges for the Préval administration were daunting: to satisfy the requirements of foreign donors and lenders without alienating the poor majority. It is in this context that the Préval administration opted for a limited land distribution as part of its agrarian reform of 1998. The Haitian Constitution of 1987, article 248, provides for agrarian reform and the establishment of a land tenure administration in the context of a national land use plan. The land distribution also emanated from two presidential decrees. The first decree established a National Institute for Agrarian Reform on April 29, 1995. A subsequent presidential decree authorized the National Institute for Agrarian Reform to appropriate land in conflict across the national territory for redistribution (*Le Moniteur*, 1996). On February 7, 1997, President Préval awarded the first group of 1,600 peasant families a half-hectare of land each. This land allotment was complemented by the allocation of agricultural credit to beneficiaries.

The international community demonstrated its willingness to cooperate with the cabinet formed by decree by President Préval in March 1999 in spite of the absence of legislative imprimatur. This period saw the elimination of sheer state terror and greater respect for human rights. The new prime minister, Jacques-Edouard Alexis, has announced the formation of a new nine-member provisional electoral council charged with the organization of legislative and local elections. A majority consensus seems to hold credible elections as the best means to revive the democratic process in Haiti. But the holding of elections by itself is not a guarantee that the culture of peace will take root. After a temporary lapse, the traditional politics of greed and authoritarianism resurfaced.

THE THIRD ARISTIDE ADMINISTRATION (2000–2004)

The elections of the year 2000, which brought Aristide and a Lavalas-dominated legislature to power, created a political crisis. The 34-nation Organization of American States and the Caribbean Common Market (CARICOM) took turn in negotiations aiming to normalize the political panorama. These institutions and others kept the general secretariat of the United Nations aware of difficulties in reaching a compromise between the Aristide administration and the opposition and of the deterioration of the situation in terms of governance, respect of the rule of law, and aggravation of the economic and social conditions of the population. Haitian political culture is characterized by a winner-take-all attitude, which impedes the attainment of compromise between competitors and therefore political stability. This pattern also deprives elected government the stability, legitimacy, and authority that would allow them to govern effectively. At some key points of national life, Aristide was the best-positioned actor capable of unifying the country and catalyzing energies for national advancement. He declined to follow this path.

The Haitian state has not achieved a transformation of its structure, operation, and methods to satisfy the requirements of local civil society and the modern world. It continues to neglect the requirements of the majorities, in terms of democracy, justice, progress, and development. The state sector has not reached, in spite of modern influences, the capacity to manage itself and society or even to stimulate energies susceptible to usher national advancement. The main contention of this book is that the state operates against the nation rather than collaborating with the nation to stimulate energies for national advancement.

The Haitian state has historically been weak in its function of organization of society, functioning on a basis of extortions and violence. Over the years, the Haitian state seemed to have reneged on its responsibilities in matters of health and education. Public investments in social infrastructures play an important role in poverty reduction, with the betterment of indicators of human welfare. In the educational sector, throughout the 1980s, public investment oscillated between 5 and 6 percent of global public investments. Demand for education is so high that private institutions have emerged in the past two decades to fill the gap left by the public sector. The private sector has increased its control of the educational sector at the primary, secondary, and university levels. The number of private educational establishments, religious institutions, and nongovernmental organizations has grown significantly since the 1980s. The private sector has also made some inroads in the provision of vocational, technical, and higher education. As a result, the State University of Haiti no longer holds a monopoly over higher education.

The state seems to be reneging even on its police role, which is one of the rare missions it purported to fill from the time of its creation. It has failed to pick up steam and generate a political direction likely to propel democracy, development, and progress. This leads to an endless democratic transition and creates a situation in which local actors are seeking international assistance to solve a situation that the normal dynamics of local forces cannot resolve.

THE SECOND PRÉVAL ADMINISTRATION (2006–PRESENT)

Security remains the core challenge for the second administration of President René Préval. The new government faces the daunting task of confronting illegal armed gangs and addressing drug trafficking and kidnapping. Kidnappings were once rare in Haiti, the poorest country in the Western Hemisphere. The trend flourished after Aristide's departure. Urban enclaves of violence and kidnappings have emerged in Haiti (Cité Soleil), which is also prevalent in other Caribbean countries such as Jamaica (Trench Town), Trinidad and Tobago (Laventille), and Guyana (Buxton). The engineering of gang violence can also be politically motivated. Urban gangs have shown no restraints in engineering violence for personal and political purposes, and the distinction between criminal and political violence is becoming more and more difficult to ascertain. The Haitian National Police face difficulties in containing threats such as drugs, weapons, contraband, and human trafficking. The weakness of the Haitian National Police is reflective of the weakness of the Haitian state in general, which no longer enjoys the monopoly on legitimate use of force, which a functioning state must have. The Haitian National Police is rivaled by unknown numbers of urban gangs, which often possess superior armament.

There is a danger that the emerging urban gang culture could persist as it has in Latin American and larger Caribbean cities of the hemisphere. A positive development, however, is the bipartisan nature of U.S. support for the Préval government, something that was nonexistent under Aristide. Such support was evident in the recent decision of the U.S. State Department to license the commercial sale of weapons to the Haitian National Police. The main difficulty is that uprooting gang violence cannot be complete in the absence of education and job opportunities.

THE ENVIRONMENT

Both state and civil society sectors are attempting to reverse centuries-old pattern of environmental devastation. The history of farming practices in the Haitian countryside is manifested in progressive and considerable destruction of the Haitian forest cover; the encroachment on forests by local peasants in search of new agricultural land, combined with tree cutting to satisfy the needs of service enterprises, such as the dry cleaning industry, has been the leading causes of deforestation. Tree cutting for construction and energy reasons and the reduction of time that the land is laid fallow result in the rapid erosion of the topsoil. The cover of the Haitian forest, for instance, decreased from 20 percent in 1956 to 9 percent in 1978 and to 2 percent in 1989 (Vernet, 1998, 95). Unless otherwise reversed, this process will lead to greater desertification. Moreover, some 25 percent of 20 of the country's 25 major water reserves are now bare of forest cover, which means severe erosion and the endangering of water levels.

In sum, Haiti encounters serious problems of soil conservation resulting from deforestation, which, combined with unfavorable natural conditions, intensifies the erosion of the soil and reduces the availability in water. Eroded mountains decrease the availability of sweet water, impede agricultural production, and cause the clogging of the estuaries and coral reefs. This process also causes periodic inundations and agricultural losses, particularly in the rainy season, which spreads from May to October. During this period, the abundance of water combined with serious drainage problems and an inefficient system of canals can provoke inundations of gardens, houses, and public infrastructures.

Moreover, on the maritime coasts, the alluvial deposits are causing significant damages to the aquatic habitat. To illustrate, let us consider the eloquent case of the Macaya Peak (Pic Macaya), which feeds more than seven watershed basins. The unregulated management of the environment has caused inundations, water rarity, and decrease of irrigation-driven energy.

The weakening of the ecosystem has resulted in a diminution of underground water levels, regressive and linear erosion, the deterioration of riverbanks, and the weakening of land surfaces. It has become evident that further deterioration of the ecosystem will affect the future of the entire island of Hispaniola, not just Haiti.

The two nations forming Hispaniola have a joint ecosystem, with shared water systems. At 200 miles in length, the Artibonite River is the longest watercourse in the Republic of Haiti. It rises in the town of Restauración, Dominican Republic, and flows first southwest and then northwest before passing through the Grand-Saline, or salt plain, to a muddy outlet on the Gulf of Gonâve (Dorsainville, 1932, 189). The degradation of local forests undermines the basis for agricultural production and causes a deterioration of other natural resources in Haiti. For instance, the whole area from Camp-Pérrin to Roseaux in the southern department has sustained a process of degradation. The amount of exposed soil nearly doubled from 9.4 percent in 1956 to 18.6 percent in 1978. The rate at which forest cover was lost and the rate at which the area with unprotected soil increased were 1.3 percent per year. Unless otherwise reversed, this process will lead to greater desertification. In most localities in southern Haiti, the annual loss of arable land varies from 0.1 to 2.47 metric tons per acre per year. In some watershed basins, such as the Acul du Sud Watershed Basin, the loss of arable soil has reached 1,852.50 tons per acre per year (Roose, 1991).

Because the ecosystems are connected, this process also affects the Dominican Republic. In February 2007, the Ecological Society of the Cibao (SOECI) expressed its concern about the degradation of the environment on the Haitian side of the island, which displays rapid and rampant desertification, and recommended the establishment of a common program of protection and preservation of the environment. This statement reflects recognition that the ecosystems are interdependent, given that desertification in one side of the island affects the other.

Environmental degradation undermines not only food security, but also electrical output. The hydroelectric dam at Péligre once furnished 48 MW of hydroelectric energy (roughly 99 percent of the total national source of energy). It lost 59 percent of its capacity as a result of sedimentation and poor water management.

Both public and private sectors in Haiti display awareness of these problems and attempt to address the country's environmental problems. However, conservation policy is undermined by limited expenditures and the absence of coordinated state action in the environment. Whether conservation efforts will work remains to be seen. What remains clear is that the accumulated experiences of previous projects indicate that there will be no restoration of the environment without authentic peasant participation. Solutions have to be immediately rewarding for the farmers for them to be viably adopted. Projects related to soil and water conservation must be conceived as part of reforms of land systems, capable of improving agricultural productivity and the welfare of the Haitian peasantry. Effective remedial action rests on a better understanding of the socioeconomic logic as well as the know-how of the Haitian peasantry.

The quality of life declined significantly at the beginning of the twenty-first century. Haiti continues to be characterized by wide disparities between incomes of the rich and the poor. Whereas many wealthy Haitians have second homes, the average Haitians face a difficult battle for survival. Most Haitians rely on public transportation.

Stories of Haitian boat people intercepted at sea are often broadcast in American and other foreign media. Since the middle of the 1980s, the Haitian diaspora living abroad has been estimated at 1 million individuals. The history of relations between the Haitian diaspora and the central government has been characterized by deep-seated antagonism. Significant migration flows occurred in the period preceding and following the assumption of power by François Duvalier. The diaspora assumed a prominent role in exposing the brutality of the Duvalier dictatorship to the world. The diaspora played a similar role during the period of the coup d'état that deposed the democratically constituted government of Jean-Bertrand Aristide.

Middle-class Haitians still make shopping trips to Miami. The capital city of Port-au-Prince witnessed a construction boom that created million-dollar homes for the newly rich in the hills, complete with swimming pools and security. More Haitian women have filled the ranks of the Haitian National Police and have professional careers than ever before. Census data show that women represent 52 percent of the total Haitian population (Alter Presse, 2006, 1). Many Haitian families send their children to private schools and universities. Literate Haitians are typically conversant about national and international affairs.

SOCIAL ISSUES

The Labor Code recognizes the right to form unions. Many assembly-industry firms hire mostly women because they are deemed likely to accept lower wages than men. Many Haitians live with the anxiety of not knowing where their next meal will come from because unemployment is high.

Tourism

There has been a surge in tourism across the border between Haiti and the Dominican Republic, not only to visit tourist sites but also to permit family members to be reunited with loved ones. International tourists come to Haiti more frequently during Carnival, which takes place typically in February and during the holiday season. The fact that Haiti has only 1,200 hotel rooms that conform to international standards undermines the expansion of tourism. Moreover, the political instability that affected the country in the past few years dampened the inclination of national and foreign investors to invest in Haitian tourism.

However, thousands of tourists are brought regularly by international cruise lines to visit the Haitian resort of Labadie. Tourism to Labadie is marketed differently abroad, with Labadie presented as an exclusive territory. The Haitian government aims to broaden sites visited by inducing cruise goers to visit historical sites in the north of the country, notably the Citadel, which has been admitted to the world historic heritage. Another major tourist destination is the city of Jacmel, which receives a huge influx of visitors because of its easy access by land and air, the variety of its products, the high quality of handicraft, the variety of local culture, the Carnival celebration, the security, and the overall creativeness and dynamism of residents of this locality. Tourism in Jacmel serves as a model for other Haitian towns in the provision of a vibrant art scene, cultural events, well-known Carnival festivities, safe streets, and beautiful natural attractions. Jacmel offers commodities unparalleled in other Caribbean destinations: a unique, vibrant, and potent cultural and historical experience and a beautiful land untouched in most places by the kinds of commercial development found in places such as Jamaica, Puerto Rico, and Cancun.

THE DOWNFALL OF THE LAVALAS REGIME (2003–2004)

The accelerated deterioration of the political climate at the end of the year 2003, with massive popular demonstrations and the emergence of irregular armed forces, strengthened the position of powerful member-states, notably France, concerning the possible involvement of the United Nations in a humanitarian or peacekeeping mission in Haiti. Indeed, the surge of henchmen brought back the question of the right to interfere. Murders and the exactions of all sorts, in an alarming environment of increased misery, created a situation of a "population in danger," which incited international interference. Such a decision ensued from the systematic destruction of the institutions, which reached its climax with the weakening and demoralization of the Haitian National Police. The state appeared completely incapable of assuming the responsibilities and requirements of the democratic order. The UN Security Council referred to the threats to human lives and private assets in the country and the dangers that Haiti represented for the security of the region. In an unusually overheated climate, the Haitian population, in a state between relief, humiliations, and indignations, resigned itself to the arrival of foreign troops to reinstate order. Such a scenario was not at all new.

As described earlier, in 1915, in a local context of violence and chaos, an infantry of marines from the United States of America disembarked at Port-Au-Prince, and that American occupation lasted 19 years. Its rationale was to restore democratic order in Haiti in a regional context of expansionism and interference. The only constant is the vigilance of the American superpower, always attentive and keen to correct all disorder in its backyard. This time, this preoccupation was shared by France, which beyond all competitive attitude, showed a clear coincidence of interests.

In spite of enjoyment of popular support at the beginning of his mandate, Aristide did not succeed in satisfying the elementary demands of the masses. He favored the maintenance and multiplication of gangs of heavily armed men in popular districts that served as a rampart against the assault of his enemies, assumed or declared. Aristide purchased loyalties and constituted his own bases of action with the goal of exercising leverage on the balance of power. In the end, rather than building a national consensus for development and political trust for catalyzing national progress, Aristide did not trust anybody and recruited foreign security guards for his own protection. It is this legacy that culminated in the events of February 29, 2004, when Aristide fled the country. Rather than strengthening the state and society and promoting collaboration between the two spheres, the apparent goal of this political movement seems to have been the reconquest of power on the ruins of the state and society.

After Jean Bertrand Aristide's departure for exile, the president of the Court of Cassation, Supreme Court judge Boniface Alexandre, took oath at the Office of the Prime Minister, in the presence of the retiring prime minister, as Provisory President of the Republic of Haiti.

QUALITY OF LIFE

The Haitian population was officially estimated at 8.4 million inhabitants in 2006. This reflects a significant growth in population, considering that in 1990, the population was estimated at 6.5 million inhabitants, of whom 1.92 million (30 percent) lived in urban areas (Economic Intelligence Unit, 1993, 34). That means that roughly 2 million people were added over the course of 16 years. But some gains have been made. A small portion of the Haitian population has access to basic social services. Factory workers, who rarely achieve middle-class status, are a small minority of the workforce.

The bottom segment of the population, which is the majority of the country, continues to live in hardship. Nationally, the illiteracy rate continues to fall, with 63 percent of men and 58 percent of women now able to read and to write (Fourth Census, Government of Haiti, 2006 cited in Alterpresse May 10, 2006). But "the maternal and infantile death rate in Haiti is the most elevated of all of the Americas. For every 100,000 living births, 523 women do not survive, and 1 child out of 8 dies before the age of 5 years," according to Hernando Clavijo, Haiti representative of the UN Population Fund (cited in Alterpresse May 10, 2006).

The quality of life has deteriorated significantly. The Republic of Haiti figures among the world's poorest countries. In fiscal year 2006–2007, Haiti's gross domestic product was estimated at US$3 billion, of which US$1 billion comes from small cash remittances from the United States and Europe (United Nations and the World Bank, 2007, 23). The money that emigrants in search of better employment opportunities send to their families in their countries of origin has served to alleviate poverty in home countries. Migration from Haiti and the Caribbean has increased drastically since 1965. Some factors leading to the exodus have been political instability, few good-paying jobs, devastation from natural disasters, and huge wage disparities between the northern and southern hemispheres.

The rural sector employs two-thirds of the workforce but contributes only one-third of the gross domestic product. The population per acre of arable land is the densest in the Western Hemisphere, but the output ranks among the lowest. The culture of coffee, which has been Haiti's most important export commodity, has been on a decline. Inequities in taxation on export products undermined the production of coffee. Tariff data suggest that from 1957 to 1961, the Reynolds Mining Corporation spent only 7 percent of its revenues on taxes, which represented 100,000. In the same time period, the production of bauxite increased from 150,000 to 400,000 tons. In contrast, the Haitian state levies an average of 12 dollars on every bag of coffee worth 30 dollars. This tax is passed along to coffee producers. This high level of taxation discouraged coffee production, during and after the Duvalier regime (CEPAL, 1989). In addition to discriminatory tax policy toward coffee exports, other factors explaining the decline of coffee are underinvestments in human capital in the countryside as well as deficiencies in support services. Only 5 percent of coffee growers use improved technologies to obtain a superior production of 2,470 kilograms per acre per year. The remaining 95 percent are not interested in increased production because of the lack of effective support systems and coffee infrastructures. Moreover, disincentives abound with the lack of market outlets for eventual surpluses.

Land, labor, and cash are crucial factors in peasant farming decision-making. However, access to land seems to be the dominant factor. The conditions of access to the land determine the level of security of farmed plot. When this security is weak, the farmer doesn't have an interest in capital or work investments that may benefit either the owner or the other farmers.

There has been some movement of coffee between Haiti and the neighboring Dominican Republic in response to exchange rate fluctuations. In the past, quota considerations may have played a function. It is likely that cross-border movement happens in both directions.

Haitian coffee can be of excellent quality. The most popular type of coffee cultivated in Haiti *(Coffee arabica)* is commercially classified as a mild coffee. In the 1990s, new ameliorated coffee varieties were introduced on the national market, such as the Caturra, Catimor, and Catuaï. A new brand of Haitian coffee, Haitian Blue, has recently been marketed on the international gourmet coffee market. This brand distributes the coffee "Arabica Lavé" produced by peasant producers with membership in Coopérative Caféière Natives. This cooperation tends to offer its members a price equal or above that offered by spéculateurs. An additional benefit to peasant producers who maintain membership in the cooperative is that this institution reinvests in coffee infrastructure, a major departure from the coffee export companies that take profit out of the coffee market and seldom engage in reinvestments. Cooperative members also receive premiums based on quality and benefit from profits made by the cooperative.

Haiti produces both wet and dry processed coffee. The warm reception received by the Haitian Blue brand in the international market is expected to open a new era in the production of specialty coffee for niche markets. However, the creation of a brand image requires a long-term commitment and a well-conceived marketing strategy, as was adopted by other coffee brands from the Caribbean, such as Bleu Mountain of Jamaica and the Yacuo Selecto of Puerto Rico. The washed coffee has an excellent market position in Japan, where it is said to be used as a substitute for the vastly more expensive Jamaican Blue Mountain coffee. Specialty roasters in Italy and Belgium have also purchased the Haitian Blue brand.

Maintaining this market position requires, however, maintaining the quality of the product itself. The warm reception received by Haitian Blue will fade if the product does not fulfill the following three requirements: (1) maintenance of the inherent quality of the coffee; (2) the capacity of exporters to furnish a homogenous quality of coffee, whose characteristics are predetermined; (3) and regularity of the deliveries with determined timetables. The specialty coffee sector pays important rewards but in return expects rigor in terms of quality.

In the past, the experience of American coffee importers with Haitian coffee has been negative because of the lack of conformity between the sample and the delivered coffee stock. Rigor in terms of quality is necessary if Haitian specialty coffee is to remain competitive with other specialty brands from the Caribbean, which have maintained, if not enhanced, their standing in the coffee market.

In addition to coffee, Haiti exports vetiver to world markets. Vetiver is a perennial grass with broad uses from perfume to the medicine. The stems are typically tall and the leaves are long, thin, and often rigid. Vetiver is widely cultivated in the tropical regions of the world. The culture of vetiver is practiced in Haiti as it is practiced in all other countries that produce it (India, Java, Reunion Island, and Brazil). Because of its extensive character, its robust nature, its limited needs for fertilizers, its great resistance to sickness, and the weak finances of the Haitian peasantry, the production of vetiver does not require much care and only limited labor investments in plantation and harvest. As an essential oil, vetiver is widely used in the production of perfume. In addition to vetiver, extracts from lemon grass, citronella, petit grain, sweet basil, and citrus fruits are exported to perfume, after-shave lotion, and pharmaceutical manufacturers.

Many Haitians believe that education is a major challenge. In 1986 the monthly wage of public school teachers was $16.25 at the rate of 20 gourdes for a dollar. This wage level was lower than that received by cargo haulers, who made 15 to 20 gourde per day. This reduced incentives for teacher performance. After a strong campaign to improve teachers' wages in 1986, the government of General Henri Namphy raised the monthly wage from 325 gourdes to 900 gourdes.

The educational system requires that students take exams that test their capacity to memorize knowledge. Because the public educational system is unable to accommodate the high demand for education, private educational institutions have sprung up to address the shortfalls. Haiti possesses one of the youngest populations of all the Americas, with 50 percent of its people being under 20 years old. Roughly 190,000 of these youths enter the labor market every year where the unemployment rate is 32.7 percent.

OUTMIGRATION

The deterioration of the economic conditions, in the context of the acute underdevelopment that characterized Haiti, partially explained the acceleration of the Haitian emigration at the end of the 1970s and the phenomenon of Haitian "boat people." Haitians seeking better opportunities abroad opted to migrate by sea or by crossing the border with the Dominican Republic. The Haitian government recognizes that immigration is an important source of remittances. Haitian migrants abroad have usefully contributed to the economic development of their native country.

However, undeclared immigration provokes intense concerns in receiving countries. A 1981 agreement between the Reagan administration and the Haitian government authorized U.S. patrols to seize and forfeit vessels used for illegal boatlifts, interdict boatlifts on the high seas, and repatriate seaborne Haitians.

Haitian Migration to the Dominican Republic

From the standpoint of the Haitian government, Haitian emigration yields positive outcomes. Emigration was seen as a means to reduce demographic growth and unemployment, but also as an important source of foreign currencies for country because of the importance of remittances from Haitian migrants abroad. Demographic growth is the result of several factors, including increase in life expectancy; levels of reproduction that are superior to desires in matters of procreation, as expressed by female respondents; and important illegal immigration, which is a source of problems not only for the migrants themselves but also for the receiving countries. Class factors also affect maternal reproduction. To the bourgeoisie, which often lament the fertility and the economic obstacles posed by demographic explosion, a lower-class mother often responds, "C'est le Bon Dieu qui Donne des enfants, les enfants sont la richesse des malheureux" (It is God that grants children, children are the wealth of poor people). In any case, the worst of it is that the peasant economy, which for a long time partially absorbed the population growth, is less able than before to cater to the essential needs of the growing Haitian population.

The first legal recruitment of Haitian workers occurred in 1918 when the North American occupation of the Dominican Republic and Haiti was in full swing. This workforce was concentrated almost exclusively in the sugarcane industry, the mainstay of the economy of the Dominican Republic. Recruitment was managed first by the American marines them and then by members of the armies of both sides of the island.

Emigration constituted a direct source of income for the government of Duvalier. In 1965 the Haitian government negotiated an agreement with the Dominican Republic to provide every year, against remuneration, between 10,000 and 15,000 workers to engage in the sugarcane harvest of that country (Veras, 1983). The treaty on recruitment of Haitian workers was ratified in 1966. After 1971 a noticeable increase occurred in terms of irregular migration to the Dominican Republic, notably between 1973 and 1975 and again with a hike in the price of sugar in 1979–1981.

Moreover, until 1979, the government drew substantial revenues from foreign emigration. The cost of a passport and an exit visa from the territory, renewable after every trip, was placed at 100 dollars, to which were added the cost of travel insurance and airport taxes (Allman and May, 1982).

With the adoption in 1979 of a new law on immigration and emigration, the situation of the Haitians going abroad improved somewhat. Exit visas were still required, but it was possible to obtain visas for several exits over a maximum period of one year. However, a return visa was required for any Haitian who has sojourned abroad for more than three months. Such visas can be obtained at Haitian embassies and consulates abroad.

With the creation in 1989 of a Commissariat for Haitians Living Abroad, emphasis has been placed on fostering greater participation of Haitians living abroad in the development of their country and return migration. This Commissariat has been the primary instrument of exchange and communication between Haitians living in the Diaspora and those living in the homeland.

Many of the Haitians migrating to the Dominican Republic did not hold passports, but some had either a carnet or other documents specifying a contract with particular companies. In the middle of the 1980s, the sugar industry began to decline, and the Haitian workforce broadened its presence in the economy given that workers were no longer restricted to the agricultural sector. The late 1980s witnessed an expansion of the Haitian presence in non-agricultural sectors such as construction and informal trade. Greater irregularity and informality in recruitment arose as well.

There was also greater diversity in terms of the population migrating to the Dominican Republic. Middle-class Haitian students numbering at more than 11,000 began their studies in the Dominican Republic since the late 1990s. There is also greater Haitian investment in the country aimed at export toward Haiti. A novelty is the presence of Haitian workers in the tourist industry, which, at this moment, is the most dynamic sector in the economy of the Dominican Republic.

Significant problems exist in the Dominican Republic regarding the treatment of Haitian migrants in that country. Migrants from the most African country of the Caribbean face violent forms of xenophobia in the Dominican Republic. Haitians in the Dominican Republic serve a deep symbolic function, one that has profoundly affected the very notion of Dominican identity.

In his book *Haiti and the Dominican Republic,* former Haitian ambassador to the Dominican Republic Jean-Price Mars exalted the African origins of Haitian cultural identity, while observing Dominican pride in adapting to Spanish culture. Based on historical evidence, this analysis takes this observation a step further.

Media plays a crucial role in the construction of imagined communities and identities and as an instrument of political power and cultural radiance. Significant ownership of the media by the tiny white minority in the Dominican Republic has been associated with diffusion of whiteness as the frame of reference and with related depreciation of African ancestry.

It has been established that the primary means of establishing specified relationship to the group is generally by exclusion. After a lengthy and complex historical process, Dominican society has chosen to promote cultural affinity with the Spaniards and the exclusion or marginalization of both African and Haitian influences. This socially constructed identity in which everything from Spain is deemed better is used to help justify the unequal treatment of black Dominicans and Haitians. Various xenophobic ideologists played a decisive role in creating this framework of imagined Hispanic consciousness. This value system persists because the media actively promotes its reproduction within Dominican society.

In June 2005, the Dominican secretary of state for labor publicly commented in the media that the Dominican government plans to "de-Haitianize" the country. This discourse was similar to the state-sanctioned prejudicial discourse toward Haitians that resulted in the bloody massacre of 1937. The perceived need to cleanse the country is part and parcel of a process of social control. Dominican society is bombarded by uncontrolled advertisement that conforms to the dominant elite's view that "whiteness is the frame of reference." However, beyond the high levels of anti-Haitian xenophobia that fed the massacre, there is a need to recognize in the 1937 massacre a strategy of war against civil society in the Dominican Republic. The employment of naked and sheer violence was a key element of the imposition of Trujillo dictatorship. The end purpose was to instill fear in civil society. Fear affected day-to-day activities and permeated life, thinking, the psychology, and the overall feel of the society. The absence of organized response and resistance to sheer state violence opened the way to the political consolidation of the Trujillo regime. The weakness of the reaction and the feeble resistance to the slaughter of the popular classes provided evidence of the might of Trujillo. The slaughter demonstrated Trujillo's capacity to impose his logic and force on Dominican society.

The logic was one of Eurocentric ideology, which called for the purification of the country's Hispanic identity and rejection of African heritage. The Trujillo regime's obstinate and well-funded promotion of a notoriously Eurocentric view of Dominicanness looked to the Spanish conquerors and colonial settlers to find the ethno-racial foundation of the nation while excising any cultural form evidently associated with the African heritage (Torres-Saillant, 2006, 64). The Eurocentric view of Dominicanness lends itself to racism because it distinguishes bodies of people from each other by introducing issues of superiority and inferiority within Dominican society.

With the 1937 massacre, anti-Haitianism took on a political character that shaped Dominican society and culture. According to Joaquín Balaguer (1983) and Manuel A. Peña Batlle (1988), two outstanding intellectuals of Trujillismo, the central concept of Trujillismo was that the Dominican people were a community of Hispanic and Taíno origins, a community that is threatened by the constant degrading contamination of "the African thing," that "black and Haitian thing." The concept of the "Indian" is an anthropological and juridical fiction, which still persists. The "Indian" is a nonwhite Dominican who is not black. As a social construction, the Indian label accommodates the nonwhite persons and makes them accomplices to this ideological setting.

As the Eurocentric view has become the main frame of reference, black Dominicans have been marginalized. It is undeniable that black Dominicans face prejudice in Dominican society. The writings of Afro-Dominican sociologist Carlos Dore Cabral certainly indicate a situation that preoccupies some sectors and personalities engaged in the fight for social equality in the Dominican Republic.

The Dominican elite also seek to give the Haitian presence in the Dominican Republic the dimension of an ethno-cultural threat. The marginalization Dominicans of African descent and the deportation of Haitians are part of the same process of imposition of white-dominated values in the Dominican media. It is not a coincidence that, for instance, the *Diario Libre* newspaper is part of the collection of companies owned by the wealthy Dominican Vicini family.

ECONOMIC CONTRIBUTIONS OF HAITI TO DEVELOPMENT OF THE DOMINICAN REPUBLIC

The Republic of Haiti and the Dominican Republic share the Caribbean island of Hispaniola. The two countries share a border of some 248.54 miles There is dynamic trade between the two nations at several border cities, including Pedernales, Jimaní, Elías Pinas, and Dajabón. This trade brings millions of dollars to the Dominican Republic annually. In 2007 Haiti became the third largest importer of Dominican goods, worth US$300 million. Dominican exports to Haiti nearly doubled from 2005 to 2007, standing at 161 million dollars in 2005 according to the CEI. Foodstuffs and building supplies are the principal exports, especially flour, eggs, cement, and tin roof sheeting. The 2005 figure did not include exports from free zones. Near 90 percent of Dominican exports to Haiti pass though Jimaní and Dajabón. Finally, millions of dollars of imported merchandise are directed to Haiti through the ports of the Dominican Republic, which are better suited for large international containers. They arrive to their final destination in Haiti through the different border points. These amounts raised through transshipment are not included in the CEI figures.

Dominican exports to Haiti are responsible for job creation and family incomes in border regions. The families living on or near the border sell goods, offer services, or simply save by buying the cheaper products that the Haitians sell. According to a survey carried out in the city of Dajabón, 51 percent of the families received revenues from the trade, and 95 percent declared substantial savings for their purchases in the same place, mainly used clothes, oil, and rice. That means that border trade with Haiti impacts positively on Dominican poverty reduction. According to CEI figures, from 1993 to 2002, border trade accounted for a reduction of poverty on a scale of 12 to 18 percent in border cities where commercial fairs take place.

In spite of these contributions, Haitians living in the Dominican Republic face intolerance and persecution. Recently, increased tension made it more difficult to manage conflict through pragmatism and peaceful means. In May 2005, the regrettable incidents at Hatillo Palma in the Dominican Republic spurred a cycle of heightened persecution of Haitians and Dominican-Haitians. No arrest was made for the killing of a Dominican woman, but an angry mob of Dominicans went on a rampage, beheading two Haitians. The Dominican government deported at least 2,000 Haitians and Dominican-Haitians in May 2005 alone, although Dominican president Leonel Fernandez recognized that the process of deportation was fraught with human rights violations. Fernandez promised that this would not "continue under his administration." Unfortunately, human rights groups continue to report mistreatment and deportation of Haitian migrants, legal residents, and Dominicans of Haitian descent.

Since May 2005, there has been an intensification of deportations. According to official numbers released by the Dominican Office of Migration, some 25,000 Haitians were deported in 2006. In the first two months of 2007, the number of deportees had already reached 10,000. The total number of deportees is expected to be much higher for 2007, especially in light of recent accusations made by Dominican nationalists toward Sonia Pierre. Pierre, a 2006 recipient of the Robert F. Kennedy Human Rights Award, has been the subject of attempts by members of the Dominican congress to revoke her citizenship, despite the fact that she was born and raised in the country. In addition to the Dominican government, the Dominican people are also opposed to the establishment of a formal policy governing economic exchanges and migration between the two nations forming Hispaniola (Cedeno, 1992, 137).

Xenophobic politicians and organizations use the mass media to spread hatred toward Haitians. Politicians such as Pelegrin Castillo and Vincho Castillo consistently fan the flames of hatred against Dominicans of Haitian descent and Haitian immigrants in the Dominican Republic. Their xenophobic discourse, which portrays the Haitian presence as a "burden" for the Dominican Republic, has been widely publicized by the national media. It seeks to create a sense of fear of a "Haitian invasion," which then breeds irrational violence against Haitians. In the absence of any investigative reporting, Dominican media often divulges accusations of Haitians for any act of violence, whether founded or unfounded.

As a result, hardworking Haitian immigrants become the target of mob violence in the Dominican Republic. On March 12, 2006, Jako Medina, one of two innocent Haitians who were burned alive by residents of the Yabonico community, died in Santo Domingo, the capital of the Dominican Republic. After the clubbing death of the regional mayor, Manuel Bolivar Lopez Mora, on March 7, 2006, a son of the victim went out to "hunt" for Haitians accompanied by a crowd and found the two Haitian immigrants, including Medina, who were not involved in the earlier incident, and proceeded to tie them up and burn them alive using flammable substances. No one was ever arrested or punished for his murder.

On December 12, 2005, student protesters disrupted a one-day visit to Port-au-Prince by Dominican president Leonel Fernandez. The demonstrators stood in solidarity with the brethren facing persecution in the Dominican Republic. Student protestors threw stones at Fernandez's presidential motorcade and burned tires in the streets as Fernandez left a meeting with the interim prime minister and president. In reprisal for the disruption of the Dominican president's visit, the Dominican police summarily arrested hundreds of Haitian nationals studying in the Dominican Republic. More than 6,000 students are currently enrolled in various campuses of the Dominican Republic. These students are but a small fraction of the 800,000 Haitians who live in the Dominican Republic, which has a population of 8.8 million.

Overt xenophobic attacks against Haitian-looking individuals have remained unpunished, sending a signal to armed gangs that the Dominican state condones impunity. This creates a situation of chain reactions where towns openly attacked Haitians after criminal acts against them have remained unpunished in other towns. For instance, after the May 6, 2005, incidents at Hatillo Palma remained unpunished, attacks against Haitians were reported in Dajabòn (August 5–6, 2005); Higuey (September 7, 2005); Baranca (September 8, 2005); and Villa Trina (December 10, 2005). Waves of reprisals have been inflicted on innocent Haitians after crimes have been broadly attributed to Haitians without any form of police investigation. Even when proper investigations have cleared Haitians from the crimes as in the case of Hatillo Palma, no reparations have been offered to victimized families.

This led Amnesty International to denounce discrimination against Haitians. In the wake of the 36th General Assembly of the Organization of American States that took place in Santo Domingo, Amnesty International denounced racial discrimination and intolerance against Haitians and

Dominicans of Haitian origin in the Dominican Republic. The organization reported that, "many deportees, including women and children, revealed stories of their being robbed, beaten, and subjected to sexual violence by military personnel. In many cases, their houses have been pillaged, destroyed and burnt. Documents and identification papers are routinely confiscated from deportees by military authorities while no word is left with remaining family members as to their forcible removal from the Dominican Republic." P. José Núñez of the Jesuit Service for Migrants and Refugees also found repeated indications of coerced labor in the Bateys of Dominican Republic.

Moreover, contrary to bilateral agreements and international laws governing the repatriation of migrants, some deportations have occurred at night and at unofficial border points. In addition to violating protocols, nightly deportations endanger the lives of the deportees and Dominican military personnel and are known to cause transportation disasters, such as the incident of September 25, 2006, in which a vehicle transporting migrants at night had a major accident.

Ethnic groups typically try to differentiate themselves from other groups, particularly their neighbors. Given that Haiti shares the same island with the Dominican Republic, it is no wonder that Dominicans define themselves in opposition to their neighbors, the Haitians.

The Dominican elite imposed an ethnic configuration that sees the imposing majority of blacks in Haiti as a threat to the social fabric of the Dominican Republic. In pursuance of its xenophobic agenda, the Dominican media typically inflates the number of Haitians and Dominicans of Haitian origin living in the Dominican. Reported numbers are typically above 1 million people. Regino Martinez, coordinator of the Border Solidarity Organization in Dajabòn, finds this number to be exaggerated. Martinez placed the total number of Haitians living in the Dominican Republic at a maximum of 800,000 (personal communication, New York, October, 2007). Martinez linked the exaggerated numbers to the will of the Dominican elite to give to the Haitian presence the dimension of an ethno-cultural threat.

Organizations and individuals that have historically helped Haitian immigrants are the target of intolerance as well. For instance, Belgian priest Pedro Ruquoy, who advocated harmonious relations between the two countries for 30 years, was forced to leave the Dominican Republic after numerous death threats from the Dominican military. A similar fate befell Christopher Hartley, a Catholic priest. Hartley was forced to leave the Dominican Republic in late 2006 under what he says was pressure from the Dominican government and the wealthy and politically powerful Vicini family. The Vicinis control the Batey dos Hermanos, a sugar-growing territory in San Jose de Los Llanos, Dominican Republic.

INTOLERANCE AND XENOPHOBIA IN THE COURTS

For years, domestic and international human rights organizations have decried the denial of Dominican citizenship to children of Haitian descent born in the Dominican Republic. In a press conference on November 23, 2005, Luis Schecker Ortiz of Citizen Initiative, a civic movement in the Dominican Republic, stated that "government denial of citizenship to Haitian children born in the Dominican Republic is contrary to the United Nations Charter, which is signed by the Dominican Republic." The ruling of the Inter-American Court reinforced that position. In the historic verdict of October 7, 2005, an international court strengthened a fundamental right of immigrants by ruling that their children can gain the nationality of the country where they are born. The Inter-American Human Rights Court verdict rejected Dominican authorities' refusal to issue birth certificates to two girls of Haitian ancestry who were born in the Dominican Republic. The high court stated that "the condition of birth in the state territory is the only thing that needs to be demonstrated to acquire nationality." The court ruled that the Dominican state had violated the right to nationality and the right to equality before the law, as well as articles 3, 5, 19, 20, and 24 of the American Convention on Human Rights Pact of San Jose. The court ruling pressed the Dominican government to guarantee the rights of citizenship and education to all children born in their territory, irrespective of their ethnic origin.

That decision of the Inter-American Court of Human Rights reinforced that, in its denial of citizenship to persons born within its borders, the Dominican Republic was in violation of article 11 of its own constitution, which guarantees Dominican citizenship to all those born within its territory save for those "in transit" and the children of foreign diplomats.

On the heel of this favorable decision, several civic organizations along with the Jesuit Service for Refugees and Migrants petitioned the Dominican Supreme Court in a bid to change the law on behalf of Haitians born in the Dominican Republic. In December 2005, the Supreme Court upheld the exclusionary Dominican law, stating that children born in the Dominican Republic whose parents are illegal migrants are "in transit" and therefore not eligible for citizenship. In response to the court decision, P. José Núñez declared, "Although the constitution provides that everybody who is born in the country is a citizen, with the exception of those people in transit or diplomats' children, many reports exist on the cases of children born in Dominican Republic to Haitian parents who were denied the possibility to register as citizens, on the basis that their parents are 'in transit,' even after they have resided in the country after several generations." In Núñez's view, the Supreme Court made a mistake in declaring that the condition of "in transit" applied to the children of "illegal immigrants." The proof that the disposition of article 36 of the Law of Migration aims to exclude from Dominican nationality the children of illegal aliens is evident in the following ruling: "Those that are non residents are considered in transit, for purpose of implementation of Article 11 of the Constitution of the Republic" (article 36, paragraph 10).

In 2006 the Dominican newspaper *El Caribe* reported a statement by the chancellor Carlos Morales Troncoso that the Dominican Republic would comply with the sentence of the Inter-American Court of Human rights, which established that this country should reimburse two girls of Haitian origin who were denied the right to have the nationality of the Dominican Republic.

During the dialogue of Chiefs of Delegation with representatives of civil society of the continent, which occurred during the session of the Organization of American States in Dominican Republic in 2006, the Dominican secretary of external relations stated that, by virtue of his attachment and respect to the responsibilities of the state, the country accepted the jurisdiction of the referred court, and he assured that the country would comply with the disposition made by the same court.

> I want to comment in a special way with regards to one of the recommendations resulting from the deliberations of civil society. This concerns their demand that it be requested to the Dominican Republic that it complies with the verdict of the Inter-American Court of the Human rights, in the case Yean and Bosico, stated Morales Troncoso. "As per their request, they can be calm, and from now on they can take out that topic from the list of their preoccupations," he assured.[1]

This verdict referred to in Troncoso's statement was an October 2005 ruling of the Inter-American Court of Human Rights, which ordered the Dominican Republic to pay monetary damages to two girls and their families. Dilcia Yean and Violeta Bosico had been refused birth certificates even though they were born and raised in the Dominican Republic. They remained without birth certificates and stateless until September 2001. One of them, Bosico, was prevented from attending school for one year as a result.

The Inter-American Court of Human Rights also ordered the government to reform the country's birth registration system and create an effective procedure to issue birth certificates to all children born within the national territory regardless of their parents' migratory status; open school doors to all children, including children of Haitian descent; publicly acknowledge its responsibility for the human rights violations committed against the girls within six months of the sentence date; and widely disseminate the sentence.

Since the statement made by Troncoso, the Dominican Government paid $22,000 in indemnification but has not yet implemented the other measures contained in the Court sentence.

MARGINALIZATION OF BLACK DOMINICANS
IN THE DOMINICAN REPUBLIC

The Dominican elite created a profile of the "Haitian" based on African physical features. As a result, black Dominicans face deportation if they are believed to be Haitian. Any "Haitian-looking" person can be picked up on the street, in their workplace, and in their home throughout the Dominican Republic. This unfair profiling splits parents from children and deprives deportees of any opportunities to claim properties and wages earned. Conservative estimates indicate that roughly 80 percent of the Dominican population is black as a result of the African presence at the time of colonization, Haitian migration. and the migration of black Americans and Caribbean blacks to the Eastern region of the Dominican Republic in the past century. Evidently, a meaningful percentage of the Dominican black population is of Haitian origin. The mere fact that any "Haitian-looking" person can be deported places a significant portion of the black Dominican population at risk.

According to P. José Núñez of the Jesuit Service for Refugees and Migrants, "In raids directed at illegal immigrants, the authorities pick up and expel from the Dominican Republic many black Dominicans besides legal Haitian residents, without granting them the opportunity to refute the expulsion decision. Such conditions violate their fundamental human rights of deportees."

The whole emphasis on "whiteness as the frame of reference" is detrimental to a large segment of the Dominican population. It depreciates the many contributions of black Dominicans to the development of the Dominican society. Black Dominicans contributed to the artistic, cultural, and athletic promotion of the country. This is why the names of Johnny Ventura or Pedro Martínez act as frames of reference when speaking of the existing ethnic mixture. We cannot forget the remarkable television producer Rafaël Corporel de los Santos, whose programs were transmitted by satellite to many countries of the world. At the political level, the role of José Francisco Peña Gómez was also remarkable.

The first massive wave of repatriation of Haitian migrants from the Dominican Republic began in 1985 under the Duvalier regime. Since May 2005, there has been an intensification of deportations of Haitians from the Dominican Republic. According to official numbers released by the Dominican Office of Migration, some 25,000 Haitians were deported in 2006. In the first two months of 2007, the number of deportees had already reached 10,000. The volume of deportation is expected to be much higher for 2007 overall, especially in light of the issuance in March 2007 of a circular by the civil registrar's office instructing officials "to thoroughly examine birth certificates when issuing copies or any document related to civil status," given that documents "were issued irregularly in the past (to individuals) with foreign parents who had not proven their legal residency or status in the Dominican Republic." The issuance of the circular has been associated with an increase in discriminatory treatment by Eddy Tejada, a member of the Regional Network of Civil Organisations on Migration (cited in Pina, 2007).

HAITIANS IN THE UNITED STATES

The richest Haitian families have always had second homes in Miami, Paris, or New York. Celebrities such as Sweet Mickey and Wycleff Jean have a home in Haiti, with another in Florida or New York. Many wealthy Haitians have left the country for Miami because of the rising rate of kidnappings for ransom, which seems to affect almost every sector of the society but particularly families with money. Millions of Haitians reside in the United States, many of them having overstayed their tourist visas in search of better economic opportunities or simply to escape violence in Haiti. With so many Haitians residing in Brooklyn, New York, Eugène Mathieu, the first native of Haiti, was elected to the New York City Council in April 2007. Chain migration helps explain the settlement patterns of Haitian immigrants in Brooklyn. New immigrants from particular towns in Haiti benefit from the existence of kinship networks and established regional associations in New York City. Hundreds of Haitians operate retail ethnic businesses in Brooklyn, many of which cater to fellow Haitians.

Haiti has a long legacy of monopoly power. This makes difficult the emergence of negotiated solutions and the collaborative management of public affairs. However, in the past two decades, a national conscience has been timidly emerging. There has been a recent increase in official awareness about the necessity to have better relations with local bodies and civil society. What is lacking is a consensus on the way things should change. The 1987 constitution has set the tone by defining the main institutional and territorial parameters necessary for decentralized governance. Civic and popular sectors seek to establish new relationships with the state based on awareness of the common good. It is increasingly believed that attainment of the common good requires policies that reflect the interests of the entire population. This view corresponds to the sentiment of the nation. In other words, the very process of power-sharing strengthens the concept of the nation.

Overall, this book favors a new configuration of power between the state and civic society based on cooperation and reciprocity rather than state coercion and unilateral action. The analysis promotes consensus-building for collective action. If incentives for cooperation exist, outcomes can be rewarding for both government and civil society actors.

NOTE

1. "República Dominicana acuerda indemnizar niñas de Haití: El canciller Morales Troncoso afirma que el país cumplirá dictamen de Corte," *El Caribe*, June 5, 2006.

REFERENCES

Allman, James, and John May. "Haitian Migration: 30 Years Assessed." *Migration Today* 10, no. 1 (1982).

Alter Presse. "Haïti: Une population officielle de 8.4 millions d'habitants, Fort déséquilibre démographique et socio-économique." May 10, 2006: 1.

Balaguer, Joaquín. *La Isla al revés, Haití y el destino dominicano.* Santo Domingo, Dominican Republic: Fundación J. A. Caro Alvarez, 1983.

Bernier, Barbara L. "Democratization and Economic Development in Haiti: A Review of the Caribbean Basin Initiative." *The International Lawyer* 27 (1993): 455–469.

Cedeno, Carmen. "La nacionalidad de los descendientes de haitianos nacidos en República Dominicana." In Wilfredo Lozano, ed., *La Cuestión Haitiana en Santo Domingo* (pp. 137–144). Santo Domingo: FLASCO; Miami: North South Center, 1992.

CEPAL. *Boletín Estadístico de América Latina* (1969).

Compa, Lance. *Labor Rights in Haiti.* Washington, DC: International Labor Rights Education Fund, 1989.

Dorsainville, Luc. "The Rivers and Lakes of Haiti." *Bulletin of the Pan-American Union.* Washington, DC: Union of American Republics, March 1932.

Ebert, Allan. *Corporate Duvalierism: Haitian Workers Hit with Massive Union Busting.* Washington, DC: Washington Office on Haiti, 1987.

Economic Intelligence Unit. *Country Report: Cuba, Dominican Republic, Haiti, and Puerto Rico* 3rd Quarter (1997): 44.

———. "Cuba, Dominican Republic, Haiti, Puerto Rico, Country Profile." *Economic Intelligence Unit* 1 (1993): 32–52.

El Caribe. "República Dominicana acuerda indemnizar niñas de Haití: El canciller Morales Troncoso afirma que el país cumplirá dictamen de Corte." June 5, 2006.

Franklin, James. *The Present State of Hayti (Saint Domingo) Remarks on Its Agriculture, Commerce, Laws, Religion, Finances and Population.* Westport: Negro University Press, 1970 (originally published in 1828 by John Murray and reprinted in 1970).

Garrity, Monique P. "The Assembly Industry in Haiti: Causes and Effects, 1967–1973." *The Review of Black Political Economy* 11 (1981): 203–215.

Hayes, Margaret D., and Gary F. Wheatley. *Interagency and Political-Military Dimensions of Peace Operations, Haiti: A Case Study.* Washington, DC: National Defense University, Institute for National Strategic Studies, 1996.

Hooper, Michael. "Model Underdevelopment." *NACLA, Report on the Americas* 21, no. 3 (May/June 1987): 32–39.

Institute for Agriculture and Trade Policy. "Haitian Agriculture: Exports, Imports and Food." *NAFTA and Inter-American Trade Monitor* 3 (March 1996): 1–3.

Maingot, Anthony P. *The United States and the Caribbean: Challenges of an Asymmetrical Relationship.* Boulder, CO: Westview, 1994.

Le Moniteur (Port-au-Prince). "Loi Portant Sur L'Organisation de la Collectivité Territoriale de Section Communale." April 4, 1996: 1.

Núñez, José. *Aporte y Discriminación Dentro del Fenómeno Migratorio Haitiano a República Dominicana.* Powerpoint document presented at the International Conference, Dominican-Haitian Representations: Migrations, Citizenship and Human Rights at John Jay College, February 2007.

Peña Batlle, Manuel Arturo. *Historia de la cuestión fronteriza dominico-haitiana,* Second edition. Santo Domingo: Sociedad Dominicana de Bibliófilos, 1988.

Pina, Diógenes. "Dominican Republic: Children of Haitians Fight for Birth Certificates." Inter Press Service, August 28, 2007.

Roose, Elise. *Introduction à la gestion conservatoire de l'eau et de la fertilité des sols.* Montpellier: CNEARC/ORSTOM, 1991.

Shin, Doh Chull. "On the Third Wave: A Synthesis and Evaluation of Recent Theory and Research." *World Politics* 47 (October 1994): 135–170.

Torres-Saillant, Silvio. *An Intellectual History of the Caribbean.* New York: Palgrave Macmillan, 2006.

United Nations and the World Bank. "Crime, Violence and Development: Trends, Costs and Policy Options in the Caribbean." *A Joint Report published by United Nations Office on Drugs and Crime and the Latin America and Caribbean Region of the World Bank.* Report No. 37820 (March 2007).

Veras, R. A. *Inmigración, Haitianos, Esclavitud.* Santo Domingo: Edición Taller, 1983.

Vernet, Joseph. "La situation actuelle des bassins versants d'Haïti et les différentes approches d'aménagement." In *La Gestion de l'Environnement en Haïti: Réalités et Perspectives.* Port-au-Prince, Haïti: PNUD Haïti/Econet, Edition Spéciale, 1998, 162–169.

Notable People in the History of Haiti

Acaau, Jean-Jacques. A peasant turned leader who led the Piquets war, which refers to a peasant rebellion originating in the southern peninsula (Camp-Perrin, Tiburon, and Grande Anse) in 1843.

Alexis, Jacques Stephen (1922–1961). This writer, poet, activist, historian, and diplomat published several reviews, before founding La Ruche, a group dedicated to creating a literary and social critique in Haiti in the early 1940s. In 1955 his novel *Compère Général Soleil* was published by Gallimard in Paris. This superb novel has recently been translated into English as *General Sun, My Brother.* He also authored *Les Arbres Musiciens* (1957), *L'Espace d'un Cillement* (1959), and *Romanceros aux Etoiles* (1960).

Jacques Stephen Alexis actively participated in social and political debates of his time. In 1959 he formed the People's Consensus Party (Parti pour l'Entente Nationale-PEP), a left-oriented political party, but he was forced into exile by the Duvalier dictatorship. In April 1961, he returned to Haiti, but soon after landing at Mole St. Nicholas, he was captured by Tontons Macoutes. He was taken to the town's main square where he was tortured and then assassinated.

Audubon, John James. Legendary, revered bird watcher and art enthusiast in America. The Audubon Society is named after him.

Basquiat, Jean Michel. Famous New York City artist of Haitian and Puerto Rican descent who performed graffiti art and later became one of the most successful, controversial, and glamorous artists in the world.

Bellegarde, Dantès (May 18, 1877–June 16, 1966). Born in Port-au-Prince, Haiti, Bellegarde served as both historian and diplomat. He is known for his works *Histoire du Peuple Haïtien* (1953), *La Résistance Haïtienne* (1937), *Haïti et ses Problèmes* (1943), and *Pour une Haïti Heureuse* (1928–1929). Bellegarde also served as a diplomat in Paris in 1921 and Washington, DC, in 1930. He did not reach moving beyond his ambiguous attitude towards France. He wrote, "I am certain to remain...in the tradition of this French culture, made of clarity, sociability and sympathy, and of which Mr. Daniel-Rops, in a recent article in the Present Time of Paris, recognizes Mr. Sténio Vincent, Mr. Léon Laleau, Mr. Clément Magloire, Mr. Abel Leger, the doctor Price-Mars, and myself, among others, as counting among faithful advocates in Haiti."

Boyer, Jean-Pierre (1776–1850). President of Haiti from 1818 to 1843. Some of the founding elements of the Haitian sociopolitical structure were established during his rule.

Christophe, Henry (January 1807–March 1818). A valiant commander in the independence army who proclaimed himself king in northern Haiti after the death of Dessalines. He built the Citadelle in Haiti as a fortress representing freedom.

Danticat, Edwidge. Haitian American author of such revered novels as *Breath, Eyes, Memory*; *The Dew Master*; *The Farming of Bones*; and *Krik? Krak!*

Déjoie, Louis. This well-known planter was defeated in Haiti's mulatto-versus-black presidential elections in 1957. After his defeat, Déjoie traveled to Havana, Cuba, where he announced a unity pact with former President Daniel Fignolé, a New York–based exile, and Dr. Clement Jumelle to unseat Duvalier.

Dessalines, Jean-Jacques (September 20, 1758–October 17, 1806). First led the Haitian Revolution and then proclaimed himself Emperor of Haiti (1804–1806) under the name of Jacques I.

Dumas, Thomas-Alexandre. The son of a Haitian slave woman and a French soldier, Thomas-Alexandre Dumas was the father of the French writer Alexandre Dumas, who authored *The Three Musketeers* and the *Count of Monte*

Cristo. Though it is known that Alexandre Dumas was born on March 25, 1762, at Jérémie, Saint-Domingue, it is not known with certainty how long he lived in the colony. Because his arrival in France is attested as November 1776 after about one month of navigation, it is possible to establish that he lived 14 years and 7 months on Saint-Domingue, which means one-third of his existence given that he died at 44 years old.

Durant, Oswald. This well-known poet composed "Choucoune," which would later become the lyrics for the song "Little Bird" by Harry Belafonte.

Duvalier, François (April 14, 1957–1971). President of Haiti from October 22, 1957 to April 21, 1971. He was born in Port-au-Prince. After studying medicine, he was admitted to the Bureau of Ethnology, which was founded in 1942. From his marriage to Simone Ovide on December 27, 1939, four children were born: Marie-Denise, Nicole, Simone, and Jean-Claude. To maintain his power and the allegiance of the United States, he exploited the phobia of Communism.

Firmin, Anténor. Best known for his book *The Equality of the Human Races,* which was published in 1885 as a rebuttal to French writer Count Arthur de Gobineau's *Essay on the Inequality of Human Races.* Gobineau's essay advocated the superiority of the Aryan race and the inferiority of blacks and other people of color. In contrast, Firmin's book made a convincing argument that all men are endowed with the same qualities and the same faults, without distinction of color or anatomical form. This book became a model for Haitian sociology.

Jean-Baptiste, Nemours. This noted saxophonist, bandleader, and composer made significant contributions to Haitian music. He is credited with the creation of Compas, a musical rhythm in Haiti in the 1950s that fused fundamental Haitian rhythms and the Tipico musical genre. Although artists Rodolphe Legros and Guy Durosier achieved popular appeal at the time of the emergence of Compas, their music, which was rooted in Haitian culture, never reached the level of popular attraction that was attained by Compas.

Lange, Elizabeth Clarisse. This freed slave migrated from Saint-Domingue to Cuba and then to Baltimore, Maryland. In Baltimore, she founded the first Catholic school for black children, the Saint Francis Academy. She is currently being considered for canonization by the Vatican.

L'Ouverture, Toussaint (1743–April 7, 1803). The early leader of the war of independence was a former slave named François Toussaint. He first joined the service of François Biassou and quickly proved to be a courageous strategist. He was nicknamed L'Ouverture because of the bravery with which he forced openings in breaches. Toussaint quickly became a political and military leader on par with the greatest rulers of the time in Europe and North America. Toussaint L'ouverture displayed rare intelligence as an administrator and exceptional qualities of military strategy. This former slave with a peculiar destiny perished roughly one year after his deportation to France in a lugubrious prison at the Fort de Joux, in the Jura.

Nérette, Joseph (1924–2007). Extra-constitutional provisional president of Haiti from October 8, 1991 to June 19, 1992. He was a former judge at the Court of Cassation, the highest judicial level in the country. He was ejected from the political scene in June 1992.

Péralte, Charlemagne (1886–1919). A rebel leader of the Cacos War, which pitted Haitian peasant rebels against the U.S. occupation. He is known for starting guerilla warfare against American troops. Charlemagne Péralte was betrayed by one of his officers, Jean-Baptiste Conzé, who led disguised United States Marine Corps (USMC) second lieutenant Herman H. Hanneken to rebel territory. Péralte was killed, and U.S. troops took a picture of his body tied to a door and distributed it in the country to demoralize Haitian resistance to American occupation. The effect was the opposite. Péralte became a martyr for the Haitian nation.

Pétion, Aléxandre (March 9, 1807–March 29, 1818). Promoter of Latin American independence who gave the liberator, Simon Bolivar, weapons and soldiers with the promise of freeing all the slaves he liberated.

Pointe Du Sable, Jean Baptiste. This freed man from Haiti became a successful trader in America. He established the first permanent settlement of the city of Chicago. In 1779 he established a trading post on the north bank of the Chicago River mouth. His business prospered and became the center of a permanent Chicago settlement. His trading post was the main supply station for white trappers, traders, and the natives. He is known today as the founder of that city.

Préval, René (January 17, 1943–). Born in Port-au-Prince, Haiti, from a black middle-class family. His father, Claude Préval, was government minister under President Paul Magloire, beginning in 1950. He studied agronomy in Belgium and went into exile for close to 10 years in the United States, where he practiced small professions.

Upon his election as president, Jean-Bertrand Aristide named René Préval prime minister in February 1991. After the coup d'état of September 1991, René Préval took refuge at the residence of the French ambassador. He then joined Aristide in exile in Washington. The American troops brought back Jean-Bertrand Aristide to the presidential palace in fall 1994, and René Préval headed the Economic and Social Action Fund, which managed projects financed by the international community. In December 1995, René Préval was elected president with 88 percent of the votes. Préval launched a late bid for the presidency in 2005, at the head of a coalition named "The Hope" ("L'Espoir"). The Provisional Electoral Council proclaimed Préval the winner of the elections with 51.15 percent of the votes on February 16, 2006.

Price-Mars, Jean (October 15, 1876–1969). This scholar was born in northern Haiti. After attending the national school of medicine, he helped found the Society of Haitian History and Geography. He held several cabinet posts and served as Haitian ambassador to France, the Dominican Republic, and the United Nations. He authored several books, including *Ainsi Parla l'Oncle* (1928), which was translated into English as *So Spoke the Uncle*; *La Vocation de l'Elite* (1919); *La République d'Haïti et la République Dominicaine* (1953); *De Saint-Domingue à Haïti* (1957); and *Silhouettes de Nègres et de Négrophiles* (1960). His writings embraced the cultural identity imported from Africa while noting the pride of the neighboring Dominican Republic in adapting to the culture of Spain.

Roumain, Jacques (June 4, 1907–August 18, 1944). A major Haitian literary figure and one of the founders of *La Revue Indigène,* a magazine that sought to articulate an authentically nationalist voice in the face of the U.S. occupation of the country. Jacques Roumain was born in Port-au-Prince, Haiti on June 4, 1907. His best-known novel, *Masters of the Dew,* was published posthumously in 1944 in Port-au-Prince and in 1946 in Paris by United French Publishers. The book was later translated in several languages. He also published several other important works, such as *La Proie et L'Ombre, La Montagne ensorcelée* and *Les Fantômes.* He was jailed in 1933–1934 just after founding the Haitian Communist Party, which he served as secretary general. His publication of *Schematic Analysis 1932–1934 (Analyse schématique 1932–1934)* sent him to jail for three years, after which he departed for Europe, weakened. He traveled a lot but chose to stay one year on the side of Cuban poet Nicolás Guillén in Havana. The election of President Lescot, in 1941, allowed him then to return to Haiti. Upon his return, he founded the Bureau of Ethnology of Republic of Haiti, which he also served as director. His research culminated in the publication in 1942 of several studies, including *Autour de la campagne anti-supersti-tieuse* and *Contribution à l'étude de l'ethno-botanique précolombienne des Grandes Antilles.* In 1942 the Haitian government granted him a diplomatic post in Mexico City. Roumain died in his homeland. In 1943 he published a book titled *The Sacrifice of the Assoto Drum.* Roumain's work influenced many Haitian writers, including Jacques Stephen Alexis, who authored the novels *Compère Général Soleil* (General Sun, My Brother) and *L'Espace d'un cillement* (In the Flicker of an Eyelid).

Simon, Antoine. Loyal collaborator, he did not take arms against Nord Alexis in spite of his order to fire him. Winner in the elections, he did not unleash any vengeance upon former president Alexis and his assistants. The liberal and even debonair pace of Antoine Simon during the first year of his Presidency had won him general sympathy. On September 7, 1909, in visit in Jacmel to re-establish concord between two rival factions, he declared:

"I served under Hyppolite and North Alexis; there was not only one exile in my region. One will never see under my Government any authority making a summary execution. That person will be judged in accordance with the law for the acts for which he is blamed. This sword that I carry is for the defense of my brothers, the safeguard of the national autonomy, not to hit unjustly" (cited in Paul, 1923, 11).

Toussaint, Pierre. This Haitian-born slave is under consideration by the Vatican for canonization for his humanitarian work in New York.

REFERENCE

Paul, A. Pierre. "A la mémoire du général Antoine Simon," [microfilm], *ancien président de la république d'Haiti*. Port-au-Prince: Chenet, 1923.

Glossary of Selected Terms

arrondissements: Precincts that were established for administrative purposes.

carreau: Land measurement unit used in former French colonies. One carreau is the equivalent of 1.29 hectares, or approximately 3.1 acres.

commune: An administrative subdivision of the arrondissement.

don de leta: Land grant that implies a transfer from state to private ownership. Traditionally, the state gave land to supporters and officers of the army in return for their services or support.

FRAPH: French acronym for the Front Armé pour l'Avancement et le Progrès d'Haïti, which was a paramilitary group.

gourde: Haitian monetary unit.

lavalas: A Haitian Creole word meaning a sweeping flood that washes away everything in its path.

Macaya Pic: The tallest peak in the Massif de la Hotte, which is one of the few sites with remaining cloud forest in Haiti.

Madam Sara: A name given to market ladies who travel through communities in the plains and the mountains to purchase agricultural commodities, which are then sold in urban markets.

manman pièce: Master deed to a piece of land.

notè: Notary. The Haitian notary performs a wider variety of functions than notaries in the United States, including the registration of property transfers.

resu: A formal or informal receipt signed by parties involved in a land transaction.

soup joumou: Pumpkin soup, traditionally cooked on the first of January to celebrate Haitian independence.

spéculateurs: Licensed buying agents who usually operate on behalf of coffee export companies.

Bibliographic Essay

There are many good sources on Haiti, including a growing number of Web sites and collections of documents on the Internet. Web sites constantly change, but some of the best include LANIC (http://lanic.utexas.edu/la/cb/haiti/), NYIHA MEDIA (http://www.nyiha.com), and Bob Corbett's Haiti Page (http://www.webster.edu/~corbetre/haiti/haiti.html). Those with the ability to read French, of course, will find a range of books and articles in that language. The list below is intended as a starting point for important sources on Haiti.

For background, see Dupuy, Alex. *Haiti in the World Economy: Class, Race, and Underdevelopment since 1700.* Boulder and London: Westview Press, 1989; Dupuy, Alex. "Peasant Poverty in Haiti." *Latin American Research Review* 24 (1984): 259–271; Fass, Simon. *Political Economy in Haiti, the Drama of Survival.* New Brunswick, NJ: Transaction Books, 1984; Mintz, Sidney W. "Can Haiti Change?" *Foreign Affairs* 74, no. 1 (January/February 1995): 73–86; Dorsainville, Luc. "The Rivers and Lakes of Haiti." *Bulletin of the Pan American Union.* Washington, DC: Union of American Republics, March 1932; Simpson, George E. "Haitian Peasant Economy." *The Journal of Negro History* 25, no. 4 (October 1940): 498–519; Lundhal, Mats. *The Haitian Economy: Man, Land, and Markets.* New York: St. Martin Press, 1983; Mackenzie, Charles. *Notes on Haiti, Made during a Residence in That Republic,* vol. 2. London: Henry Colburn and Richard

Bentley, 1830; Heinl, Robert D., and Nancy G. Heinl. *Written in Blood: The Story of the Haitian People, 1492–1971.* Boston: Houghton Mifflin Company, 1978; Métraux, Alfred. *Making a Living in the Marbial Valley (Haiti).* Paris: UNESCO, Occasional Papers in Education, 1951; Ardouin, Beaubrun. *Etudes sur l'Histoire d'Haïti.* Port-au-Prince, Haiti: Editions Fardin, 2004; Madiou, Thomas. *Histoire d'Haïti.* Port-au-Prince, Haiti: Editions Deschamps, 1988.

For an examination of nineteenth-century Haiti, consult Logan, Rayford Whittingham. *The Diplomatic Relations of the United States with Haiti, 1776–1891.* Chapel Hill: University of North Carolina Press, 1941; Courlander, H. *The Drum and the Hoe: Life and Lore of the Haitian People.* Berkeley: University of California Press, 1960; Lacerte, Robert K. "Xenophobia and Economic Decline: The Haitian Case, 1820–1843." *The Americas* 37 (April 1981): 499–515; Leyburn, James G. "The Making of a Black Nation." In George P. Murdock, ed., *Studies in the Science of Society.* New Haven: Yale University Press, 1937; Logan, Rayford Whittingham. *The Diplomatic Relations of the United States with Haiti, 1776–1891.* Chapel Hill: University of North Carolina Press, 1941; Lacerte, Robert K. "The First Land Reform in Latin America: The Reform of Aléxandre Pétion, 1809–1814." *Inter-American Economic Affairs* 28, no. 1975; d'Ans, André-Marcel. "Institutions paysannes, constitution, légitimation et gestion de l'héritage foncier dans la plaine de Port-à-Piment." *Annales des pays d'Amérique Centrale et des Caraïbes* Numéro 4, Presses Universitaires de France, Presses Universitaires d'Aix-Marseille, 1984; Lepkowski, T. *Haití.* La Habana: Casa de las Américas, vol. 1: 1968, vol. 2: 1969; Pierre-Charles, Gérard. "Génesis de las naciones haitiana y Dominicana." In *Política y Sociología en Haití y la República Dominicana.* México: Coloquio Dominicano-Haitiano de Ciencias Sociales, UNAM, 1974; Lepelletier de Saint-Rémy, R. *Saint-Domingue: Etudes et solutions nouvelle de la question haïtienne.* Paris: Arthur Bertrand éditeur, 1846.

For the twentieth century, consult Pierce, John C. "The Haitian Crisis and the Future of Collective Enforcement of Democratic Governance." *Law and Policy in International Business* 27, no. 2 (1996): 477–512; Constable, Pamela. "A Fresh Start for Haiti." *Current History* 95 (February 1996): 65–69; Cox, Ronald W. "Private Interests and United States Foreign Policy in Haiti and the Caribbean Basin." In David Skidmore, *Contested Social Orders and International Politics.* Nashville, TN: Vanderbilt University Press, 1997; Doyle, Kate. "Hollow Diplomacy in Haiti." *World Policy Journal* 11, no. 1 (Spring 1994); Maingot, Anthony P. "Haiti: Problems of a Transition to Democracy in an Authoritarian Soft State." *Journal of Interamerican Studies and World Affairs* 28, no. 4 (Winter 1986–1987): 75–102; Pierce, John C. "The Haitian Crisis and the Future of Collective Enforcement of Democratic Governance." *Law and Policy in International Business* 27, no. 2 (1996): 477–512; Garcia-Zamor, Jean-Claude. "Obstacles to Institutional Development." In Derick W. Brinkerhoff and Garcia-Zamor, Jean-Claude. eds., *Politics, Projects and People: Institutional Development in Haiti.*

New York: Praeger Special Studies, 1986; Fass, Simon M. *Political Economy in Haiti: The Drama of Survival.* New Brunswick, NJ: Transaction Books, 1984; De Young, M. *Man and Land in the Haitian Economy.* Gainesville: University of Florida Press, 1958; Fatton, Robert A. "The Rise, fall and Resurrection of President Aristide." In Robert I. Rotberg, ed., *Haiti Renewed: Political and Economic Prospects.* Washington, DC: Brookings Institution Press and Cambridge: The World Peace Foundation, 1997; Ridgeway, James. *The Haiti Files: Decoding the Crisis.* Washington, DC: Essential Books, 1994; Laguerre, Michel S. *The Military and Society in Haiti.* Knoxville: University of Tennessee Press, 1993; Farmer, Paul. *The Uses of Haiti.* Monroe, ME: Common Courage Press, 1994; Plummer, Brenda Gayle. *Haiti and the United States: The Psychological Moment.* Athens: University of Georgia Press, 1990.

For an examination of Toussaint Louverture and the influence of the Haitian Revolution, see Césaire, Aimé. *Toussaint Louverture.* Paris, 1961; Lacroix, Pamphile, vicomte de. *Mémoires pour servir à l'Histoire de la Révolution de Saint-Domingue.* Paris: Pillier aîné, 1819; Fick, C. *Black Masses in the San-Domingo Revolution.* Montreal: Concordia University, 1979; Geggus, David Patrick. *Haitian Revolutionary Studies.* Bloomington: Indiana University Press, 2002; Lachance, Paul. "The Repercussions of the Haitian Revolution on Louisiana." In David Patrick Geggus, ed., *The Impact of the Haitian Revolution in the Atlantic World.* Columbia: University of South Carolina Press, 2001; Zuckerman, Michael. "The Power of Blackness: Thomas Jefferson and the Revolution of Saint-Domingue." In *Almost Chosen People: Oblique Biographies in the American Grain.* Berkeley: University of California Press, 1993; Matthewson, Tim. "Jefferson and Haiti." *Journal of Southern History* 61 (1995): 209–248; Dubois, Laurent. *Avengers of the New World: The Story of the Haitian Revolution.* Cambridge, MA: Belknap Press of Harvard University Press, 2004; Bénot, Yves, and Marcel Dorigny. *Rétablissement de l'esclavage dans les colonies Françaises, 1800–1830: Aux origines d'Haïti: Actes du colloque international tenu a l'Université de Paris VIII les 20, 21, et 22 Juin 2002.* Paris: Maisonneuve et Larose, 2003; Paquette, Robert. "Revolutionary Saint-Domingue in the Making of Territorial Louisiana." In David Barry Gaspar and David Patrick Geggus, eds., *A Turbulent Time: the French Revolution and the Greater Caribbean.* Bloomington: Indiana University Press, 1997; Sidbury, James. "Saint-Domingue in Virginia: Ideology, Local Meanings, and Resistance to Slavery, 1790–1800." *Journal of Southern History* 63, no. 3 (August 1997); Alfred de Lacaze in *Nouvelle biographie générale depuis les temps les plus reculés jusqu'à nos jours* (..), edited by M. le Dr Hoefer, Paris: Firmin Didot Frères, 1860, t. 32, pp. 38–44; E. Regnard in *Nouvelle biographie générale depuis les temps les plus reculés jusqu'à nos jours.*, sous la direction de M. le Dr Hoefer, Paris: Firmin Didot Frères, 1865, t. 44, pp. 184–185; Gragnon-Lacoste, Thomas Prosper. *Toussaint Louverture, Général en chef de l'armée de Saint-Domingue, surnommé le Premier des Noirs.* Paris and Bordeaux, 1877; Schoelcher, Victor. *Vie de Toussaint Louverture.* Paris: Paul Ollendorf, 1889; Sannon, Pauleus. *Histoire de Toussaint-Louverture,* 3 vols. Port-au-Prince, 1920–1933; James, Cyril L. R. *Les Jacobins noirs: Toussaint-Louverture et la Révolution de Saint-Domingue.* Gallimard, 1949 (réédité aux Éditions Caribéennes, Paris, 1984, XXVIII-375 p., coll. Précurseurs noirs); Césaire, Aimé. *Toussaint-Louverture. La Révolution française et le problème colonial.* 1960; Debien, G. "Les vues de deux colons de Saint-Domingue sur Toussaint Louverture (octobre 1797-février 1800)." *Note d'Histoire coloniale* 149; Debien, G., M.-A. Menier, and J. Fouchard. "Toussaint Louverture avant 1789. Légendes et réalités." *Note d'Histoire coloniale* 134 (1977); Pluchon, Pierre. *Toussaint Louverture. De l'esclavage au pouvoir.* Paris, 1979; *Dictionnaire d'Histoire de France,* Librairie Académique Perrin, Paris, 1981, à l'article *Toussaint-Louverture; L'état de la France pendant la Révolution (1789–1799),* sous la direction de Michel Vovelle, éd. La découverte, Paris, 1988, pp. 444–446; Champion, Jean-Marcel. Notice biographique consacrée à Toussaint-Louverture dans le *Dictionnaire Napoléon,* publié sous la direction de Jean Tulard, Fayard, 1989, pp. 1645–1646; Pluchon, Pierre. "Toussaint Louverture d'après le général de Kerverseau." In *Revue française d'histoire d' outre-mer,* 1989; Pluchon, Pierre. *Toussaint Louverture. Un révolutionnaire noir d'Ancien Régime.* Fayard, 1989; Pluchon, Pierre. *Histoire de la colonisation française,* t. 1, *Le premier empire colonial, des origines à la Restauration.* Fayard, 1991; Dorsainville, Roger. *Toussaint Louverture.* Paris: Editions Lulliard, 1965; Pluchon, P. *Toussaint Louverture: de l'esclavage au pouvoir.* Port-au-Prince, Haiti: Editions Caraïbes, 1979 and Paris, France: Edition de l'Ecole, 1979; Pluchon, P. *Toussaint Louverture, fils noir de la Révolution Française.* Paris, France: Bibliothèque documentaire de l'école des loisirs, 1980; Pluchon, P. *Toussaint Louverture: Un révolutionnaire noir d'Ancien Régime.* Paris, France: Edition Fayard, 1989; James, C.L.R. *Les Jacobins noirs, Toussaint Louverture.* Londres, Angleterre, réédition française, Paris, France: Les Editions caribéennes, 1983.

For an examination of Duvalier's legacy, consult Ferguson, James. "The Duvalier Dictatorship and Its Legacy in Haiti." In Anthony Payne and Paul Sutton, eds., *Modern Caribbean Politics.* Baltimore: Johns Hopkins University Press, 1993; Rotberg, Robert, and C. Clague. *Haiti: The Politics of Squalor.* Boston: Houghton Mifflin Company, 1971; Trouillot, Michel-Rolph. *Haiti, State against Nation: The Origins and Legacy of Duvalierism.* New York: Monthly Review Press, 1990.

For good surveys of religion in Haiti, consult Desmangles, Leslie G. *The Faces of the Gods: Vodou and Roman Catholicism in Haiti.* Chapel Hill: University of North Carolina Press, 1992; Greene, Anne. *The Catholic Church in Haiti: Political and Social Change.* East Lansing: Michigan State University Press, 2003.

Index

About the Author

STEEVE COUPEAU is a professor in the School of Continuing and Professional Studies at New York University and a media consultant with the Gerson Lehrman Group Media Council. Dr. Coupeau has written several books and articles about Latin America and the Caribbean. In particular, he is the author of "Legacy of the Haitian Slave Revolt" published by Greenwood Press (2006) in the *Encyclopedia of Slave Resistance and Rebellion* (edited by Junius P. Rodriguez). His media company, NYIHA MEDIA (www.nyiha.com), recently released "Human Rights in Quisqueya," a documentary on human rights matters on the island shared by Haiti and the Dominican Republic.